Studying Abroad 2016

university for the **creative arts**

Canterbury
New Dover Road
Canterbury
Kent
CT1 3AN

Tel: 01227 817314
Fax: 01227 817300
e-mail: librarycant@ucreative.ac.uk

Studying Abroad 2016: A guide for UK students

4th edition

Cerys Evans

trotman | **t**

Studying Abroad: A Guide for UK Students 2016

This fourth edition published in 2015 by Trotman Publishing, a division of Crimson Publishing Ltd, 19–21C Charles Street, Bath BA1 1HX

© Trotman Publishing 2015

Previous editions published in 2012, 2013, 2014

Author: Cerys Evans

British Library Cataloguing in Publication Data
A catalogue record for this book is available from the British Library

ISBN 978 1 84455 618 2

Typeset by IDSUK (DataConnection) Ltd

Printed and bound in Malta by Gutenberg Press Ltd, Malta

Acknowledgements

This book would not have been possible without the help of UK students at universities across the world who were happy to tell their stories. Many got involved in order to share their experience of a life-changing opportunity. Particular thanks go to Mark Huntington (A Star Future), Stefan Watts (Study Options), Jamie Dunn (US-UK Fulbright Commission) and the many university staff who took the time to talk to me and who put me in touch with their students.

Finally, Matt, Alice and Oscar deserve my heartfelt thanks for their understanding and support.

Contents

Contents

Contents

Contents

Introduction

Britain has had a long tradition of welcoming international students to its universities, yet far fewer UK students venture overseas to study. All that is changing and there has never been so much interest in the possibility of studying abroad.

The three-fold increase in tuition fees in England in 2012 prompted some young people to start looking for alternative, affordable ways to study. Many students are still unaware of the degrees available to them overseas, taught in English and at a range of prices. Although fees outside England are subsidised, students from Wales and Northern Ireland will also be able to find comparably priced, and sometimes cheaper, opportunities than those available at home. Scottish students can find free courses available elsewhere in Europe, at undergraduate and even at postgraduate level.

But price alone is not enough to drive people to study overseas. A more competitive marketplace for graduate employment is leading students to make themselves more attractive to potential employers and studying overseas provides the opportunity to produce a more dynamic CV.

However, choosing to study overseas is not a decision that should be made lightly. There are many aspects to consider and many questions to ask before you get to that stage. Higher education is a global market and, although there is a lot of information available online, the challenge is making sense of it, ensuring that it is genuine and being able to make meaningful comparisons between the different options available.

This book will help you to determine whether studying a degree abroad is the right option for you. It will tackle the costs, risks and benefits of studying abroad. It will enable you to compare the merits of different countries and their education systems. You can read about the trials and the tribulations of a variety of students, as well as learning about their highlights of overseas study. The book will help you to navigate the plethora of information available, guiding you through the decision-making process by providing answers to the essential questions.

This book is only the starting point of what could be a life-changing educational and cultural adventure.

Note

The following exchange rates were used throughout the book (sourced in February 2015).

- £1 to €1.35 (Euro)
- £1 to $1.54 (US Dollar)
- £1 to C$1.93 (Canadian Dollar)
- £1 to A$1.96 (Australian Dollar)
- £1 to NZ$2.05 (New Zealand Dollar)
- £1 to DKK10.09 (Danish Krone)
- £1 to CZK37.25 (Czech Koruna)
- £1 to NOK11.58 (Norwegian Krone)
- £1 to SEK12.90 (Swedish Krona)
- £1 to CHF0.69 (Swiss Franc)
- £1 to S$2.09 (Singapore Dollar)

- £1 to HK$11.95 (Hong Kong Dollar)
- £1 to ¥9.65 (Chinese Yuan Renminbi)
- £1 to JPY183.28 (Japanese Yen)
- £1 to ZAR17.90 (South African Rand)
- £1 to MYR5.62 (Malaysian Ringgit)
- £1 to JA$177.30 (Jamaican Dollar)
- £1 to SAR5.78 (Saudi Arabian Riyal)
- £1 to QAR5.61 (Qatari Riyal)
- £1 to BRL4.42 (Brazilian Real)

Student story
Simran Gill, Fontys University
of Applied Sciences, Venlo, the
Netherlands

Simran Gill is in the second year of a bachelor's degree in International Marketing. He originally decided to study outside England due to the high tuition fees, but he was also very keen on the added benefit of being able to experience life and study in Europe.

'The tuition fees in Holland are nearly €1,800 (£1,330) a year, and the cost of living, including accommodation, is much cheaper than in the UK.'

His search for a university started at the Student World Fair. 'The Netherlands were well represented and knew how to cater for British students.' He later went on to visit his chosen institution and felt well supported throughout the research and application process. 'It was considerably easier than UCAS, but this could depend on the university. Fontys was extremely quick and helpful as and when questions needed to be answered. Studielink, Holland's equivalent of UCAS, is simple to navigate and free.

'The university assigned me a buddy who was a second-year student and who was able to guide me through the process of registration and also help in matters regarding student life in the city and university. When I have required information, Fontys has been extremely informative and when I needed help with accommodation the support given was fantastic.'

Simran's experience of studying has been positive, although there have been some adjustments that he has had to make. 'Well, there were several modules which I had not studied for since GCSE so when it came to statistics and maths, for example, it was difficult for me to adjust. The other subjects were challenging as I had to get used to a more concise way of writing, but it was more the workload that presented the real challenge for me. I did far more in my first few months in comparison to my friends at

UK-based universities. I was definitely worked hard for the money I spent, so it was worth it in that respect. I guess you are eased into it in the beginning but by the second month you are expected to be up to speed. Now that I'm in the second year, I would say that the course has become more focused, whereas last year it was rather generalised.

'The standard is extremely high. Learning is more personal and contact time with your lecturer is more than just a person standing in front of a hundred students. They know me by name and classes are no bigger than 30.'

He recommends starting early in your quest for somewhere to live. 'Be sure to look early and allow yourself to see the surroundings, as the environment where you live is also important.'

Now that he is a second year student, he's moved out of halls into a shared house with friends. 'I live with two other students, from Germany. Fontys is primarily populated by German students due to its location near the German border, which in turn has attracted many of them to study in the Netherlands. The rapport with them is great; they're very easy-going, yet focused when necessary. The university has an international influence which you can see by the many friends I have from all over the world.

'In regards to renting, there aren't many major differences from the UK. Deposits are small, and if you have friends in the year above who are moving out of their accommodation, it's easy just to continue the contract with the landlord once they have left, as I did.'

Simran didn't experience any major difficulties adjusting to his new way of life. 'Not at all, I relished the opportunity of living somewhere else and experiencing a new culture. The chance to live abroad does not always present itself, and at the age of 18 it's not common, so take it by both hands if available. Perhaps the hardest adjustment was having to slow down the pace of my English so my international peers could understand!

'Moving away from home is never easy wherever you go, but I get the chance to go back regularly, so missing friends and family has not been much of an issue.'

Simran's top tips

Living costs

'Living costs are relatively cheap. There are low-price supermarkets which offer a wide variety of products at good prices. Food is pretty much the same here as it is in the UK. Supermarkets are tremendously accessible; I live above one. I'd recommend setting a budget and making food in bulk, if necessary. Going out to party is not too expensive, as drinks are cheap in Venlo and I rarely spend over €80 (£59) a week.'

Insurance

'A European health card (EHIC) will cover anything under €200 (£147). I have also registered with the British Embassy in Holland, so in case anything happens support is provided for us.'

Working while studying

'Last year, I was the sole representative of the UK at Fontys International Business School. Partly due to my increasing involvement with the international relations team, we have gained four more new students from Britain this semester. I have subsequently earned a job with the university as an international relations consultant, working occasionally with the team to promote the university in the UK. They use my input and social media skills to help them recruit in the UK. One of the benefits of working for the university is that they are considerate of my timetable.'

Lifestyle and culture

'It's a wonderfully chilled and relaxed lifestyle, the people are friendly and their English is great. They have many celebrations at points of the year where one can become a part of their culture and tradition.'

Travel

'Travel is of no concern as bikes rule the roost in Holland, and my university is a five-minute ride away and the city centre is two minutes away. Train travel is speedy and on time and, with the country being relatively small, nothing is too far away. Germany is five minutes over the border, Belgium is 40 minutes distance and Paris is a four-hour drive.'

Options for after you finish your studies

'There are many graduate schemes which I can apply for. In my third year, a year in industry is required. Fontys has amazing connections with companies worldwide, so I feel that the option of pursuing a career in marketing is certainly attainable.

'My plans are to return to the UK with two new languages in my repertoire (Dutch and an understanding of German) and an experience which would rival that of any graduate from the UK. To become a marketing manager before 30 at a large company is the goal.'

Fontys University of Applied Sciences is the second largest institute of higher education in Holland with campuses in the south of the country.

Chapter 1
Why study abroad?

UK students don't traditionally study abroad. Far more international students come to the UK than leave its shores to study. International study might be a new thing for UK students, but across much of the world it is far more common. In fact, the number of international students around the world just keeps growing. The Organisation for Economic Co-operation and Development (OECD) and United Nations Educational, Scientific and Cultural Organization's (UNESCO) Institute for Statistics tell us that more than 4.5 million international students were enrolled in higher education in 2012. The number of students going abroad to study has more than doubled since 2000 and looks set to soar.

But how many of these are UK students? OECD reveals that 44,290 UK students were enrolled at overseas tertiary institutions in 2014. Although this figure is low compared to the global numbers, it is worth knowing that the numbers have gone up by almost 7,000 since last year, an 18% increase.

According to a 2014 report from the British Council, the number of UK students considering studying overseas is increasing substantially too. In Broadening Horizons 2014, 37% of UK respondents were considering studying overseas, an increase of 17% on the previous year. Things are certainly changing.

If you mention studying abroad, a common response is that we already have a world-class university system, so why look elsewhere? But there are benefits of moving country to go to university which is why UK students are starting to look elsewhere, and in increasing numbers. There are plenty of reasons why study abroad might be beneficial; maybe you want to avoid higher tuition fees, to have an amazing adventure or to gain a place at one of the top universities in the world.

Interest in overseas study has been steadily growing since the announcement of the fee increases in the UK. Studying abroad may be a hot topic, but is that enough of a reason to set sail for foreign shores? I don't think so. Things are changing so fast that it is hard to know what the economic, employment or educational landscape will look like in a year or two, while you might only be part-way through your overseas degree. So it makes sense to consider overseas study in far more depth as part of your wider and longer-term plans; you will need to look carefully at the pros and cons before you make your decision.

The global market

As you walk around schools and colleges in other European countries, it is normal to see international opportunities on the notice boards; summer schools, study exchanges and overseas degrees are far more commonplace than in the UK. Young people in many other countries have come to expect international experiences.

This is not always the case in the UK and this causes a problem, according to a recent report into the global skills gap. Three-quarters of board- and director-level executives and CEOs think that 'we are in danger of being left behind by emerging countries unless young people learn to think more globally'. A similar proportion (74%) are 'worried that many young people's horizons are not broad enough to operate in a globalised and multicultural economy'. (The Global Skills Gap: Preparing young people for the new global economy, Think Global and British Council, December 2011.)

The British Chambers of Commerce carried out a survey of over 8,000 UK businesses in 2012, exploring barriers to exporting and international trade. They came up with the following recommendation: 'It is important to ensure that the next generation of business owners are "born global" with language skills.'

Picture yourself having finished university and ready to look for work. If you consider the global marketplace for jobs, then you will not only be competing against UK graduates, but against the brightest and best from across the world. And while the number of graduates from western countries is starting to plateau, countries like China and India are producing more young graduates, many of whom choose international higher education. The market is starting to get even more crowded and competitive.

Many organisations now do business or seek clients in more than one country, so job applicants with international experience, and the increased cultural awareness that brings, have added value. Some students choose study abroad as the first step towards an international career. Those graduates who have spent a summer school in the States, an exchange to Sweden as part of their first degree followed by postgraduate study in Malaysia, have a head start.

A 2011 report from the Association of Graduate Recruiters (AGR), Council for Industry and Higher Education (CIHE) and CFE (research and consultancy specialists in employment and skills) examines how global graduates can be developed. 'Students have a role to play in acquiring global competencies and choosing appropriate pathways to enable them to develop a global mindset. Experience of working outside their home country and immersion in a different culture can catapult a graduate into being considered for rewarding and challenging roles.'

The report's authors worked with multinational employers based in the UK to identify the most important qualities a global graduate will need. 'Global graduates require a blend of knowledge, competencies and corresponding attributes spanning global mindset, cultural agility and relationship management and must be able to apply them flexibly.'

Studying abroad can not only give you the opportunity to study in a new country, but also to choose a degree with an international focus while studying alongside a group of students from across the world. Consider how all these aspects can help you to develop the global mindset that will prepare you for the international job market and the global economy.

> **"** I feel I am having a much more international experience here than I ever would have had in England. I am studying in a diverse environment which is reflected in the debates and classes that we take part in. My class has such a range of nationalities that makes the lessons more dynamic, but it also has a real effect on personal development. By being in these classes you develop a more tolerant attitude and change your outlook completely on some things. **"**
>
> *Clare Higgins, The Hague University of*
> *Applied Sciences, the Netherlands*

Competition in the UK

Competition for university places

In 2014, over 187,000 students applied for university in the UK without gaining a place. For some of the most competitive courses in the UK, there are tens of applications per place. You have to be truly exceptional, and perhaps a little bit lucky, to get a place for medicine or veterinary science in the UK. Yet there are internationally recognised universities offering the same opportunities in the Caribbean and parts of Europe. Although you still need to demonstrate academic excellence and the right aptitude and attitude, the level of competition for places is not as extreme as in the UK. It is not surprising that applicants, frustrated by the limits in the UK, are looking for alternatives.

The UK operates a highly competitive system, where great importance is placed on predicted grades and high academic achievement. Competition for places is one of the reasons why entry criteria are so high. Up until September 2015, a cap on the number of places available meant that the demand outstripped the supply, so the universities were able to pick and choose their candidates and ask for higher and higher requirements. The cap on places will end for most courses in 2015, although some courses, like nursing, teaching or social work will continue to be restricted.

Other countries do things differently. Some countries will accept you provided that you have achieved three A levels (or equivalent) but are not so concerned about grades. This doesn't mean that they are less stringent in their entry processes; in some cases, they are more concerned with how you actually perform at university – if you don't achieve in your first year, they may ask you to leave.

A number of countries don't have a coordinated central application process like UCAS. On the downside, this may mean having to complete more application forms. On the positive side, it also means that you aren't limited to the number of applications you make, which can keep your options open. You can even apply through UCAS at the same time as applying to overseas universities; all the while gathering the information you need to decide which option suits you best. Some students use an international university as a back-up option to their UK plans.

Competition for jobs

Many current students and recent graduates understand all too clearly the effects of the upsurge in numbers in higher education over the past decade. The increase in numbers of graduates, exacerbated by the recent economic challenges, is creating a crowded graduate job market. Yet the more graduates there are, the more pressure there is to get a degree in order to compete. A degree has become essential yet, conversely, a degree alone is not enough. Students are looking for ways in which to stand out, to make themselves different and to get an edge over the competition. Studying abroad can be a way to achieve all these things.

As Dr Jo Beall of the British Council explained in 2012: 'The good news is that people are beginning to recognise how vital international skills are for enhancing their career. Research last year revealed that more UK employers look for international awareness and experience above academic qualifications. But the bad news is that not enough people in the UK are taking opportunities to gain international experience. That needs to change if the UK will successfully compete in the global economy. Our recent research showed that while almost two-thirds of students felt they had an international outlook, they failed to see the potential career advantages to be gained from international experiences.'

> **❝** Global leaders need to be willing to work in
> different locations as an integral part of their
> career but many employers have difficulty recruiting
> graduates willing to travel or relocate. Employers felt that
> graduates with a global mindset would be more likely to
> embrace international immersion and relish the opportunity
> to work in different countries. It is essential that leaders are
> positioned where they are most needed and thus able to
> respond to market demands. **❞**
>
> *(Diamond, A., Walkley, L. et al., Global Graduates*
> *into Global Leaders, www.cihe.co.uk, [Online]*
> *accessed November 2014.)*

Financial benefits

Since autumn 2012, tuition fees of up to £9,000 per year have been
charged in England for undergraduate courses. Fees will continue
to be charged at these rates for students starting university in 2015.

At undergraduate level, Welsh students are expected to contribute
£3,810 per year in 2015, while fees in Northern Ireland (for students
from Northern Ireland) are capped at £3,805. Undergraduate study
in Scotland remains free for Scottish students, although students
from the rest of the UK studying in Scotland will pay fees of up to
£9,000 per year.

On top of the increasing fees, repayment options for student loans
are also looking less appealing. In England and Wales an interest
rate of RPI plus 3% (making a total of 5.3% at October 2014's rate)
will be charged on your loan from day one, with variable rates
charged once you graduate, depending on your earnings. The UK

is not a cheap place to live at the moment either, with the cost of living remaining fairly high. So, in addition to your hefty debts from fees, you might be looking at less reasonable terms on your loan and high costs of living.

Unsurprisingly, students and parents are now wondering whether there might be a more financially attractive proposition elsewhere. There are universities in countries like Sweden, Denmark, Norway and Finland that charge no fees to UK students. Many countries charge less than England, Wales and Northern Ireland – countries like Estonia and Ireland, for example. There are countries with considerably cheaper costs of living (the Czech Republic or Malaysia, for example) and there are universities with generous scholarships and sources of student financial support (for example, the USA and the Netherlands). Graduates from some overseas universities may come home with the ideal situation of no debt (or at least smaller debt), as well as many of the other benefits introduced in this chapter.

> **❝** Belgium offered a world-renowned university at the heart of Europe for a fraction of the tuition price at American and British institutions.**❞**
>
> *Tom Aitchison, KU Leuven, Belgium*

Academic benefits

There can be academic benefits to studying abroad, for example, the chance to try out a number of subjects before specialising; or how about the opportunity to study new subjects or specialist options not available in the UK? Some countries are world leaders in specific subjects; Australia, for example, is known for its geology and marine biology courses, among others. Other countries offer a different perspective on familiar subjects, like veterinary medicine or history. Or perhaps you relish the opportunity to study a subject in its natural setting, Arctic studies or American literature, for example.

> 66 The style of learning is very similar to A levels in that you are taking multiple subjects at once. Because of this, each of my classes feels very interdisciplinary. For example, there is a Math major in my English class, who brings a different perspective to the texts compared to a History major, for example. 99
>
> *Stephanie Addenbrooke, Yale University, USA*

Studying abroad may give you a more realistic chance of studying at a world-class university or of taking one of the competitive subjects that is becoming increasingly difficult in the UK (see Competition for university places, page 12). Outside the UK, some of the best universities in the world can be more accessible in the grades they expect and in the scholarships they offer. Different countries place different importance on entrance exams, face-to-face interviews, exam results, and hobbies and interests. You may find that what is needed by other universities across the world plays to your strengths better than what the UK asks of you.

You will have the chance to experience a different academic environment, with access to different types of campus and university facilities. Some universities offer much smaller classes than in the UK, better tutor-contact time or high-profile internships; finding out exactly what is on offer is an important part of your research.

You may even find that the styles of teaching and learning outside the UK suit you better. For example, in Australia teaching is often more informal and lecturers are approachable and accessible; in Denmark, much is made of problem-based learning, while exams are required in all subjects.

Personal benefits

Studying abroad can be a great adventure, broadening your horizons and throwing up new challenges to be faced. It is hardly surprising that so many students come home from time overseas feeling confident, mature and independent. Understanding that there are different ways of doing things can make you more flexible. Learning to cope in an unfamiliar situation reinforces your adaptability and ability to use your initiative. Most universities arrange lots of events to let international students meet one another and get settled in, so your social skills will get some practice too.

> ❝ The values and memories that studying abroad gives you are always worth it and they equip you with skills to do it again or adapt to similar alien situations in the future. ❞
>
> *Tom Aitchison, KU Leuven, Belgium*

The list of personal benefits goes on and on. Many courses delivered in English attract a wide and varied mix of international students, not just those from English-speaking countries. The chance to make friends from across the world makes you more culturally aware, but also means a wider network of contacts for future life and work.

Even if you are being taught in English, studying in a non-English-speaking country means that you will need to develop your language skills in order to be able to communicate effectively. Most institutions will offer language courses to their students. Language skills can make you more employable; Britain lags behind the rest of Europe with its foreign-language skills and this might even be having an impact on our export market.

In a 2012 survey of over 8,000 businesses in the UK, the British Chambers of Commerce discovered that 'up to 96% of respondents had no foreign language ability for the markets they served, and the largest language deficits are for the fastest developing markets. For example, only 0.4% of business owners surveyed reported that they were able to speak Russian or Chinese well enough to conduct business deals in their buyers' language. Addressing the gaps in commercial exporting skills – including language skills – must be a priority to support the growth of Britain's export sector.'

Think how beneficial language skills could be to your future prospects.

> **66** My plan is to return to the UK with two new languages in my repertoire (Dutch and an understanding of German) and an experience which would rival that of any graduate from the UK. **99**
> *Simran Gill, Fontys University of Applied Sciences, the Netherlands*

Studying in another country can also give you access to lifestyle options that aren't accessible or affordable in the UK. If you fancy a sauna in your apartment building, try Finland. Or how about surfing before lectures in Australia? If you're looking for a great place to ski, parts of the USA or Canada have much to offer.

You might get the chance to work overseas too, perhaps part-time alongside your studies or as part of an internship, co-op programme or placement related to your subject. Essentially, you will get the chance to develop a global perspective or an international outlook, which is so important in today's global society.

The employer's view

When considering overseas study as part of a longer-term plan, you need to be sure of your prospects when you return to the UK. So what kinds of competencies could you develop through overseas study that would be attractive to employers back in the UK? Here are the views of some top employers.

> ❝ Cultural dexterity is important: an ability not to impose one's own culture on another one, to be sensitive to other cultures and how to do business in different environments. There are certain ways of working with clients in the Middle East that you wouldn't adopt in Japan. ❞
>
> *PWC*

> ❝ Adaptability and self-awareness are probably the two things that we find the toughest to find . . . we want our graduates to feel they fit with our culture and hit the ground running. ❞
>
> *HSBC*

> 66 If you have people that can integrate with local teams, or who are able to move globally and take with them their experience in a seamless way, I think that can only help the business move forward. A lot of our work is very dependent on engaging with local governments [and] other local and national oil companies, and we need to be able to work with them effectively. 99
>
> *BP*

> 66 You need the mindset that says, 'The person I'm talking to isn't like me and I need to understand what they are like and then work with them.' It isn't only about having the technical knowledge, it's also necessary to understand the values, customs, cultures and behaviours that are significant to them. 99
>
> *National Grid*
>
> *(Source: Diamond, A., Walkley, L. et al., Global Graduates into Global Leaders, www.ncub.co.uk, [Online] accessed December 2014.)*

A 2013 British Council report, *Culture at Work*, considered the views of recruitment specialists at 360 large organisations from nine countries, including the UK. The employers could clearly see the benefits that intercultural skills could bring to a company's earnings. They also identified the risks, including financial risk, of not having employees with these skills, which included:

- loss of clients
- damage to an organisation's reputation
- team conflict.

If you choose to study overseas, you should develop many of the qualities that these organisations are looking for, but you will still need to be sure that you can articulate these strengths to potential employers. Think about how you could sell your international experiences, your ability in foreign languages and your intercultural skills at interview.

Why not go?

Of course, studying abroad isn't the right choice for everyone and there are a number of reasons why you might not choose to take this option. Some of the reasons that make international study ideal for one person (the chance to have an adventure or take a leap into the unknown, for example) might make it an awful prospect for another.

YouGov and the British Council asked 1,000 undergraduates why they had not worked, lived or studied abroad and some of the most common responses were:

- 'It costs too much to do so.'
- 'My foreign language skills are not good enough.'
- 'I find the idea daunting.'
- 'I wouldn't know how to go about it.'

Source: British Council and YouGov, 2011. Next generation UK. [pdf] Available at: www.britishcouncil.org/new/pagefiles/15492/ yougov_report_v3.pdf [Accessed 7 December 2014]

You do need a certain amount of confidence to take this step. It is a braver move than simply following the crowd and it does have some risks. You are further from home if things go wrong, although many students overseas talk of the support network they build up of university staff, room-mates and fellow students.

The need for thorough preparation and research

Ideally, you need to be fully prepared to take this step. Getting a place through Clearing in the UK can be a stressful process and can lead to students feeling the pressure to accept courses or institutions for which they are not suited. Imagine how it feels when you end up in a different country. After A level results day in August there is often great interest in late opportunities overseas, but not always the time and space to make an informed decision. A rushed decision doesn't always end up being a negative one, but there are benefits from taking your time with this process.

> **❝❝** The Dutch universities start earlier so I had not even enrolled, had no financial aid or plan, don't speak any Dutch and had no accommodation, so I felt very unprepared. **❞❞**
>
> *Clare Higgins, The Hague University of Applied Sciences, the Netherlands*

When considering an unfamiliar education system, you need to find out far more about the type and reputation of an institution, the way you will be taught and assessed, the qualifications you will gain, the grading system and so on; you can't assume that anything will be the same as in the UK.

Financial reasons

One of the downsides to overseas study is the lack of UK student financial support you can access. With no loans or grants from the UK government, you will need to find some money for fees and living costs before you go.

However, in 2015–2016, the Scottish government is trialling the Portability Pilot scheme to open up opportunities to Scottish students by offering 500 students the same financial support whether they study at home or take their full degree at specific institutions in Europe:

- University of Maastricht, the Netherlands
- University of Groningen, the Netherlands
- Rhine-Waal University of Applied Sciences, Germany
- University of Southern Denmark, Denmark
- Malmo University, Sweden.

You can find out more at the Student Awards Agency for Scotland at www.saas.gov.uk

If you're a UK student applying outside the EU and you need to apply for a visa, you will need to provide evidence that you have the money to study. Don't forget to factor in additional costs for application fees, travel, admissions tests, visa applications or insurance, for example.

> 66 Remember that start-up costs are a lot. Whether it is desk lamps or mattresses, it soon spirals. Your first month's living costs will likely be twice as high as a normal month. 99
>
> *Tom Aitchison, KU Leuven, Belgium*

There may be some opportunities for scholarships and occasionally even grants and loans from your host country. Even if you're lucky enough to get a scholarship or financial support from the country where you study, chances are that you'll need some money to supplement this, or in case of an emergency. If you plan to work to fund your studies, don't bank on getting work right away, particularly if you don't yet speak the language.

Language barrier

If you are studying in a country where English isn't an official language, even though your course may be taught in English, you will still need to manage away from the university. A rental agreement for accommodation or an application for a bank account, for example, will be in another language, so you will need to consider how you might cope. If most of your fellow students don't speak English as a first language, you may feel isolated in social situations.

Learning a new language is likely to be highly beneficial, but it is another commitment on top of your studies. If you are concerned about the language barrier, it is worth finding out how widely English is spoken in your chosen country and whether the institution takes many students from English-speaking countries.

Adjusting

You will need to be prepared to make adjustments if you decide to study abroad.

Education

Teaching and learning can be different (as you'll learn in Chapters 5 to 11). Expectations about what you should achieve in your first year can be very high, often determining whether you are allowed to stay on into the second year. The workload may be heavier than you would expect in the UK and terminology may be unfamiliar. It will be a steep learning curve, so you will need to use your initiative and seek help to avoid falling behind.

Lifestyle

Moving abroad means that your normal way of life will be thrown into disarray. The familiar and comforting will have disappeared, replaced by the new and strange, and the life you expect to lead at university may not always be realised. You may spend a disproportionate amount of time studying, adjusting to the new education system and working (rather than socialising). You may find that other home students from the host country are older or living at home. There will be cultural and social differences to the ways you spend your time and you will be far away from your normal support network of family and friends. In combination, these factors often lead to feelings of culture shock and homesickness. It is quite normal to feel this way, but it is an adjustment that you will need to consider.

66 There is a big restaurant scene in Doha, but a limited number of bars and they are all located in hotels. Much of student life when we are not working revolves around cultural events, socialising at the souqs, or going to the beach and malls. **99**

Benedict Leigh, UCL Qatar, Qatar

Risks

Although many people love their experience of studying abroad, it is not risk-free. You might be concerned about whether you will get a visa, have fears about how you will manage financially and worry about the distance from family and friends. International study can bring flexibility, but there may be more restrictions in the choices that you make, particularly if you need a visa. It can be problematic to change institution or course once you start. It is not always possible to change your reason for being in a country, from studying to full-time work, for example, so you need to be fairly sure of your plans before you depart.

No matter how thoroughly you plan and research, you cannot know what you will be faced with when you come to leave university, so you cannot assume that the opportunities of today will still be there tomorrow. You may find that employers do not recognise or understand your degree, even if it is equivalent to those available in the UK. Even if you're attending a world-ranked university, UK employers may fail to recognise its status. Perhaps you were planning to stay on in a country, but economic conditions made that difficult. Courses that meet certain professional standards today might not fit the bill tomorrow, so it is worth considering a back-up plan, where possible.

> **“** Before you leave home, make sure you sort how your finances are going to work from your bank back home, and how you can withdraw money abroad.**”**
>
> *Tudor Etchells, IE University, Spain*

Finally, international education is big business, so there are people out there trying to make money from bogus institutions, low-quality provision and non-existent accommodation. Be on your guard and use some of the tips and reputable sources of information found in this book.

Having gathered and considered all the information that you need, you may just get the feeling that studying abroad is not the right option for you. If it isn't the right step right now, you don't necessarily need to rule it out for ever. You might want to consider alternatives to taking your full degree abroad (see page 71) or you might choose to study or work abroad at a later stage in life.

Many of the trailblazing students who have already taken the step of taking their full degree overseas have additional reasons for going. Some have already spent some time abroad, have family members who had lived overseas or have personal links to a country before they decide to study there. This is changing; as a degree overseas has started to become more common, more attractive and more understood in the UK, students are now making the move without those personal links beforehand.

If you're looking for . . .

- If you're looking for the cheapest fees, try Europe (Chapter 5).
- If you're looking for a similar student lifestyle to that of the UK, try Ireland (page 148), the Netherlands (page 156) and many of the US campus universities (Chapter 6).
- If you're looking for accelerated degrees or tailor-made education, try a private university (page 37).
- If you're looking for a low cost of living, try eastern Europe (Chapter 5), South Africa (page 309) or China (page 297).
- If you're looking for the best in the world, try the USA (Chapter 6).
- If you're looking for a different culture, try Qatar (page 302), Hong Kong (page 280) or Japan (page 285).
- If you're looking for no tuition fees, try the Nordic countries (Chapter 5) and Germany (page 144).

- If you're looking for outdoor activities, try Canada (Chapter 7), Australia (Chapter 8) or New Zealand (Chapter 9).

- If you're looking for the opportunity to stay on after study, try Europe (page 122), Canada (page 232), Australia (page 252) or New Zealand (page 272).

Student story
Hannah Burrows, University of Southern Denmark Odense, Denmark

Hannah Burrows was already thinking globally when she headed off to Denmark to study for an MA in American Studies. 'After doing a law degree in Britain and qualifying as a lawyer in the USA, I decided that I wanted to study American Studies as a master's degree, which I felt would help me understand their system better. I looked at the courses on offer in Britain but I was daunted by the huge cost of tuition and disappointed that I did not have the opportunity to work or study abroad as part of any of the programmes. My boyfriend is Danish, and we were both looking at our options in the UK, the USA and Scandinavia. In the end, Denmark gave us both the best package of options.

'The best information resource for me was the university's Facebook page. That's how I learned the most about the university before going to see it in person. I looked through the photo albums of the local area, the videos of student testimonials, the pictures taken inside classes, and I asked questions to current students.

'The university I chose is the biggest in Denmark, and is the only one to offer a master's in American Studies. It's entirely in English, I study a full-time two-year programme to get a broad base of topics and get the opportunity to do internships and study abroad as part of the programme. The university offers accommodation for the full length of my degree, all of my teachers are recognised experts on America, and, best of all, there were no tuition fees whatsoever.

'I can work up to 15 hours a week and the Danish minimum wage is more than £13 an hour so that goes a long way to helping with living expenses. I had help from the university's career centre with finding a part-time job before I arrived in Denmark. You can also sometimes get help from the Danish government toward your rent and things like that.

'The application process was pretty simple. I applied directly to the university through their website. I had to send electronic copies of my CV, my transcript of grades from my undergraduate degree, and a copy of my diploma. I applied about a week after the applications opened, and I was accepted a month later.

'The university has an international office, so administrative aspects of moving to Denmark and general questions about being a student at the university went through them. They help with getting your social security number (in Denmark it's known as a CPR), for health insurance, for getting a bank account, for free Danish lessons, for your registration as a resident. That's probably the most complex thing I have dealt with in moving here.

'The university organises a buddy system for your arrival. They pick you up from the airport and help you move into your accommodation, and after that, they introduce you to people and help you to settle in to life in Denmark. My buddy has been one of my best friends since the day we met; the university matched us up really well. She was my shoulder to cry on when I got homesick at the very beginning!'

Hannah has had to get used to some differences in the Danish approach to education. 'The style of education is more laid back, they allow you to eat, drink and use your phone in class. Probably most strange is using first names, for your teacher right up to the vice-chancellor. It's a Danish thing, where they insist on the equality of first names.

'The teaching style is more like seminars than lectures, with a discussion by all students and the teacher together. For exams, the biggest shock for me was that you can choose your exam format. You can choose between an oral presentation, an essay or a written exam where you have access to your notes, books and the internet. They allow students a lot of independence, and in return expect you to take responsibility for your studies. If you want help, you can always get it from your teachers or the Study Board.'

Even with all the support available, there have been some adjustments for Hannah to make. 'It can be hard not speaking Danish at the beginning and you can feel left out if you don't understand what's going on. In my first week, the girls in my class would speak Danish together outside of class. I was too shy to ask them to switch to English so I could join in, but once I got the courage, they said it was no problem for them to speak in English.

'I suppose the biggest negative is that there is no Cadbury's chocolate here, and I have to wait for my mum to send it over in a package!'

Hannah's top tips

Accommodation
'You can arrange accommodation through the university. It's about £250 a month, with your utilities and internet included. You can arrange it privately with friends, but it might work out a little more expensive and be ready for all the paperwork to be in Danish!'

Food
'Food costs around the same at the supermarket as it does in England. Eating at restaurants is a bit more expensive, maybe 25% more than back home. Fast food costs roughly the same – a cheeseburger at McDonalds costs 10 kroner, just over a pound.'

Living costs
'The most expensive things about Denmark are buying alcohol, eating in restaurants and having a car. Always ask the place if they have a student discount, it's not always advertised but most places have something to offer. There are also tons of happy hour deals; because Danes start their nights out so late in the evening (after midnight), the bars generally offer free drinks if you get there between 9pm – 11pm, so you could bar-hop and get free drinks most of the night!'

Financial support for study
'There aren't that many scholarships for American Studies. There probably are for other subjects, especially if you're working in Engineering or Business, the university can match you up with a company who will sponsor your projects, research and internships, and give you a job at the end of your degree.'

Working while studying

'I can work up to 15 hours a week, and I have a job at the university proofreading English and posting on the university's Facebook page in English. If you're a native English speaker, it's not too hard to get a part-time job or two. Your first port of call in seeking work could always be the university.'

Making friends

'Denmark is a really social place that encourages a strong work–life balance, getting involved in groups and extra-curricular activities. They are big on sport teams, clubs and societies, and unions. In my first week, I ran for the board of a student society and to my amazement I was voted in! I also took up ballet classes to meet new people, started Danish classes with other students from the university and joined the Model United Nations.'

Lifestyle and culture

'The most common word you'll hear about the Danish lifestyle is "hygge" which means cosiness. They love to spend evenings together in bars, pubs, or having dinner and drinks at home. I have only been here a month, and already most of my classmates have invited me to theirs for a dinner party, or for drinks and games.

'During the day, Danes are pretty active: they're always on bikes and quite outdoorsy. They are definitely a nation of nature lovers. As for culture, this is the hometown of fairy tale author Hans Christian Andersen. His image is everywhere in the city. Pastries and hot dogs are like national symbols here, the locals will tell you that you haven't lived until you've tried the Danish version of each.'

Travel and transport

'Everyone in Denmark uses a bike. It's just unheard of not to own one! There are more bike paths than roads around Odense so it really is the best way to get around. They're safe and well lit. Just make sure you have a bike lock. You can get a student bus pass called a Wild Card as well, if you need to travel longer distances. The trains are clean, modern and on-time. Going home isn't too hard either – there are dozens of flights to several British cities every day for about £100.'

Options for after you finish your studies

'The university has a lot of links with big firms around Denmark like Lego, Nordea Bank, Novo Nordisk, Accenture and Danfoss, as well as government institutions, and you can easily get an internship organised with the help of the university.'

So, what next for Hannah? 'So far, my plan is to stay in Denmark. Although it's only been a month, I really love it here, and I could see myself applying to do a PhD at this university later on.'

And the best thing about studying overseas? 'The best thing is definitely that first step, when you see what opportunities you can get elsewhere by taking your focus away from Britain. The course in Denmark gives me several advantages over the equivalent in Britain, and I can even go further abroad for a semester without paying tuition fees as the university gives you a grant that pays you to study. I can't imagine getting the same level of benefits in an English course. A lot of degrees in Europe look to improve your employability prospects by putting you into work-like situations during your programme and getting hands-on experience in industry. When you're asked those questions in a job interview such as "when have you demonstrated leadership qualities . . .?", a degree from Denmark will give you many different instances with which you could answer, because it aims to simulate a cooperative work environment whilst doing academic study.'

University of Southern Denmark (www.sdu.dk/en) is a modern education and research institution with 20,000 students offering a range of bachelor's and master's degrees taught in English. It appears in the Times Higher Education World University Rankings Top 400 for 2014–2015.

Chapter 2

What you need to know before you go

It is normal to have concerns and to feel some anxiety about whether studying abroad is the right step for you. As we have already seen in Chapter 1, common worries concern the cost of fees and access to finance; the prospect of leaving family and friends; concerns about getting a visa; whether your qualifications will be recognised when you return home; and fear of adjusting to another country, culture or language.

This chapter aims to put your mind at rest by addressing some of the questions you may have about making the move overseas.

Education

Don't assume that education overseas will be just like that in the UK. There are lots of questions to be asked. When does the academic year start? How long do bachelor's degrees take? How do I know if my university is genuine?

Length of study and academic year

When you start to look at the options for overseas study, it is important to understand that many countries operate a four-year bachelor's degree and a two-year master's degree. When comparing the academic experience and the cost of fees and living, an extra year can make a big difference.

Other countries may also have differences in when their academic year begins and when you can join a course. Many European universities start in early September. Some universities offer more than one start date during the year, which can save you having to wait a full year for the next intake.

Differences in teaching and learning

Education systems vary across the world, so you will encounter some differences when you study in another country. University in the UK requires independent study and critical thinking. In some countries (although less so in Europe and the western world) university education can be more tutor-led, following set texts. You need to know how education works in your chosen country (and institution, see Different types of institution on page 36) and how you will be taught and assessed. If you study in a country where every course is assessed by means of an exam, you need to be able to cope under exam pressure. Before you apply, you should check whether the style of education suits your style of learning. Finding out what to expect will help you prepare for any differences when you arrive. Your university will be able to tell you more.

> **“** I would say that education in Brazil is much more tutor-led; Brazilian students have their hands held much more than in the UK.**”**
>
> *Justin Axel-Berg, University of São Paulo, Brazil*

> **“** The biggest shock for me was that you can choose your own exam format. You can choose between an

oral presentation of 45 minutes, or a 24-hour take-home essay, or a 3–4 hour written exam where you have access to your notes, books and the internet.**99**

Hannah Burrows, University of Southern Denmark

66 I have a very close relationship with all of my professors. Classes rarely, if ever, exceed 30 students.**99**

Joshua Jackson, SP Jain School of Global Management, Singapore and Australia

To prepare yourself and improve your chances of success, find out as much as you can about what to expect. Read through the course information and make a start on any recommended reading before you get there. See the chapters on 'Studying in . . .' for more details.

Different types of institution

Having local knowledge can be reassuring; in the UK, you may already understand which universities are considered to be the best, which have strong vocational backgrounds or which are seen to be weaker. It is much more difficult to make these comparisons on an international scale and where the education system is unfamiliar.

As you research your chosen countries, find out about the different types of institution and how they differ. In Finland, and in a number of other European countries, universities offer research-based education, while universities of applied science offer work-related education. In the USA, you can choose between university and community college. Reputation (but also cost and competitiveness) of the different types of institution may vary.

Although there are only a handful of private institutions with UK degree-awarding powers, it is a different case overseas. The USA has many private providers, and there are plenty to be found across the rest of the world too. Private universities offer a variety of different features; they tend to have higher fees, but often offer more generous scholarships and financial aid. They may offer a more supported or bespoke service, with accelerated programmes, low student–teacher ratio and personalised tuition and internships. Don't rule private universities out on a cost basis alone; in some cases they might end up the better-value option, because of the financial support available and the opportunities to choose a tailor-made education.

University rankings

If you are seeking out a particular type of institution, you might like to compare potential overseas universities to those that you are familiar with in the UK. Use worldwide university rankings to get an idea of how your chosen institutions fare on the world stage and how they compare to institutions that you know from the UK. Look at which international universities choose to work in partnership with a familiar university back home; it is likely that partner institutions will share some characteristics.

Here in the UK, the national league tables are familiar, but you might not know so much about worldwide rankings. Pay attention to worldwide league tables (Times Higher Education World University Rankings, QS Top Universities, and Academic Ranking of World Universities, for example) to check out how your chosen UK university measures up to the global competition. Although British universities are well-perceived, only a handful of them regularly appear at the top of the world rankings. Many universities that we might not recognise as household names are beating UK universities hands down, for example, USA's Northwestern University, Korea Advanced Institute of Science and Technology and the Swiss Federal

Institute of Technology in Zurich are all rated more highly than University of Manchester and University of Bristol in the Times Higher Education World University Rankings 2014–2015.

Try some of the following league tables:

- Times Higher Education World University Rankings
  www.timeshighereducation.co.uk/world-university-rankings
- Academic Ranking of World Universities (ARWU)
  www.shanghairanking.com
- QS Top Universities
  www.topuniversities.com/university-rankings
- *Financial Times* Business School Rankings
  http://rankings.ft.com/businessschoolrankings/rankings

If you are going to use league tables, make sure you don't use them in isolation and that you understand what they are measuring. A league table can't tell you whether a university is the right choice for you. The methods used to rank universities mean that large, research-based, English-speaking universities tend to do best. It is worth noting that many of the universities that don't make it into the top few hundred in the world can still offer you a good-quality education that might suit your needs perfectly.

An alternative to the traditional league tables is U-Multirank (www.u-multirank.eu) which allows you to compare universities based on a range of different data.

UK equivalence

There are two aspects to consider under the equivalence of qualifications. Will your qualifications be accepted by your chosen overseas institution? And, when your studies are over, will a degree from your institution be recognised when you get back to the UK?

The International Baccalaureate and A levels tend to be well-recognised overseas and often meet the entry requirements of international universities. In some cases, they exceed the requirements. In the USA, for example, you may be able to join an associate degree course at a community college without A levels. You can find out more in Chapter 6, Studying in the USA.

Other qualifications, like the new Scottish Highers, or vocational qualifications, like BTEC Diplomas, may need to be verified by one of the centres of academic recognition. Overseas universities don't tend to include Highers or vocational qualifications within their published entry criteria, but you shouldn't assume that these qualifications won't be accepted. Each country has its own system of comparing international qualifications to those in the home country. Go to ENIC-NARIC (European Network of Information Centres – National Academic Recognition Information Centres in the EU) at www.enic-naric.net to find out about academic recognition in the country where you wish to study. For countries that are not listed, try their Ministry of Education.

For all of the countries listed within this book, degrees at undergraduate and postgraduate level taken at accredited universities are equivalent to the level offered in the UK; this means that you should be able to use them to access further study or graduate-level employment on your return to the UK. You will need to do further checks to ensure that your qualifications meet any professional requirements. See Professional recognition on page 40 for more explanation.

Although an honours degree is the norm in England, Wales and Northern Ireland, many countries outside the UK don't offer honours degrees as standard; they might offer an ordinary bachelor's degree instead. Where honours degrees are available, they might require additional work and the preparation of a dissertation. You will need to check whether your degree is classed as an honours degree or not, as this may have a bearing on your future plans, particularly for further study.

A number of the students featured in this book have decided to stay on in their chosen country or move to a new country for further study or work. If you decide to do the same, you may also need to check out how your qualification compares to academic standards in your new country of residence. You can do this through one of the national academic recognition information centres (NARIC); for a list of national centres, go to www.enic-naric.net. If your country isn't listed, your overseas university or the Ministry of Education in your chosen country will be able to advise further.

Professional recognition

If you intend to practise a particular profession on your return to the UK, or intend to take further study to fulfil this aim, it is essential that your qualification is accepted, otherwise you will have wasted precious time and money.

If you know that you want to move into a particular field, you should check with the relevant professional organisations in the country where you hope to practise. So, if you want to be a doctor in the UK, you could check with the General Medical Council, while prospective architects should contact the Architects Registration Board.

> **66** The university course is exempt from Professional and Linguistic Assessment Board by the General Medical Council (find out more at www.gmc-uk.org). While it will be very competitive, it should be fairly easy for British nationals to come and work in the UK.**99**
>
> *Shakeel Shahid, Palacky University, Czech Republic*

The National Contact Point for Professional Qualifications in the UK (UKNCP) (www.ecctis.co.uk/uk%20ncp) aids the mobility of professionals across Europe. If you return to the UK with a professional qualification, UKNCP can advise you on regulations in your profession and outline the steps you will need to take before finding employment. They can also link you to the relevant authorities in other countries across Europe. To find professional bodies outside Europe, you should speak to your overseas university's careers service.

UK-regulated professions and contact details for the professional bodies can be found on the UKNCP website. These bodies should have clear guidelines on acceptable qualifications. Check before you go and then keep checking as you continue your studies. There is a risk that changes may be made to these guidelines while you are midway through your studies; some students have been affected in this way. Should this happen, there can be options for further study to make up any shortfall in knowledge or expertise.

Quality and reputation

One natural concern for many students is about the quality of the education they will receive overseas. The UK has its own systems for checking quality, but how can you be sure that international universities meet the same stringent standards? When you are making decisions from a distance, how can you be sure that your university even exists, let alone that it is a genuine provider of quality education?

There is money to be made from international students, so you need to be aware of potential scams and of discrepancies between what an institution says it will offer and what it actually delivers. You want to be sure that any money you spend is going towards a good-quality education that will deliver what you expect.

Use www.enic-naric.net to find a list of recognised universities from over 50 countries, as well as information on the various education systems. You can verify that your institution is recognised with education authorities or similar government bodies in your chosen country. Bear in mind that if you need to apply for a visa, there may well be a requirement that you are attending a recognised university. You are safer and better protected within an accredited and recognised university.

Ask your university about how it is inspected or checked for quality. Most countries will have national (or regional) organisations making sure that universities meet required standards. You may be able to read their inspection reports online. You can find further information on the quality assurance systems for higher education at www.enic-naric.net.

Using reliable and official websites, such as those included in this book, should help you to find your way to accredited and quality-assured universities. Use common sense when trawling through information and be suspicious of some of the following points:

- a purportedly official website full of errors, adverts or broken links
- an institution offering courses at rock-bottom prices
- if entry requirements are much lower than comparable institutions
- if you are being offered the chance to gain a qualification much more quickly than normal.

How to apply

Most countries don't have the equivalent of UCAS, a centralised admissions system, so give yourself time to fill out more than one application. You may have to apply on paper, rather than online, so allow time for the application to be delivered (and take copies, in case it gets lost in the post). Pay attention to the closing dates in Chapters 5 to 11, so you don't miss the chance to have your application considered.

Countries operating centralised applications include Denmark, Finland, the Netherlands, Sweden and (for some courses) Germany.

> **❝** The university application process was incredibly straightforward: a small entrance exam and a telephone interview.**❞**
>
> *Tudor Etchells, IE University, Spain*
>
> **❝** Studielink, Holland's equivalent of UCAS, is simple to navigate and free.**❞**
>
> *Simran Gill, Fontys University of Applied Sciences, the Netherlands*

There may be entrance exams and additional tests that you need to sit in order to be considered for a place. These might include the Scholastic Assessment Test (SAT), Graduate Record Exam (GRE) or Graduate Australian Medical Schools Admission Test (GAMSAT). If English is your first language and you will be studying in English, you are unlikely to be tested on your English-language skills. Check with your institution, or see Chapters 5 to 11 for more details. Once a place has been offered, and where fees are payable, you may then need to pay a deposit to secure your place.

Costs

Fees vary widely and depend on the country where you choose to study; where you are from; the type of institution you are attending; and the level of your course. In a number of countries within Europe, for example Denmark, Sweden and Germany, you will not be charged tuition fees if you are an EU citizen. Countries like France, Spain and Italy charge low fees.

> **❝** Among most EU countries, including Austria, Belgium (Flemish Community), the Czech Republic, Denmark, Estonia, Finland, France, Germany, Italy, the Netherlands, Poland, the Slovak Republic, Spain, Sweden and the United Kingdom, international students from other EU countries are treated as domestic students with respect to tuition fee charges. This is also true in Ireland, but only if the EU student has lived in Ireland for three out of the five previous years. **❞**
>
> *(OECD, Education at a Glance 2014)*

You'll need to bear in mind that although, within the EU, EU nationals tend to be treated the same as domestic nationals for fees' purposes, entitlement to student financial support for living costs does not have to be included.

Further afield, some countries, like Iceland, Japan and Korea, tend to charge the same fees for domestic and international students. Most countries will charge higher fees for international students than for domestic students. This list includes Australia, Canada, New Zealand (except on advanced research programmes), the Russian Federation, Turkey and the USA (see Chapter 6 for notable differences in the US system).

> Take out an International Student Identity Card (ISIC, www.isic. org) to enjoy student discounts and benefits across the world.

Fees are not the only consideration. Some countries have high fees, but extensive financial support systems (particularly for those with academic excellence or low-income background). Other countries have high fees but a lower cost of living. Some countries with a generally lower cost of living may still have variations within pricing, perhaps high prices for accommodation, internet access or even alcohol. If you had to pay three or four months' rent to secure accommodation, as you do in some countries, how would it affect your finances? Other costs include visas, travel and costs of application. Consider all these factors when calculating the cost of study and remember that exchange-rate fluctuations can have a great impact on any cost calculations.

Paying for your studies

One of the challenges for a student choosing to study overseas is how to fund it. With the exception of Scotland's Portability Pilot, the UK system of loans and grants can only be utilised in the UK. Although the terms of UK student loans are no longer as attractive as they once were, they do solve the problem of having to find the money to pay for tuition fees upfront.

Any financial support when studying overseas will need to come from:

- financial support from the host country
- scholarships
- savings
- earnings.

In most cases, international students have to fund themselves. Scholarships are often highly competitive. Jobs may be hard to come by, particularly if you don't yet speak the language, and some visas may restrict or deny you the opportunity to work. If you are applying for a visa, you are likely to have to prove that you have the necessary funds; you need to consider how you will fund yourself before you apply. See page 50 for information on visas.

Even if you are staying in the EU, it is recommended to have some money saved. Mark Huntington, of A Star Future, advises young people on overseas study. 'We recommend that even those who plan to work while abroad should have at least a semester's worth of living expenses covered before they go.'

Whilst those living costs and tuition fees might not always be as high as they are in the UK, they still have to be paid for. International students often use a combination of sources to pay for their studies: savings or personal loans, income from work, and scholarships.

Financial support from the host country

In EU countries, ask the Ministry of Education or your chosen institution about any opportunities for grants, loans or other benefits to students. In the Netherlands, for example, there are loans that UK students can access. In some countries, fees may include a free or discounted travel pass or free language lessons.

Scholarships

Scholarships are available, although competition can be fierce. Scholarship funding tends to be more widely available for postgraduate rather than undergraduate study. You should apply early, often a year in advance, following all instructions to the letter. Bear in mind that many applicants are unsuccessful in gaining scholarships and, even if you are successful, many scholarships do not cover the full costs of study, so consider how you will cover any shortfall.

The Ministry of Education or embassy should have information
about government scholarships, while your institution is the
best source of information for local sources of funding. See
Chapters 5 to 11 for more information. You can also search for
scholarships through websites like www.scholarshipportal.eu,
www.hotcoursesabroad.com/study/international-scholarships.html
and www.iefa.org.

Other sources of funding include:

- US-UK Fulbright Commission: www.fulbright.org.uk
- Marie Curie scheme (EU doctoral students): www.ukro.
  ac.uk/mariecurie/Pages/index.aspx
- Commonwealth Scholarships: http://cscuk.dfid.gov.uk/
  apply/scholarships-uk-citizens
- The Leverhulme Trust: www.leverhulme.ac.uk/funding/
  funding.cfm
- UK Research Council: www.rcuk.ac.uk
- UNESCO Fellowships: www.unesco.org/new/en/
  fellowships

Charities and trusts

In the UK, a range of charities and trusts offer funding in various
amounts. Each has their own eligibility criteria, deadlines and
application procedures. You could start with the Educational
Grants Services, search at www.family-action.org.uk/what-we-do/
grants.

If you are looking for postgraduate funding, approach your
university, which should have a copy of the Grants Register, a
worldwide guide to postgraduate funding. Alternatively, try the
online search at: www.prospects.ac.uk/funding_postgraduate_
study.htm.

The Association of Charitable Foundations (www.acf.org.uk/seekingfunding) has a useful guide to applying to charitable trusts and foundations.

Career development loans

If you are studying overseas because your course is not available closer to home and you intend to return to the UK, EU or EEA to work after your studies, it may be possible to get a Professional and Career Development loan. Your institution overseas will need to register your chosen course with the Skills Funding Agency in the UK before you can apply for your loan, unless they have already done so for another student. Repayments start once you complete your course, regardless of your situation. You can borrow up to £10,000 for up to two years of study, so it would be more appropriate for postgraduate students. For more information, go to www.gov.uk/career-development-loans/overview.

Life overseas

Whether you will be 100 or 10,000 miles away from home, it is important to know that you will be supported. Finding out the basics before you go can help to ease the adjustment process. Who's going to be there to help you out? What are the essentials you need to know about moving and living overseas?

Support available

The international office at your chosen university is likely to be your first, and probably your best, source of support throughout the process: from when and how to apply for a visa to finding the cheapest place to buy groceries. They should support you throughout the research and application process and will also be there for you once you arrive.

> **❝** Every question under the sun was answered by email, with quick replies. The admissions department are great. Also, upon arrival at an open day, I was welcomed with open arms, despite arriving four hours late!**❞**
>
> *Jacob Matthias Kummer, IE University, Spain*

> **❝** I received a lot of key information and support via email. I received a list of books and resources that I had to buy as well as details of where to buy them. I was sent an online orientation module to complete and this was very helpful as it included local transport and how to access your timetables and accommodation.**❞**
>
> *Anwar Hussain Nadat, University of Auckland, New Zealand*

In addition to the support from your international office and your department, making friends with other students makes settling in a lot easier and also provides a source of much-needed support. Orientation week, welcome week, *nollning* or frosh week activities can be a great place to start meeting new friends. In the UK, we know it as freshers' week, but different countries have their own names and their own traditions.

Your university might offer special activities and events to help you meet students from across the world. Try to take the opportunity to meet domestic students as well as international students; local students will give you a different perspective on life and culture in their home country; they will also have more insight into where to go, where to shop and what not to miss. International friendships are important too and may help to ease your homesickness and culture shock, as you see other people adjusting to their new environment.

> ❝ The university organises a buddy system for your arrival. They pick you up from the airport and help you move into your accommodation, and after that, they introduce you to people and help you to settle in to life in Denmark. My buddy has been one of my best friends since the day we met; the university matched us up really well. She was my shoulder to cry on when I got homesick at the very beginning!❞
>
> *Hannah Burrows, University of Southern Denmark*

There will normally be a team of staff to support you at university; this team might include careers advisers, counsellors and welfare officers. Support will vary from country to country and between institutions. If you have a disability, a learning difficulty or any health problems, you should discuss these with your university before you apply, to ensure that they can adequately support you.

Getting a visa

If you are studying outside Europe, you are likely to need a visa. You can apply for a visa once you have the offer of a place. Use the services of your university to support you through this part of the process; if they recruit lots of international students, they should be experienced at easing people through. They will also understand the reasons why some people are declined, so follow their advice. If you can't get this type of support from your university, you should speak to the embassy or High Commission.

In many cases, visas are declined because of lack of correct evidence or because of insufficient finances; in other cases, if the immigration office doesn't believe that you are a genuine student and that you intend to return home afterwards. Never lie or falsify information on a visa application; if discovered, your application will be declined and future attempts to apply will be affected. Some health conditions (TB, for example) and key criminal convictions (violent offences or drugs charges, for example) can also affect your chances.

Visa applications can be complex, but it is essential to follow each step to the letter, ensuring that you provide all the evidence required.

> 66 The process of applying for a visa was quick, but a little bit complicated. Firstly you must register and complete a form on the federal police's website before booking an appointment at the consulate. Unfortunately, my university acceptance letter was caught in a postal strike so I was rather delayed in getting documents sorted, but once I got to the consulate they were friendly and helpful and the whole process took well under a week from giving them my passport to receiving my visa. 99
>
> *Justin Axel-Berg, University of São Paulo, Brazil*

Registering within Europe

Although the EU allows its citizens free movement, there may be some red tape to go through when you first move to another European country. In many cases, EU citizens have to register with a local government office. Normally you should do this within the first week or two of arrival. Your university will explain what you need to do.

> **❝** My application for foreign residency, which is
> necessary after three months of living here, was all
> sorted by the university.**❞**
>
> *Jacob Matthias Kummer, IE University, Spain*

EU countries

Austria, Belgium, Bulgaria, Croatia, Republic of Cyprus, Czech Republic, Denmark, Estonia, Finland, France, Germany, Greece, Hungary, Ireland, Italy, Latvia, Lithuania, Luxembourg, Malta, the Netherlands, Poland, Portugal, Romania, Slovakia, Slovenia, Spain, Sweden, UK.

EEA countries

The EEA is made up of the all the countries in the EU plus Iceland, Liechtenstein and Norway. Although not within the EEA, Switzerland offers some rights to EEA citizens.

Accommodation

Safe and acceptable accommodation is essential to enable you to settle in and start adjusting to life overseas. The good news is that most universities with international students do their utmost to place them in suitable housing, often giving them priority. To enhance your chances of finding accommodation, remember to:

- apply well in advance
- be realistic about the rent you are prepared to pay
- be flexible about where you are prepared to live.

Most students want good quality, affordable accommodation in a convenient location; you may find that there is not enough to go round, so it is worth considering what you are prepared to compromise on.

Types of student accommodation

If you're counting on university-run halls of residence, you may be surprised; some countries don't offer this option for accommodation. Some universities have campus-based halls run by private companies, while others have no accommodation at all. Alternatives on offer include temporary or short-term accommodation, rental property or home-stay with a local host family.

> **❝** The university cannot guarantee accommodation because of the size of the student body, but private sector provision is excellent and catered towards students in either 'republicas' (shared houses) or individual kitchenettes or studio flats both next to the campus and further into the city. It'll be very hard to sort anything out before you arrive though, so plan on starting in a hostel for a couple of weeks.**❞**
>
> *Justin Axel-Berg, University of São Paulo, Brazil*
>
> **❝** The university provided a database for housing and the opportunity to apply for halls. Whilst halls primarily go to undergraduates, there is always a chance for postgraduate students. Housing in Leuven is a mixture of studios, rooms and shared apartments. The database is made up of registered landlords who sign up to a university-drafted contract, giving you full support if anything was to go wrong.**❞**
>
> *Tom Aitchison, KU Leuven, Belgium*

Finding accommodation from the UK

In some university towns there is a shortage of student accommodation, so some international students, particularly late applicants, find themselves in the position of leaving the UK without long-term accommodation. Arranging private accommodation from a distance can be risky. You shouldn't pay a deposit to a private landlord for unseen property.

Seek the advice of your university's international or accommodation office on the safest options when finding accommodation from the UK. They might discuss reputable short-term options with you, perhaps bed and breakfast, a local hostel or home-stay. Home-stay involves living with a local family; it can be a great way to give you time to adjust and help you to learn about life in your chosen country, as well as boosting your language skills. Securing short-term accommodation like this should then give you time to find suitable longer-term accommodation when you get there.

Check what's included

Whichever accommodation option you choose, remember to clarify what will and won't be included in your rent (water, electricity, gas, any kind of local rates, internet) and factor in travel costs; that way you can make a more meaningful comparison between properties. Check whether you will need to buy things like cooking utensils and bedding when you get there.

Practicalities

As you prepare to make the big move, you're going to need to know about the cheapest ways to phone home; how to open a bank account; how to navigate the area by public transport; the system for paying tax on your earnings; and much more. Talk to your university's international office or check out expat websites like Just Landed, www.justlanded.com. You can also ask questions on online message boards for prospective students, some of which are filled with information about accommodation, buying bikes and so on.

Once you arrive, you can start to use the network of friends that you make. This is where the local students, and those who've already studied there for a while, become invaluable. Most people are more than happy to help.

Insurance: health and belongings

It is important to make sure that you and your belongings are adequately insured from the time you leave the UK until your return.

If you are studying within the EEA or Switzerland, take out a European Health Insurance Card or EHIC. It is free and easily obtainable, normally arriving within seven days of application. It entitles you to the same treatment as a resident of the host country, but doesn't cover additional costs, like ongoing treatment or returning you to the UK in the event of an accident (www.ehic.org.uk). Conditions vary depending on your country of study, so be sure to check any time limits or restrictions carefully on the EHIC country-by-country guide.

You will need to take out additional insurance for travel and health to cover you whilst you are away. A number of UK providers offer study-abroad insurance policies, including Endsleigh (www.endsleigh.co.uk/personal/travel-insurance/study-abroad-insurance) and STA Travel (www.statravel.co.uk/travel-insurance.htm). Alternatively, you could take out a policy in your host country. If you are working alongside your studies you may be required to purchase additional insurance to cover you. Your international office should be able to advise you further.

There may be vaccinations or preventive measures, like malaria tablets, that you need to take before you travel. Talk to your GP and see the Travel Health pages of the Foreign and Commonwealth Office (www.fco.gov.uk). You may need to demonstrate that you are fit and well in order to gain a visa; this may involve a medical examination.

> **❝** Our school provided us with health insurance policies in both Singapore and Sydney. In Sydney it was mandatory to have health insurance to get the visa. **❞**
>
> *Joshua Jackson, SP Jain School of Global Management, Singapore and Australia*

Personal safety

Although studying abroad is not, in itself, a dangerous activity, visiting different countries carries different risks. The Foreign and Commonwealth Office has useful information for Britons travelling and living overseas, including travel advice by country. Find out about safety and security, health issues, local laws and customs or natural disasters before you go. The Foreign and Commonwealth Office also has a useful travel checklist to follow: see www.gov.uk/foreign-travel-checklist.

Follow the advice of your international office; they have a vested interest in keeping you safe and have an understanding of the risks in the local area. However, you do have to take responsibility for your own safety, much as you would if you were leaving home to study in the UK.

> ❝ Pickpocketing, having food stolen while on a train and witnessing mass brawls have all occurred in the two years I have spent in China. However, providing you are aware of risks and use some common sense you should be fine. On the whole, China is probably the country that I have felt safest in for travelling, living and walking home late at night. ❞
>
> *Lewis McCarthy, University of Shanghai Jiao Tong, China*

> ❝ Despite São Paulo's violent reputation, it's really quite a safe place. I've lived here for three years now, travelling all over the city at all times of night and day and never come to harm anywhere. ❞
>
> *Justin Axel-Berg, University of São Paulo, Brazil*

According to a 2012 British Council survey of students from over 80 countries, some of the safest places to study include Canada, USA, Germany, New Zealand and Singapore.

Top tips for staying safe include the following.

- Get to know your local area.
- Don't flash valuables and cash.
- Drink sensibly.
- Don't take unnecessary risks.
- Stay alert.
- Tell people where you are going.
- Keep in contact.

Language and cultural issues

However much you prepare yourself and find out about what to expect, there are going to be some adjustments to make when you move abroad. Differences in language, lifestyle, culture and cuisine may bring unexpected challenges.

> ❝ Embrace the lifestyle and culture. Live it. I admit I take a fair few siestas here in Spain and have whole meals of tapas! ❞
>
> *Tudor Etchells, IE University, Spain*

> ❝ The lifestyle in Singapore is very metropolitan, busy, and Asian; they are more traditional, hierarchical and family oriented. It is definitely a hybrid between typical Western and Eastern lifestyles, a good stepping stone between England and Malaysia, for example. ❞
>
> *Joshua Jackson, SP Jain School of Global Management, Singapore and Australia*

Culture shock is a common side effect of spending time overseas, away from family, friends and the ease of your own culture. It takes time to adjust and you will need to be open-minded and flexible as you get used to the changes a new country brings.

Your university will provide orientation events to help you to adjust and make new friends. Most universities have a range of support services (student welfare staff, counsellors, health professionals and so on) to help you if you find the adjustment process particularly challenging. If you look after yourself, by eating well, taking exercise and sleeping well, you will feel in a stronger position to tackle any challenges.

Other tips to help you deal with culture shock include the following.

- Keep in touch with family and friends back home.
- Get involved with familiar activities, like sports or cultural activities you enjoy.
- Display personal items and mementoes to make your room feel homely.
- Make an effort to meet other international students, who may be feeling like you.
- Get to know students from the host country so you can find out about your new home.

Staying on after study

After spending three or four years in your host country, you may start to wonder whether you want to return to grey old Britain. So which countries offer the most attractive welcome for students who want to stay on? Canada, Australia and New Zealand give extra points in their immigration system to students who have studied at their universities; this can make it easier to apply to stay on for work or even permanently. In many other countries, working-visa and temporary-residence systems have been simplified for international students; you may find that you have the right to stay on and work for a period of time, for example.

Other options that can aid integration include opportunities to learn the local language, work permits and internship opportunities. See the 'Studying in . . .' chapters for more information on staying on after study.

Returning to the UK

Coming back to the UK after your new experiences is not always as positive as you might anticipate. Reverse culture shock can be an unexpected side effect of spending time away. It can impact on the way you relate to friends and family and affect the way you adjust back to life at home. Try to remember how you managed to adjust to your new life overseas; you may well need to use these same skills to adjust to your return. Don't assume that returning home will be seamless; allow yourself time to come to terms with the changes.

You will need to consider how to highlight the benefits of your experience and how to sell yourself to potential employers (or educational establishments). Think about how you might articulate what you can now offer an employer, what you have learned and the skills you have developed. Consider how you could explain to an employer the type of institution you attended and how your degree compares to those on offer in the UK (or your chosen destination country). You can work with your university's careers service to prepare for this long before you leave university. Use their support to search for job vacancies and other schemes for graduates or postgraduates. Make sure that you get hold of references from teaching staff and from employers; it is much easier to do this before you leave.

There will be some loose ends to tie up before you leave, such as giving notice to your landlord, notifying your utilities' suppliers and reclaiming any deposits you have paid. Let your bank know that you are leaving and close your account; this might take a couple of weeks to finalise.

A break in residency?

If you return to the UK having been overseas for several years, this could be considered to be a break in UK residency, which can prevent you from accessing certain services like education and benefits on your return. However, if your departure is considered to be temporary and if you maintain strong links or a base in the UK, your break may be considered a temporary absence. Advice centres, like Citizens Advice Bureau (www.citizensadvice.org.uk), will be able to advise further, as this can be a complicated subject with legal implications.

Tax

Whether your absence is considered temporary or not will also affect the tax you will need to pay. If you leave the UK permanently and are not classed as a UK resident, then, on your return, you only pay UK tax on UK income. If you are returning after a temporary period of absence (the more likely scenario if you are only going for the purposes of study), you may have to pay UK tax on some foreign income if you bring it with you to the UK; this doesn't include income from employment but might include income from things like investments. Some countries have treaties preventing the need to pay double tax. This information can be complex and is subject to change, so you should make contact with HM Revenue and Customs at www.hmrc.gov.uk for current information.

You are also likely to be taxed by your host country on any money earned whilst overseas. To find out the rules on tax and whether you should be paying it, talk to your overseas university; they should be able to direct you to any specialist advice you need.

Support and networking after you leave

If you want to keep in touch with your wider network of friends from university, you could join an alumni organisation. This should also keep you up to date with events and developments. Other university services may still be available to you after you leave, including careers services.

Student story
Shakeel Shahid, Palacky University, Czech Republic

The challenge of getting into medicine in the UK, as well as the cost, led Shakeel Shahid to the Czech Republic. 'I just wanted to do medicine, regardless of location. There aren't a lot of opportunities for someone who has already obtained a degree to get into a medicine programme either, which makes it even harder for someone who is either thinking of a career change, such as myself, or someone who was either not able to get into medicine directly after their A levels.

'I decided on Palacky University mainly due to good reviews from people who had already attended the university. Before I applied, I talked to students who had attended this university, and their reviews were very good compared to other places I had looked at such as Romania or Italy.

'The university staff at Palacky are very helpful and prompt in answering questions. It is located in a university town, so it's an ideal location in terms of settling down and getting used to living in a foreign place. It's also only a couple of hours flight from Manchester and London.

'The cost of living is significantly cheaper than the UK. Food, transport and even the accommodation is cheaper than what I would pay in the UK. For example, I was paying £6,000 a year for student accommodation in UK, but here I am paying £2,400, including rent, utilities and very fast internet. Food costs for me in the UK were £200 a month, and now it's half that for two people in Czech Republic where I live with my brother.

'The fees, however, are £9,000, just like the UK. For students wanting to go to somewhere cheap, but decent, Romania is another option.

'The application process was very smooth. The staff were very helpful and made the process easier. Of course, it's nothing like UCAS. You have to be bit more proactive here. You have to keep in contact with the university staff in terms of following up on your application and learning about any deadlines and any required documents.

'Before arrival, the university gave us directions to the city from Prague, and then explained how to find the university in the city itself. When it came to things that were required, like books, the university did tell us about it, but I felt like it was at the last moment. I would have preferred it if they'd let us know that information earlier so I could have been more prepared.

'Since I've been here, one good thing is that the students that are already studying here are very helpful, so I haven't found the need to ask much of the university staff.

'Other than moving to a new place, and all the apprehensions and stresses that come with it, there haven't been any difficulties. You are so caught up in the work right away that you don't really have time to think about any difficulties.

'The education is not that difficult, but the teaching it is very different because English is not everyone's first language. The dates of the exams are not set. They are taken orally, which is very different from the UK. There are tests that have to be taken every week, in order to sit the final examination. So we have to work every single day ensuring we keep up. There is no respite!'

Shakeel's top tips

Accommodation

'University accommodation rooms are usually shared with someone else but you can ask the university in advance if you want to share your room with a friend. If you want to rent your own flat, you can easily find good quality accommodation in the city centre for around £448 for two people, including bills and utilities. But you have to be very proactive and confident, because people here don't always know much English, and you have to make sure that you're very careful in checking out the accommodation because all the agreements are in the local language. It's better to take someone who knows the language to help you out when signing the contract.'

Food

'There are high quality restaurants if you're into dining. There are all kinds of cuisines here, like Italian, Chinese or Mexican. You can always try out the local food as well. There are a lot of grocery stores, including a Tesco. Groceries are very cheap here.'

Living costs

'Make sure you keep a record of your spending, that way you can keep track of costs and not waste money. If you spend sensibly the monthly costs are not that high – £100 for two people in my experience so far.'

Working while studying

'Unless you know the local language really well, there is no point working. And even if you know the language you won't have any time to work because of the workload.'

Making friends

'Join Facebook groups. Get to know the people that are going to start with you. You can get to know a lot of people even before you arrive in the country. Living in the university accommodation helps making friends easier than living in private. But, from personal experience, you have to be confident and talk to people. It's not really hard making new friends as everyone else is in the same boat as you so you find a lot in common. A lot of the older students will volunteer to help you around in the city, so take that opportunity to meet new people.'

Lifestyle and culture

'The people are extremely friendly. Everyone is very respectful of other cultures, and it's a very Christian but secular city at the same time.'

Travel and transport

'Trains and taxis are extremely cheap here. For travel within the city it's advisable to get a tram card. It's about £7 for three months.'

Options for after you finish your studies

'If you really like the place, you can always stay here. But for British students, it's very easy to go back to the UK. The university course is exempt from PLAB by the General Medical Council (find out more at www.gmc-uk.org). While it will be very competitive, it should be fairly easy for British nationals to come and work in the UK. I plan to go back to the UK and finish my Foundation training there.'

In addition to the opportunity to study medicine, Shakeel has experienced a number of benefits of studying abroad. 'You get to meet a lot of different people from other countries that you would not otherwise meet. You get to learn a new language. You get to experience a new culture. You get to travel. And living on your own for five years is a very good life learning experience.'

Palacky University (www.medicineinolomouc.com) is one of a number of European universities offering degrees in medicine and dentistry taught in English.

University of Twente: Profile

General information

The University of Twente has over the past 50 years grown to become one of the world's leading universities. Consistently, the institution features in the QS World University Rankings top establishments. Twente specialises in developing cutting-edge technologies to positively impact society – 'high tech, with a human touch'. 9,500 students a year are drawn to study at Twente for its world-class facilities, academic rigour, social and sporting atmosphere and the price – in contrast to other countries fees per year are approximately €1,950.

But, it is the university's interdisciplinary approach and social consciousness that makes it different. Courses combine fascinating scientific exploration with behavioural research, social sciences and economics. To this end, the university hopes to inspire responsible and cooperative leaders who will solve the most pressing human and environmental challenges.

A student city to call home

Enschede just wouldn't be the same without its students. Hardly surprising when you consider that almost a third of the town's 157,000 inhabitants are living the student life. This border town is home to no less than three higher education institutions: the University of Twente, Saxion University of Applied Sciences and the ArtEZ Institute of the Arts. The centre of student life is undoubtedly the University of Twente campus, with its modern buildings, laboratories, student residences, sports centres, bars, restaurants and theatre. Here you can hear languages from all over the world but settling in and making new friends couldn't be easier thanks to the university's compact layout and the wide range of leisure activities on offer in the city.

Bachelor of science degree programmes

The University of Twente offers 20 Bachelor's programmes in fields ranging from engineering and natural sciences to behavioural and management sciences. Each of our English-taught Bachelor's degree programmes is accredited by the Accreditation Organization of the Netherlands and Flanders; on graduation, students are entitled to calling themselves Bachelor of Science. The Netherlands enjoys international acclaim for its problem-based learning methods, for training students to analyse and solve practical problems independently, and for emphasising self-study and self-discipline. By emphasising these principles, we will give the students the best possible preparation for a challenging and exciting career.

Project-based education

The so-called Twente Educational Model of the University of Twente offers an innovative approach to academic training. It is all about challenging students to get the best out of themselves. The academic year is divided into modules of ten weeks each. In each module, all of the classes, practical assignments and projects are centered on a single theme. In projects, students are challenged to use their knowledge for solving real problems, often related to current issues. It is a great way of making sure students have acquired all the necessary knowledge related to that particular theme. The themes in the programmes usually touch on a range of different disciplines. The advantage is that students get a broad foundation and will be able to operate successfully in a lot of different fields later.

English-Taught Bachelor of science programmes

University College Twente
Technology and Liberal Arts & Sciences (ATLAS)

ATLAS is the only Honours Bachelor's programme in the Netherlands that combines Technology with Liberal education. It takes a revolutionary approach to engineering education aspired to educate different kind of engineers and global citizens who are capable of addressing global challenges and designing solutions in a wide range of social, cultural and political contexts.

Unlike other Liberal Arts colleges, ATLAS has a unique technological profile. Drawing from a diversity of academic fields – from psychology and politics to engineering and physics – our curriculums are cantered on real-life themes and project-based education. Moreover, a part of your curriculum is a 'personal pursuit' that focuses on developing your personal interest:

music, sports, a second language, development work or attending an international summer school. As a result, you will acquire a solid foundation in both engineering and social science concepts, as well as develop your creativity, flexibility, leadership and communication skills to become an academic all-rounder.

Our aim at ATLAS is, therefore, not just to deliver academic champions, but influencers, leaders, drivers of change – holistic problem solvers, who understand what society needs and can bring about the kind of change that will make the world a better place. Besides, with an ATLAS BSc. Honours degree you will be eligible for prestigious technical or social science Master's programmes in the Netherlands or abroad.

Advanced Technology

Advanced Technology is a one-of-a-kind programme, taught only at the University of Twente. It is a broad technical Bachelor's programme that is finely tuned to society's needs. Its multidisciplinary approach combines different engineering and natural science disciplines, giving you the scope to come up with innovative and unexpected solutions to new problems without being confined to a single area of science. An internationally recognised Bachelor's degree in Advanced Technology is an excellent preparation for a number of different Master's degrees at the University of Twente or other universities in the Netherlands or abroad.

Electrical Engineering

This programme focuses on developing and improving electronics-based systems. Electrical Engineering teaches you how modern technology works and how to use it to improve, accelerate or scale down electronics-based systems. Your work will result in high-tech applications that are based on nanotechnology, device physics, robotics, electronics and communication technology. The specific developments we work on include lab-on-a-chip technology, methods for producing faster and better computers, more energy-efficient cars and batteries, a chip-based pregnancy test and communication sensors. As an Electrical Engineer, you are highly employable and able to apply your knowledge and skills in almost all technological areas.

Creative Technology

How can you use cutting-edge technology or new media to create user interaction? This programme challenges you to develop innovative applications using the latest technology. You will learn to adapt state-of-the-art technology or new media in an original and appealing way to create interaction with or between users. You will work on applications that make life healthier, easier and more fun. Think of a staircase that is so inviting that people would prefer taking it rather than using the escalator. You will distinguish yourself through your technical expertise, knowledge of design, creative processes and how technology affects human beings.

European Public Administration

This programme combines European Studies and Public Administration to help you study the causes of and solutions to complex problems on a local, national, European and global level.

We will give you a solid foundation in economics, political science, sociology and law, while equipping you with an awareness of policy and public management. Building on this, you will go on to specialise in European Studies, Public Administration or both.

Your knowledge of both national and international governance will make you an ideal candidate for jobs in national and international government, public sector organisations and consultancy firms.

International Business Administration

This programme gives you the practical and theoretical knowledge about business strategies you'll need for a successful career in our complex and demanding globalised world.

You will receive a solid theoretical grounding in finance, human resource management, procurement, corporate strategy & development and marketing.

You will devise solutions, develop entrepreneurial skills and work on cases for real companies, gaining invaluable work experience while studying for your Bachelor's degree.

Upon completion of the programme you might go to work for a major multinational, a consultancy or a trade union, or go on to pursue a Master's degree.

Contact details:

www.utwente.nl/go/dutch-bachelor

Please note that some Bachelor of science degree programmes are currently taught in Dutch. In the future all our programmes will be taught in English. Please keep an eye on our website: www.utwente.nl/go/ce-en for up-to-date information.

Chapter 3
Alternative options

If you feel that a full degree overseas is not right for you, you need not necessarily rule out all of the benefits of education outside your home country. Whatever the reasons swaying you against taking a full degree abroad, there may be an alternative choice for you to consider.

'I don't feel ready to take my full degree overseas'

Studying for a full degree overseas is a big step, but have you considered taking part of your UK degree course overseas instead? There are a range of schemes offering you the chance to study abroad without always lengthening your degree; some of these choices even bring their own financial benefits.

> **❝** I love to travel and I have always wanted to see the world. I chose my university partly based on whether they offered study abroad or exchange opportunities as I knew that I would like to go abroad for part of my degree. I enjoy experiencing new cultures and going to new places, and studying overseas just makes it convenient. **❞**
>
> *Angela Minvalla, exchange student at*
> *RMIT University, Australia*

As you research UK universities, look into the types of study-abroad option they offer. Perhaps you like the look of the University of Bath's BSc Chemistry, which features a year in Europe, North America, Asia, Australia or New Zealand; BA Economics at Durham University with the option of a year in a selection of countries including South Korea; or maybe LLB European Law at the University of Warwick with a year in France or Germany. It is important to find out whether your degree course will be lengthened by this experience and which years of study count towards your final degree classification.

More and more UK universities now have overseas campuses offering courses taught in English and mirroring some of the courses available back in the UK. The latest figures from the UK Higher Education International Unit suggest that around half a million students are studying for a UK degree overseas. These campuses are often set up to attract international students, but an added benefit for UK students could be the chance to study for a semester or a year at the international campus.

Check out which courses and in which countries you can study this way. University College London (UCL) has campuses in Qatar and Australia, while Newcastle University, University of Southampton and University of Reading all have a presence in EduCity, Malaysia. The University of Nottingham, University of Central Lancashire and Heriot-Watt University have a number of campuses overseas. The UK government is keen to see UK universities establish teaching outposts abroad, so there may be even more choice for UK students in the future.

If you prefer the familiarity of a UK university name on your degree certificate, you could always opt for a full degree course at a UK overseas campus. Fees might be the same or a little lower than you'd expect at home, but the costs of living are often considerably less. In some cases, you might even gain a degree from the UK and from the country you will be studying in.

> **❝** My tutor at University of Birmingham will come out to visit after a few months to see if we are happy with the work and our lifestyles. He also asks for a summary update every couple of months. **❞**
>
> *Madeleine Prince, Cawthron Institute*
> *(professional placement abroad), New Zealand*

What will I pay?

If you are studying overseas for part of your course, you will often continue to pay tuition fees to your university at home, rather than to your overseas university. If you choose to spend a year at certain US universities, for example, this may mean studying at a fraction of the full cost of tuition. If you are studying for a full year overseas, your UK tuition fees should be reduced. The rules vary from country to country, with a maximum of 15% charged in England and a percentage payable in Wales, Scotland and Northern Ireland. Your UK university will be able to tell you more.

You will still be able to access the normal UK system of grants and loans, with a higher overseas rate of loan for living costs available. In some cases, you may be able to apply for a travel grant to assist with the costs of travel, medical insurance, visas and so on. There may be additional bursaries or scholarships which you can apply for. For example, the British Universities Translatlantic Exchange Association (BUTEX) offers awards to students studying in the USA or Canada for at least one semester, www.butex.ac.uk. Third Year Abroad suggests some other sources of funding: www.thirdyearabroad.com/before-you-go/money-matters.

Find out more from your UK university or from your national organisation for student finance:

- Student Finance England (www.gov.uk/student-finance/overview)
- Student Awards Agency for Scotland (www.saas.gov.uk)
- Student Finance Wales (www.studentfinancewales.co.uk)
- Student Finance NI (www.studentfinanceni.co.uk).

> **66** As tuition in Scotland is free, the cost of tuition on my year abroad was covered by the Scottish government. Living costs proved to be far less expensive in the south, so the only real expense was the flights (as well as all the travelling I did in the USA). **99**
>
> *Rosie Hodgart, University of South Carolina (exchange), USA*

If you are studying outside Europe, you are still likely to need a visa in the same way as if you were taking your full degree course; your university will be able to get you started with this process.

With these options, you can gain a degree from a familiar university along with the benefits of international experience, but without so many of the risks. You may get some financial support throughout the process, with the benefit of personal support from both institutions too. It should be reasonably straightforward to transfer any credits achieved internationally back to the UK; your university should have planned for this to happen.

Erasmus

Through the European Union Erasmus scheme, you have the opportunity to study in another European country for between three and twelve months. This is completed as a part of your course, so counts towards your degree.

You will receive an Erasmus grant to put towards the additional costs of studying abroad, but you will still be expected to fund your own living costs. For 2014/2015, an Erasmus grant of €350–€400 (£259–£296) per month is available.

You will not be expected to pay fees to your host university and shouldn't have to pay more than 50% of tuition fees back home. In some cases, if you opt for a full year overseas you won't pay tuition fees at all, although this ruling varies from year to year. Some universities offer additional bursaries to students opting for an Erasmus placement.

For more information, talk to your UK university's study-abroad or international office and go to www.britishcouncil.org/study-work-create/opportunity/study-abroad/erasmus and www.erasmusplus.org.uk.

The Erasmus+ Joint Master's degree scheme allows students to study joint programmes in multiple countries, some outside the EU, at postgraduate level. Scholarships are available. Find out more at www.erasmusplus.org.uk and www.britishcouncil.org/study-work-create/opportunity/study-abroad/erasmus-joint-masters-degree.

> **66** The Erasmus scheme is really big in Denmark – they have a market where previous international students sell their furniture or Danish-plug electronic items, and they organise trips to see tourist attractions around Denmark. **99**
>
> *Hannah Burrows, University of Southern Denmark*

English-language assistant

Once you have two years' worth of higher education under your belt, you could consider working as an English-language assistant. These opportunities are normally open to language students in the UK, giving them the chance to work in an overseas school for a year (and get paid).

You should pay reduced tuition fees to your UK institution, or sometimes no fees at all, and may qualify for the overseas rate of maintenance loan. If you choose to stay in the EU, these opportunities can attract Erasmus funding.

This option would lengthen your study by a year, but should give you some valuable experience of education and life overseas. Your university's study-abroad office should be able to tell you more. Third Year Abroad at www.thirdyearabroad.com has lots of useful information.

Short-term study overseas

Shorter options to study overseas include summer schools and short placements. You could spend a summer learning a language or testing out international education, to see if you are ready to commit to further study abroad. Check out the costs and visa requirements well in advance of making final arrangements.

Opportunities include:

- Study China: a two to three week programme for existing undergraduate or foundation-degree students, www.studychina.org.uk
- INTO China: Chinese language summer programmes, www.intohigher.com/china

- IAESTE: summer placements for full-time HE (Higher Education) science, technology and engineering students, www.iaeste.org/students
- pre-university summer schools at US universities like Harvard and Stanford, www.fulbright.org.uk
- short-term exchanges in the USA, www.educationusa. state.gov/your-5-steps-us-study

Talk to staff at the study-abroad office at your university to find out more.

'I want to gain a degree from an international university without leaving the UK'

There are a couple of choices if you want to gain an international degree from within the UK: either distance learning; or choosing a UK-based overseas university.

Distance learning

Online and distance learning is on the increase. With thousands of international universities offering degrees by distance learning, you need not set a foot out of the house to gain an international education. Of course, you will need to be disciplined and focused, and you won't gain the experience of living in another country, but you may end up with a degree from a top university at a fraction of the cost. It is worth noting that not all universities allow you to complete a full degree by distance education; they might offer blended learning, a combination of distance and face-to-face learning.

The benefits of distance learning are affordability, convenience, flexibility, choice and support (from tutors and classmates). On the other hand, you need to be truly disciplined and aware of the fact that you will lose the face-to-face interaction that you would get on campus. It can be more difficult to assess whether distance-learning providers are reliable, without a physical presence to assess them by.

How do I know that my distance-learning provider is genuine?

You need to be even more thorough when researching a distance-learning provider. See page 41 for some questions to ask of potential institutions. Remember, if it sounds too good to be true, it probably is.

There may be some warning signs to look out for when checking out a distance-learning institution's website. If the organisation only provides a PO Box address, if it has a similar name to other well-respected institutions or if you can gain a higher-education qualification purely on the basis of previous experience, you might need to dig a bit deeper to ascertain whether it is genuine and accredited.

You may find it easier to be sure of the provenance of your qualifications from a traditional university that happens to offer distance-learning courses. Many traditional, accredited universities across the world, and as many as 90% in the USA (according to EducationUSA), offer distance-learning provision. If the institution claims to be accredited, double-check this with the accrediting organisation. You can find out more at the Ministry of Education of the country you hope to gain your qualification from. Check out these websites too.

- International Council for Open and Distance Education (ICDE), www.icde.org
- Study Portals (search for a distance-learning course in Europe), www.distancelearningportal.com

- Distance Education Accrediting Commission (USA), www.deac.org/Student-Center/Directory-Of-Accredited-Institutions.aspx.

Free online international education is on the increase. Prestigious universities including Harvard and the Massachusetts Institute of Technology (MIT) have set up edX (www.edx.org), while Stanford, Princeton and others have set up Coursera (www.coursera.org). Both offer online and interactive learning and the chance to gain university credits with no entry requirements and currently with no fees. Although it might be a slow process to achieve all the credits needed for a bachelor's degree, it could give you the chance to experience US-style teaching and check out your interest in particular subjects.

UK-based overseas universities

Campuses for a number of overseas universities can be found in the UK, most commonly in London. A number of these are American universities, offering US degrees. Although these universities recruit students from all over the world, only a small percentage currently attend from within the UK. This may change, with the fee hike in parts of the UK now making the fees at these universities appear much more reasonable.

In the case of Richmond, the American International University in London, you can gain a dual degree from the UK and USA, while experiencing an international university and accessing the UK system of loans and grants. With undergraduate fees set at £7,900 for 2015–2016, costs are lower than most of the top UK universities although, as these are private institutions, your maximum tuition-fee loan will be capped at £6,000.

International universities with a campus in the UK include the following.

- Richmond, American International University
  www.richmond.ac.uk
- Hult International Business School
  www.hult.edu/en/locations/undergraduate/london
- Azad University, Oxford
  www.auox.org.uk
- Limkokwing University of Technology
  www.limkokwing.net/united_kingdom.

You can find out more about courses, fees and how to apply on their websites.

Student story
James Connington
University of Bonn, Germany
(exchange)

James Connington, a BA Geography student at University College London, first considered a study abroad programme for a change of scene. 'I viewed studying abroad as a chance to escape reality for a few months. I'd say it was the idea of a change of scenery that got me hooked, then all the other reasons started to pile up, such as experiencing a new culture, meeting people from all around the world and adding to my CV.'

He took advantage of his university's study abroad programme to spread his wings. 'I chose Germany for a few reasons. First of all (and by necessity for me), the University of Bonn offered the chance to study in English. German universities also have a great academic reputation, the quality of life is great and it provides a good base for travelling throughout Europe. I also knew that the majority of Germans can speak English, so I wouldn't have too many difficulties living here.

'I liked the chance to study Masters level modules before I had finished my BA, which seemed like something too good to pass up. Most of my courses are from an international MSc programme (MSc Geography of Environmental Risks and Human Security) organised in conjunction with the United Nations, which was a huge selling point. I've realised since being here that the opportunity to tackle a different system of learning should be a major selling point of any study abroad programme. It greatly increases your adaptability and challenges your own established ideas about how university should be "done".

'I pay normal home tuition fees; however, if I was here for my full degree (whether as an undergrad or on the MSc course), then I'd be paying no tuition fees at all! Most German universities have no tuition fees and a small semester fee, but the quality of education is directly comparable to the UK. The semester fee of 280 euro gives you unlimited travel (trains, trams and buses) in the whole of this state of Germany, and even lets you take a friend on evenings and weekends.'

James had no problems applying for his term abroad. 'The study abroad team told me everything I needed to do for the UCL application, basically answering questions about why I thought I should go and what I planned to get out of it. I had to get a couple of references and meet UCL's grade average requirement also (2:1 or above).

'The Geography department international coordinator at the University of Bonn was exceptionally helpful. She helped me out with module choices, the application to Bonn itself and answered any other questions that I had. The Studentenwerk (university accommodation) people also put up with rather a lot of emails from me, although in that case the language barrier made things a bit more difficult, as I had very specific questions. A lack of communication actually resulted in me not being able to get access to my room on my first night, and ending up in a hotel at my expense.

'There was a very well organised Erasmus welcome week for all departments, which was a great opportunity to meet new people. They took us through processes such as enrolment and how to use the library. We had tours of the university and our own departments, a quiz on German culture and a couple of nights out, ending with an ESN (Erasmus Student Network) party in a club on the Friday. Since then the ESN have arranged a weekly Stammtisch (informal gathering) at a bar in the city centre, multiple trips to other countries, as well as parties on nights such as Halloween. The institution has felt very inclusive and there are multiple people to ask questions or voice any concerns to. A lot of students get the option of having a German "student buddy" to help them adjust and many students have acquired a "tandem" partner, which is a form of language exchange.'

As he's studying within the EU, James didn't need a visa, but there were some formalities to take care of. 'I had to register with the city of Bonn within 7 days of arriving and get a proof of health insurance certificate to be able to enrol at the university.

'I've had relatively little contact with UCL since I've been here. I had to send back a confirmation of arrival form and let my tutor know how I'm getting on, but other than that they leave you to get to grips with your new environment. There were a lot of problems with the Erasmus grants however, due to the new Erasmus+ system, so most of my contact with UCL was with regard to that.'

There were some differences in teaching and learning that James had to get used to. 'In the UK I have been used to weekly lectures, long reading lists and tutorial or coursework essays, followed by end of year exams. Far more classes here take the form of classroom based seminars, with active discussion, group work and presentations, compared to the large group lectures I have been used to in the UK. In Germany there is much more emphasis on active participation in classes and discussions. The reading lists are shorter and you are told exactly what to read, as opposed to being given a large list and being expected to identify what you need. Discussions and classes are often based largely on the reading that you are expected to do in between each class, so active preparation for each class is essential, as there is far less room to hide compared to a large group lecture in the UK. Some lecturers have encouraged us to just focus on them speaking rather than taking endless notes, and far less people use a laptop to take notes during class than in the UK. I have also never had to present so frequently, which has been great as previously I have found getting up and talking in front of a group to be quite difficult. It is worth mentioning that if I was here taking undergraduate courses I would probably still be having some large group lectures.'

On the whole, the exchange has been a positive experience for James. 'I've had very few bad experiences and certainly no more than I might have had at home during the same time period. I did get an egg thrown in my face and the situation with my accommodation on my first night wasn't pleasant, but aside from a few embarrassing moments in shops and the odd angry bus driver, everything has gone pretty smoothly.'

James's top tips

Accommodation
'Do your research and try to find someone who has lived there before to talk to (Facebook groups exist for most halls). Try to get accommodation

sorted as early as possible; there were many other Erasmus students who had nothing arranged before coming to Bonn, who went through weeks of stressing and living in a hostel before finding anywhere.'

Food

'Don't be surprised if the choice isn't quite what you're used to. The UK is massively multicultural so we're used to cheap and readily available Indian, Thai or Chinese ingredients. In Germany the supermarkets seem very much geared towards German-style food for German people, and the foreign ingredients that are available cost a lot more, unless you go to a specialist shop. Trying new foods from both your host country and international friends is probably one of the best parts of studying abroad.'

Insurance

'Get some! You're at far more risk than you are at home, and there may be insurance requirements from your home/host institutions. Endsleigh offer a study abroad insurance package that lets you add exactly what items and cover you want and varies the price accordingly, which I highly recommend.'

Living costs

'You will spend more than you think! Having said that, food costs will feel fairly similar to home, and whether or not the rent is cheaper depends which city you're coming from in the UK and which you're going to abroad. Going from London to Bonn, rent seems exceptionally cheap.'

Financial support for study (loans, grants or scholarships)

'If you're on a term abroad you will still get your normal student loan, but you do need to let Student Finance England know that you're heading abroad, as it may change the amount you get. Sticking with Erasmus rather than looking further afield is by far the most affordable option. The Erasmus grant is a big bonus, although don't rely upon it to survive – my grant came in more than two months later than expected.'

Working while studying

'No Erasmus students I know are working whilst they are studying here, mostly due to the financial benefits I mentioned. For those on a full year abroad a job may make sense, but for those on a term abroad I would try to avoid it, as you already have a very limited amount of time to make the most of the experience. Working and saving the summer directly before you go is a much more sensible option.'

Making friends

'Be open-minded and say yes a lot. It's incredibly easy to make friends on study abroad programmes, as everyone is keen to meet people and you all have at least one thing in common. You will find yourself spending time with nationalities that you have never encountered before.

'The best form of cultural exchange I've found and a great way to make friends is through food. One of my most enjoyable experiences here so far has been a weekly dinner at my flat, with a varying group of people of different nationalities, where each week we cook food from a different country. Don't slip into the comfort zone of just spending time with other Brits.'

Lifestyle and culture

'You will find some aspects of your host country completely baffling, but just embrace them and get on with it. In Germany, people will wait for the green man before crossing the road even when there is absolutely no traffic in sight, but will happily barge in front of you in any form of queue. You often find there are genuine reasons for these cultural quirks and even if there aren't, it's part of their nationality identity, not yours. The best way to get yourself acquainted with the culture of your host nation is to speak to people. If you're not sure about something, then just ask someone. Things like being punctual, shops all closing on Sundays and being wary of how you approach certain historical topics are all important points to remember.'

Useful websites

'GoAbroad (www.goabroad.com) and Viveras (www.viveras.com), an Erasmus social network, are both useful tools. GoAbroad is very comprehensive and incorporates a program review function which provides great insight.'

James's experiences prove that international experience, no matter how short, can offer many benefits. 'Studying abroad genuinely provides you with useful skills that are much harder to attain at home. You will learn to work with people from varying cultures and backgrounds, many of whom won't speak English as a first language; you will become more adaptable and less flappable in the face of change or uncertainty; lastly you will become more open minded and dispel many of the international stereotypes you never realised weren't true.

'You end up with friends from all over the world and they are just as keen to learn about your culture as you are about theirs. I'm spending Christmas with a new Italian friend's family just outside of Turin. That kind of thing doesn't happen if you stay at home.'

James's future plan is to become a journalist and he's already making a great start by writing articles about his experiences in Bonn for the *Telegraph*.

University of Bonn (www3.uni-bonn.de/the-university) was founded nearly 200 years ago and is a top 200 university in the Times Higher Education World University Rankings 2014-2015.

HKU: Utrecht University of the Arts

The City of Utrecht is the fourth largest city in the Netherlands. HKU University of the Arts Utrecht is at the heart of Utrecht's cultural and student life. With over 4,000 students, HKU is one of the largest universities of art in Europe. HKU offers bachelor and master programmes and research degrees in fine art, design, media, games and interaction, music, theatre and arts management.

Courage is something HKU appreciates and fosters. The courage to keep a critical eye on the content and boundaries of your own work. What HKU asks of you is an explorative attitude, an enterprising spirit and the will to pursue your individual passion. HKU offers you the chance to discover and develop your talent.

As an HKU student, you are given the opportunity during your course to work on projects for customers in the work field. These may be commercial companies, non-profit organisations or cultural initiatives. That way, you learn hands on where your strengths lie and what you can offer the world as a designer, lecturer, producer or performer. HKU produces creative professionals and entrepreneurs with initiative who know where their chances lie, both nationally and internationally. HKU works with renowned art and cultural educational institutions all over the world, so you have a wide choice of opportunities for exploring international developments in your discipline.

It's important for you to learn to present your work in a professional setting. HKU has its own Academy Theatre, concert halls and an Academy Gallery in Utrecht's city centre. Experimenting in presenting your work in these venues during your course gives you the opportunity to evolve yourself into a professional.

www.hku.nl/english

University of Groningen

400 Years of Passion and Performance

Founded in 1614, the University of Groningen is one of the oldest universities in Europe. We offer over 100 degrees in English at undergraduate, graduate and PhD levels in virtually every field and belong to the Top 100 universities in the world.

The University is located in the heart of Groningen city: a true student city with a bustling reputation, while retaining a safe community character. With 1 in 4 of its inhabitants being a student and over half its population being under 35, Groningen is the youngest city in the Netherlands and completely catered to the student way of life.

Facts and figures

- 30,000 students
- 4,100 international students
- # 83 NY Times Employability Ranking
- # 117 Times Higher Education Ranking
- # 82 ARWU Ranking (Shanghai Ranking)
- # 90 QS World University Ranking
- 23 English-taught undergraduate degrees
- Over 100 English-taught graduate degrees

Fields of study

- Economics & Business
- Medical Sciences
- Life Sciences
- Sciences & Technologies
- Arts & Humanities
- Behavioural & Social Sciences
- Spatial Sciences

- Law
- Philosophy
- Spatial Sciences
- Theology and Religious Studies
- Liberal Arts and Sciences

Facilities

The **University Library** (UB) consists of one central library and seven faculty and institute libraries at various locations in Groningen. Together they contain a total of three million books and periodicals.

The **Student Service Centre** offers different kinds of support to (international) students.

- Open office hours for international students
- study support workshops and courses
- counselling & psychological support
- individual support for students with performance disabilities

Accommodation: in Groningen students live throughout the city and among the locals or 'Stadjers' as they call themselves. As such there is no campus or campus accommodation, but to help international students to find proper housing, the University of Groningen cooperates with the SSH, a provider of students accommodation for international students.

Student organisations: studying at the University of Groningen is more than just attending lectures and passing exams. Groningen is famous for its rich student life and there are many student associations you can take part in.

Student sports: Groningen has a wide variety of sports clubs, part of these are exclusively aimed at students.

Website: www.rug.nl
Online information pack: www.rugmagazine.nl

Facebook: /universityofgroningen
Twitter: /prospectivesRUG
Instagram: /universityofgroningen

Chapter 4

Researching your options

There are so many questions to ask about yourself, your chosen country and your chosen university before you even apply. In the early stages, it is even hard to know what those questions should be. If you thought that narrowing down your UCAS choices to five was tricky, imagine choosing from the whole world. If that all sounds like too much hard work, consider that somewhere out there may be the perfect course for you at the perfect price; it's got to be worth a little bit of work to find it.

Getting started

With almost the whole world to choose from, the first step should be to research the countries that you are interested in. The chapters on studying in various countries will give you an overview of the different education systems, costs and financial support, how to apply and the visa system. Each chapter will also feature the most useful and reliable websites where you can find out more. This should help you start to compare what is on offer and how it fits in with your plans.

Where to study

This book focuses on opportunities taught in English, so the
Republic of Ireland, USA, Canada, Australia and New Zealand
are likely to have the largest choice of courses. Many other
Commonwealth countries use English, including Singapore,
Malaysia and certain Caribbean, Pacific and African nations. Find
out more at the Association of Commonwealth Universities, www.
acu.ac.uk.

Universities in many overseas countries are now actively
recruiting UK students in a way that was unheard of only ten
years ago. Events like The Student World Fair feature university
exhibitors from all over the world, as far apart as Malaysia,
Grenada and Canada, all keen to attract UK students. You might
have seen the news stories about universities in the Netherlands,
in particular, and the increase in applications from UK students.
Although the introduction of courses taught in English was
originally aimed at international students from other countries,
many UK students are now starting to take advantage. Some
universities overseas have even started to teach all their courses in
English.

In a number of countries where English isn't widely spoken, the
government or the institutions are keen to recruit international
students so offer a high proportion of courses taught in English.
These countries include:

- the Netherlands
- Denmark
- Sweden
- Finland.

According to the OECD's Education at a Glance 2014, there will be some courses taught in English available in countries such as:

- Belgium (Flemish)
- the Czech Republic
- France
- Germany
- Hungary
- Iceland
- Japan
- Korea
- Norway
- Poland
- Portugal
- the Slovak Republic
- Spain
- Switzerland
- Turkey.

The OECD tells us that very few programmes are taught in English in:

- Austria
- Belgium (French)
- Brazil
- Chile
- Greece
- Israel
- Italy
- Luxembourg
- Mexico
- the Russian Federation.

However, it is worth noting that even these countries will feature private or international universities with a curriculum in English. Others may well be moving towards recruiting more international students, so watch this space.

How to choose

Many people choose a country for emotional, rather than practical, reasons. Maybe you have always longed to spend time in a particular country or you've fallen in love with a place that you've visited. Perhaps your family or friends have links with an area of the world or you have a boyfriend or girlfriend who lives overseas.

In other cases, the decisions are much more measured and logical. Some have a particular type of course in mind and their decision is driven by the availability of that course. Others have a set of requirements, in terms of prestige, entry requirements or world university rankings.

Others don't even choose a specific country, but make a shortlist of institutions that meet their particular criteria. John Magee, who studied in Norway, took a very structured approach to his search for opportunities across Europe.

> **66** Firstly, the schools had to be ranked on the *Financial Times* European Business School Rankings, so they were internationally recognisable to future employers. Secondly, the schools had to offer my desired degree, an MSc in International Business/ International Management. Thirdly, a more selfish criterion of being situated in a mountainous country that offered easy access to alpine activities. Lastly, it was preferable if the

> course offered an exchange semester, to help me secure the maximum amount of international experience. **99**
>
> *John Magee, BI Norwegian Business School, Norway*

In many cases, access to student financial support or scholarships is a deciding factor.

> **66** The full cost of study would be about US$20,000 (nearly £13,000) a year. I have a 100% scholarship on my tuition fees but pay for accommodation. This is conditional on the basis that I get within the top 25% of the class throughout the year. **99**
>
> *Joshua Jackson, SP Jain School of Global Management,*
> *Singapore and Australia*

It is also worth considering the cost of living, how welcoming the country is to international students (for example, how easy it will be to get a visa and whether there are opportunities to gain employment afterwards) and how well your degree will be recognised when you return to the UK.

Essentially, you need to determine what matters to you and what your priorities are. Consider some of the following factors and weigh up how important each one is to you:

- subject availability
- length of study
- professional recognition of qualifications
- university ranking
- type of institution

- size of university
- style of teaching and assessment
- specialist options (for example, internships or specialist subjects available)
- drop-out rates
- pass rates
- destinations of ex-students
- cost of tuition fees
- cost of living
- availability of loans or grants
- availability of scholarships
- opportunities to stay on and work after completion of studies
- interest in specific countries
- opportunity to learn particular languages
- lifestyle factors
- distance from home.

What type of university will suit you best?

Whether you see yourself as an academic aiming for postgraduate study or you want a route straight to work, you'll find a university to suit you. Many countries have polytechnics, community colleges or Universities of Applied Sciences where you'll be taught with a more vocational, work-related focus; these institutions share some characteristics with the post-1992 universities in the UK. If you are looking for a more traditional style of teaching from lecturers with a research background, try a research-based or research-intensive university. Make sure that you always find out what type of university you are applying to; it could have a big impact on what you get out of your university experience and which doors will be open to you when you finish.

Carefully considering what matters to you, much as John Magee did, helps to focus on the essential and desirable criteria. A final list of criteria might look something like the following.

- Essential: a city-centre, research-based university in the Times Higher Education Top 200, offering low cost of living and the possibility of a scholarship.
- Desirable: flight time of less than eight hours, opportunity to stay on and work.

> What we describe as a course in the UK might be called a programme or program in some countries, with course used to refer to the modules you study as part of your degree.

Researching the options

There is no wrong or right way to choose where you want to spend the next few years. Just make sure that you discover the realities of life there, not just the pictures from the glossy brochure. It is not unusual to see universities overstating their position to international students, so make sure that you look for a secondary source of evidence (particularly if a university is telling you that they are among the best in the world).

Just as in the UK, courses with the same title may be really diverse. You should ask about course content, course structure, how you will be assessed and so on. You might find that the course you are looking for doesn't exist in your chosen country; there are limited history or English literature courses taught in English in continental Europe, for example. Courses where your learning relates specifically to practice in a particular country don't always travel well so they might not be available: social work or teaching, for example. Titles may vary from country to country; whereas UK university courses often have quite broad academic titles like biology or mechanical engineering, vocational universities in other countries might use titles that are more specific and job-related. Look out for courses in econometrics, interaction design or human ageing.

Ask the universities about additional factors, such as the ratio of students to lecturers, drop-out rates, student-success rates, library services and internet access. If you have the opportunity to visit a country or campus, take it. This can be a great chance to find out more, meet the staff and ask questions. Many students talk about the feeling they get from being on a particular campus and it is hard to 'virtually' recreate this if you have very little contact with the university before making your choices.

There are other ways of finding out more. If a visit isn't possible (and let's face it, it often isn't), try visiting recruitment events in the UK. There are a number of events that take place in the UK: the Student World Fair, USA College Day, QS World Grad School Tour, and the Study Options Open Days. At these events, you can meet representatives from universities who are actively seeking UK students. To make best use of these events, find out the exhibitors beforehand, highlight whom you want to speak to and take your list of essential questions to ask. Note down or record any responses you get, so you can consider them later.

Don't want to restrict yourself to just one country? Can't decide between Los Angeles, Hong Kong or Milan? There are a number of options where you can study in two, three or even four different countries and even gain more than one degree. Take a look at the World Bachelor in Business partnership (http://wbb.usc.edu), SKEMA's EAI Bachelor (www.skema.edu/international/eai-transfers) or SP Jain's

Bachelor of Business Administration (www.spjain.org/BBA), for example.

Online research

Most of the countries interested in attracting international students have their own official websites; you can find these in the 'Studying in . . .' chapters. For information on European opportunities, start at www.ec.europa.eu/education/study-in-europe.

All universities looking to attract international students will have their own websites with English content. Many universities have a number of other ways to engage with their potential students via social media like Facebook, Twitter or YouTube, where you can search directly for the universities you are interested in.

Following some key organisations on Facebook or Twitter when you start your research helps to keep you up to date with new developments, events and key deadline dates. You can also attend virtual student fairs and web chats from the comfort of your own home. Hobsons Virtual Student Fairs at www.internationalstudent.com/hobsons-virtual-fairs is one example; although it is not specifically aimed at UK students, it should still provide some useful information on study in the USA. Other websites, like the Student Room (www.thestudentroom.co.uk), have discussions on international study. Bear in mind that information from chat rooms can be useful, but isn't always correct, so you need to double-check any facts you get from sources like this.

From summer 2015, UK students will be able to apply to certain European universities through UCAS. Any European university wanting to be featured will first need to show they meet equivalent standards to their UK counterparts. Not every university planning to use UCAS will be using it for applications; some universities have indicated that they will use the service to promote their courses instead.

Course search

The 'Studying in . . .' chapters include some of the best websites to search for courses and institutions in a specific country. If you want to search for courses before you decide on a country, try websites like Study Portals (www.studyportals.eu), EUNICAS (www.eunicas.co.uk), A Star Future (www.astarfuture.co.uk/what_to_study.html) or Hot Courses Abroad (www.hotcoursesabroad.com).

Is the website you need opening up in another language? Look out for the Union flag or the letters EN to select the English version. If not, try a translation website like Google Translate, www.translate.google.com.

Organisations to like on Facebook

- EducationUSA
- US-UK Fulbright Commission
- The Student World
- A Star Future for Brits Studying Abroad
- Dutch Degrees
- Study in Holland
- Maastricht Students
- Study Options
- CUCAS-Study in China
- Campus France Paris
- Study in New Zealand
- Study in Finland

- Study in Australia
- Study in Estonia
- Study in the Czech Republic
- Study in Germany
- Study in Sweden
- Study in Norway
- Study in Denmark
- INTO China
- EUNICAS
- Hotcourses Abroad
- Venture.

Organisations to follow on Twitter

- @CUCAS_CHINA
- @TheStudentWorld
- @astarfuture
- @StudyOptions
- @CampusFrance
- @StudyInHolland
- @StudyinNorway
- @StudyinSweden
- @EdUSAupdates
- @USUKFulbright
- @studyinde
- @EduIreland
- @StudyinDenmark
- @nzeducation
- @FutureUnlimited
- @studyinestonia
- @INTO_CHINA.

There are some great blogs and diaries out there too. Take a look at some of these:

- Third Year Abroad, The Mole Diaries: www.thirdyearabroad.com/before-you-go/the-mole-diaries.html
- A Star Future Testimonials: www.astarfuture.co.uk/testimonials.html
- Samuel Knight in Groningen: www.samstudyingabroad.tumblr.com
- Maastricht Students: www.maastricht-students.com
- The University of Nottingham in North America: http://universityofnottinghamnorthamerica.blogspot.co.uk.

Websites like iAgora (www.iagora.com/studies) allow international students to rate their experiences at an institution based on categories for housing, student life, academic, costs and so on. SteXX, the Student Experience Exchange (www.stexx.eu), allows students to review and rate European universities. Use sites like these to get a student perspective on your chosen institution. Perhaps you will decide to rate your experiences too, after studying overseas.

Many schools, colleges, universities and public libraries have access to Venture (formerly known as Exodus), an international careers-information database. The online database features lots of useful information on studying overseas, including country profiles. Ask your UK institution for a username and password.

Students interested in postgraduate study or research should find the Prospects website useful, as it features profiles of around 30 countries (www.prospects.ac.uk/country_profiles.htm).

Using an agent
Some applicants choose to use the service of an agent or an educational consultant to help them navigate the plethora of information out there. Many like the reassurance of working with

an organisation that understands the education, application and visa system of a particular country or countries. Check whether you have to pay for the service they provide and what you will get in return. Some organisations charge no fees. It is always worth asking about the affiliations of any organisation: whether they are linked to specific universities, for example.

There are a number of organisations operating in the UK, all offering different types of support and service. Some of these are listed here.

- A Star Future: www.astarfuture.co.uk
- Study Options: www.studyoptions.com
- EUNICAS: www.eunicas.co.uk
- The Student World: www.thestudentworld.com
- PFL Education: www.preparationforlife.com
- Degrees Ahead: www.degreesahead.co.uk
- Mayflower Education Consultants: www.mayflowereducation.co.uk
- M & D Europe: www.readmedicine.com
- Study International: www.studygo.co.uk
- Pass 4 Soccer Scholarships: www.pass4soccer.com.

> 66 After results day, my teacher recommended that I get in touch with A Star Future because she knew that I would be really interested in their information on clearing places at foreign universities. 99
>
> *Clare Higgins, The Hague University of Applied Sciences, the Netherlands*

> ❝ I applied through Study Options. They were fantastic and made the process so easy. They copied all of my transcripts for my A level results and sent off passport, results, organised the visa, the course, everything! ❞
>
> *Kadie O'Byrne, Murdoch University, Australia*

Getting a different perspective

Of course, the websites listed here barely scratch the surface of the information out there. The students I spoke to share some great ways to get a different perspective.

> ❝ I did some rather intense research, checking out the university website, the city website and the online literature available. I also used more creative methods such as searching for YouTube videos of the campus and the city, listening to the local radio station online and reading the local paper online to try to get a better grip of what my future life might be like. ❞
>
> *Simon McCabe, University of Missouri, USA*

Finalising your choices

Let's recap the steps to finalising your choices.

- Consider your priorities.
- Write a list of essential and desirable criteria.
- Write a list of questions to ask each institution.
- Start to research in more detail.
- If you're struggling, write a pros-and-cons list.
- Narrow down your choices to a shortlist of five or six.

It is important to contact the university direct, talking to admissions staff as well as course leaders or professors. When you come to apply, this can have the additional benefit of making your name known to the recruiting staff, as well as improving your understanding of what those staff are looking for.

You should clarify the application process, documentation required and the visa requirements, as well as establishing a timescale for the process. The university should then send you the necessary paperwork or a link to the information online.

Try to apply to a number of institutions, while still considering the work required to produce a good-quality application, as well as any associated costs. Applying to a number of institutions gives you a better chance of a selection of offers to choose from.

Student story
Jacob Matthias Kummer, IE
University, Segovia, Spain

'I have always had, and most likely always will have, a desire to travel. I think there is a big world out there, which of course one can explore travelling, but travelling does not always mean experiencing another culture. Not wanting to take a gap year to travel, but still with a need to get out of the UK and experience something different, I decided to pack my bags, to live and study abroad.

'I chose Spain for many reasons. Firstly, I had a strong basis in the language, which certainly helps. Secondly, having travelled through Spain a lot in my life, I had only seen the tourist side of it. I had fallen in love with the country, and certainly had a desire to experience it from a more local level. Also, it wasn't too far from home, in case I had to return for emergencies, or if it didn't work out.

'One day, three months before I was supposed to start at Nottingham Trent University, having just returned from a language exchange trip to Santa Cruz de Tenerife, I had a slight panic. I realised that there was something more. I had experienced certain aspects of student life, and also everyday life in Spain, and I wanted more. Suddenly, the thought of moving up to Nottingham was one which I did not want to make a reality. The following day, I went online and googled "international university Spain". As it turned out, IE was the first result. Obviously, further research into the institution was carried out afterwards to make sure it was a good fit, but a week later, I had booked my flights to come and visit.'

Once he had decided to apply for a bachelor's degree in Architecture, Jake didn't have any difficulties with the process. 'It was very simple and straightforward. I downloaded the application form from the university website, whilst in constant email contact with the admissions department, which helped me out step by step. It involved completion of an application, submission of a portfolio, and then an interview, which I did over the telephone. Then, I had to wait for my exam results. Shortly after the results came out, I received confirmation that I was accepted. I then applied for financial aid, and found out the result a couple of months later.

'The fees are €18,000 (£13,300), but I am on scholarship of 50%, making it €9,000 (£6,650), which actually works out to be a similar price to universities in the UK nowadays. I do not have a loan, which I would get in the UK, but I am fortunate enough to be able to survive without. Living costs in Segovia are a lot cheaper than back in the UK.'

Jake felt that he got lots of support from his institution before he arrived. 'Every question under the sun was answered by email, with quick replies. The admissions department are great at IE. They really take you step by step through the process. It made the process a lot smoother than I thought it would be. Also, upon arrival at an open day, I was welcomed with open arms, despite arriving four hours late. They accommodated me with a campus tour, even though the open day was over!'

The support has continued now that he is a student. 'Professors and heads of departments are available frequently to discuss any problems, so really, whenever there is a problem, it is always addressed in a short period of time. Also, there is a student office which offers help with other problems unrelated to academics. They are always a huge help and offer great support. My application for foreign residency, which is necessary after three months of living here, was all sorted by the university.'

Jacob's top tips

Educational differences

'In IE University, the teaching is more personal. Professors and staff know who you are, and they really help you to succeed. You are not just a number.'

Adjusting to life overseas

'I have never been homesick, apart from when I have been ill. It is a different culture, and the norms of life will soon come to be second nature. I think after a period of four months, you tend to feel quite settled.'

Accommodation

'Plan ahead. If you can get there to visit flats, do it at least two months before, or get yourself into a residence.'

Food

'Most places in Spain provide great food, although it is always worth learning some of the vocabulary for food so you know what you're eating!'

Working while studying

'Whether you can work while you study depends on the course. If you have time, then do it. It's a great way to get into the local community.'

Options for after you finish your studies

'Hopefully, after I finish my studies, I'll take a few months to relax and maybe travel. Then I hope to find a job or internship either in Spain or abroad elsewhere, and then consider graduate study options.'

Jake certainly doesn't regret choosing an international university for his bachelor's degree. 'The best thing about studying overseas is the people you meet. Meeting people from different backgrounds really changes the way you think, on both a personal and professional level. International contacts are always a big plus. Do it! You can always return home if you don't like it!'

IE University (www.ie.edu) is a private university offering its students tailor-made education with an international, humanistic and entrepreneurial perspective.

Norwegian School of Economics: Profile

NORWEGIAN SCHOOL OF ECONOMICS

NHH is ranked among the top 40 business schools in Europe, and it is the leading centre for research and education in economics and business administration in Norway. It is the first choice for Norwegian students and for the Norwegian business community. NHH has a faculty of high standing in the international research community.

The MSc in Economics and Business Administration is the key element in NHH's portfolio of programmes. It consists of eight distinctive profiles, of which six are offered for international students:

- Economics (ECN),
- Energy, Natural Resources and the Environment (ENE),
- Finance (FIE),
- International Business (MIB),
- Marketing and Brand Management (MBM) and
- Strategic Management (STR).

CEMS Master's in International Management (CEMS MIM)

Students in the MSc programme at NHH can seek to combine their degree with the CEMS MIM, enabling them to graduate with two internationally recognised qualifications. The combination of these two prestigious programmes provides a solid foundation for students seeking an international business career. Ranked as one of the best in the world by the *Financial Times* since the ranking began in 2005, the CEMS MIM is the ultimate academic – corporate bridge programme.

Admission to the MSc programme

Competition for admission to NHH is tough, with only one in ten applicants being offered a place to study in our international master's programme, and the students who are admitted must have excellent academic qualifications.

Deadline for receipt – 15 February

We accept applications from 1 November 2015 for the autumn semester of 2016. We encourage early submission of applications.

As a NHH-student you will also enjoy benefits like:

- No tuition fees (state funded).
- Guaranteed accommodation.
- Granted work permission.
- Free Norwegian language courses. International career center.
- The possibility to combine your MSc with excellent international opportunities, such as exchange programs, Double Degree programs and CEMS – Master's in International Management.

'The NHH portfolio is unique because it has acquainted me with students from a myriad of cultures and different working styles through engaging projects and group work. The broad scope of the curriculum allows specialisation in one discipline, but also gives flexibility to experiment with other courses.'
SURYADEEP SEAL, MSc Student from India

'Surrounded by seven mountains, living in Bergen means living in one of Europe's most naturally majestic but cosmopolitan cities.'
JOHN BYRNE, MSc Student from Ireland

'I came to NHH and Norway to get a radical change from Southern Europe, and I definitely got what I wished for! I never thought I would meet so many different people and I am very surprised by the pool of international students.'
KENZA TAOUFIK, MSc and CEMS student from NOVA Lisbon, Portugal

'The Double Degree programme provides you with a great opportunity to specialise in two complementary areas of expertise while experiencing life and work in different cultural settings.'
LAURA HERZIG, MSc and Double degree student from HEC Paris, France

'Energy, Natural Resources and the Environment (ENE) is a unique specialisation that gives you an in-depth understanding of how the economy

works in the energy sector. NHH has strong ties to the energy industry and is one of few schools in the world that offer this kind of specialisation.'
KAI ERSPAMER, MSc Alumni from USA

'Due to increased globalisation companies need to hire more individuals with international experience and knowledge on cross-cultural communication. With the MIB degree you acquire the analytical skills needed.'
SARAH YUYAN SOON, MSc student from Singapore

KEA – Copenhagen School of Design and Technology: Profile

Copenhagen School of Design and Technology is an Academy of Higher Education which offers over 30 different educational programmes at Bachelor degree and Academy Professional degree levels.

With a degree from KEA – Copenhagen School of Design and Technology you get a practice-oriented, higher education at Academy Professional level and/or Professional Bachelor's level, developed in close cooperation with the region's business community and educational institutions in Denmark and abroad. We are in constant dialogue with companies and industry associations to keep education programmes updated in both form and content.

This ensures that the education meets the current requirements and needs of a dynamic labour market. You are therefore well prepared when choosing a future with KEA.

We are established as an international educational institution with many exchanges both to and from KEA by both students and teachers. This gives you a wealth of international contacts that are crucial in a globalised marketplace.

KEA offers programmes at 3 different levels of education:

* ACADEMY PROFESSION DEGREE PROGRAMME (AP)
* TOP-UP BACHELOR DEGREE PROGRAMME (BA)
* BACHELOR DEGREE PROGRAMME (BA)

At KEA the international element is of great importance and we pride ourselves of an inter-cultural environment. Each semester, KEA welcomes a large number of international students intending to complete a full degree at KEA. In 2015, KEA offers 13 different programmes taught entirely in English and 18 taught in Danish.

All study programmes are developed in close partnership with businesses to ensure students gain insight into real-life situations and industry needs. Tuition is project based and businesses take an active part in evaluating student skills. An internship placement (of a minimum duration of 10 weeks) is mandatory, allowing students to test their knowledge and skills in a real-world work environment.

KEA – Copenhagen School of Design and Technology: Case Study

Why KEA?

Ever since I started studying in a bilingual school in Budapest, I knew that I would be studying abroad one day. As a Hungarian, Denmark was the best choice for me, not far from my homeland, family and friends, but far from its education system.

I was looking for programmes in a creative field, something new and innovative. At KEA, I got practice-based knowledge with many international friends and connections. I became more confident working in groups, holding presentations and public speeches. I started with a 2-year AP course in Multimedia Design and Communication, and currently I am studying Sustainable Communication, which is one of the specialisations of the top-up BA in Design and Business. What I really like about being a student at KEA is the brand new campus in the heart of the city, the modern facilities and the cosy library where I can make my projects come true.

At the Design and Business programme, we have many common projects with the fashion designers, purchase students and collaborations with companies and organisations. Lately, we had to work for the Danish Red Cross, present our solution without using power point. Our classroom looked really inspiring, like an exhibition with 3D models, business origami and moodboards lying around. Some of my fellow classmates even acted out their solution, which was quite funny to see. And of course the client, Red Cross, was present giving feedback, being amazed by the new way of presentations. That was my favourite assignment.

If you want to challenge yourself, I can truly recommend studying at KEA.

Szabina Kun, 22
Design and Business, 6th semester student

Chapter 5
Studying in Europe

UK students are lucky to have such a diverse range of countries right on their doorstep. Flights to some European cities can be as cheap or as quick as a train journey within the UK. European study brings the benefit of cultural and language differences, without having to travel too far.

One myth about studying in Europe is the need to have brilliant language skills. Increasingly, European universities are offering entire courses in English. Of course, living in a different country will also enable you to immerse yourself in the language, thereby developing new language skills as a bonus. Some universities will offer you the chance to take language lessons alongside your studies.

This chapter focuses on EU (European Union) or EEA (European Economic Area) countries where UK students at public universities are charged the same fees as those for home students. The countries featured offer a range of courses available in English. The European countries that aren't listed in this chapter will still have opportunities for study in English (most European countries do) but you may find that some are more limited, perhaps restricted to private or international institutions.

In the Times Higher Education World University Rankings 2014–2015, a listing of the top 200 universities in the world, you will find universities from many European countries – Switzerland, France, Germany, Ireland, Sweden, Finland, the Netherlands, Italy, Belgium, Denmark, Spain, Norway and Austria are all represented.

Compatibility in the education system

Although there are differences in the education systems across Europe, a system known as the Bologna process has helped to make higher education more compatible and comparable across much of the continent. With transparent, mutually recognised systems and a clear credit framework, studying across Europe is now much simpler.

The Bologna process covers the European Higher Education Area (EHEA), an area much wider than the EU or EEA. It includes some countries applying for EU membership (Montenegro and Turkey, for example) and some post-Soviet states (Armenia, Ukraine and Azerbaijan, for example).

The process of studying for an entire degree abroad is sometimes known as 'diploma mobility'.

Bachelor's degrees, master's degrees and doctorates in these countries are all comparable in level. The European Credit Transfer System (ECTS) is used to measure workload and allows comparison between degrees in different countries. This makes it fairly straightforward to study a first degree in one European country and a postgraduate degree in another; some students even move part-way through their studies. Credit can be awarded for academic study, relevant placements and research, as long as they are part of the programme of study. Sixty credits equate to one full-time academic year. You may see bachelor's degrees of 180 or 240 credits, for example.

Another benefit of the coordinated system is the diploma supplement, a detailed transcript used across Europe and the EHEA which outlines any studies you complete and gives full details of the level, content and status of your achievements. It is particularly helpful if you intend to work or study in another country as it provides a recognisable context to any attainments.

The coordination of quality assurance standards means that higher education across all these countries has to meet minimum requirements. It is important to note that this doesn't remove the need for thorough research into what you will receive at your European university. You will find a range of different types of opportunity on offer. Just as in the UK, universities across Europe vary in their prestige, research, teaching and facilities. Ensuring that you find a good match to your needs is a key part of the research that you undertake.

It is important to note that most bachelor's degrees outside the UK are not classed as honours degrees as standard; extra study is normally required to gain an honours degree.

Finding a course and institution

From summer 2015, you should come across European universities when you search for courses through UCAS (www. ucas.com). Not every institution will be listed, just those which choose to be featured and which meet the requirements set by UCAS. In some cases, you'll be able to apply through UCAS too.

If you want to search more widely, A Star Future (www.astarfuture. co.uk/what_to_study.html) and EUNICAS (www.eunicas.co.uk) feature course listings for undergraduate courses taught in English. Another option is to use the Study Portal websites, www. bachelorsportal.eu, www.mastersportal.eu and www.phdportal. eu, but make sure that you select English as the language of instruction. You can use PLOTEUS (Portal on Learning Opportunities throughout the European Space) at www.ec.europa. eu/ploteus/home-en.htm. EURAXESS has a database of research opportunities across Europe (www.ec.europa.eu/euraxess).

Different websites often bring up a different range of courses, so it is worth searching more than one website. Although these websites are a good starting point, the information on application deadlines and fees can sometimes be incorrect, so you should turn to the institutions for the latest information; you will be able to clarify any details with them.

ENIC-NARIC (European Network of Information Centres – National Academic Recognition Information Centres) has information on the education system of 54 countries, within Europe and beyond. The website also lists higher-education institutions for each country, so you can be sure that your chosen institution is recognised (www.enic-naric.net).

Entry requirements

Entry requirements vary between countries and between institutions. Similarly, competition for places varies as well. Most European countries do not have such a competitive system as we have in the UK, where the cap on numbers means some students won't gain a place, even when they have the academic ability to cope with the course. Many European countries ask that you have completed A level study, without asking for specific grades; they are often more concerned with your performance at university than beforehand, so some students will lose their place after the first year if they cannot cope with the academic demands. It should be noted that the drop-out rate amongst international students tends to be considerably lower than from home students.

Some European countries expect a wider range of subjects than UK students would normally take. It is standard practice in some countries to ask for a qualification in maths or a foreign language at A level standard. If you haven't studied these subjects, look closely at the entry requirements to be sure that you will be considered.

Certain courses in some countries are subject to selective recruitment; look out for the terms *numerus clausus* or *numerus fixus*, which might indicate a competitive system for restricted places. Your nationality should not prevent you from accessing education in any EU country, although you will need to ensure that you meet any entry requirements.

What is your UK qualification equivalent to?

Unless you have taken an internationally recognised qualification, like the International Baccalaureate, it is possible that your UK qualifications will need to be compared to the qualifications in the country where you wish to study. A levels tend to be understood overseas, but many other UK qualifications will require further evaluation. Each country has its own system for ensuring the adequate comparison of academic qualifications. Your chosen institution will be able to advise you further on any information that they require, so it is best to speak to them initially. You may later need to contact the ENIC-NARIC organisation in your host country for formal comparison of your qualifications (www.enic-naric.net). There will be a fee for this service.

Applying

Each European country has its own system and timescale for application. In some countries this is centralised, a bit like UCAS, but in other cases you have to apply individually to each university. The country guides will give you an idea of the different systems and deadline dates for application. Remember to check whether you can apply to your chosen university through UCAS.

Registering your stay

Although UK students studying in the EU or the EEA will not require a visa, you will need to register your stay if you are going to be in the country for longer than three months. In most countries, you simply need to take your passport to a police station or immigration department. It is advisable to do this early; in some cases it must be done in the first week of your stay. Some countries charge a small fee for this service. Your university's international office will be able to tell you more.

Costs and help with finances

For course fees, UK nationals studying at public universities in other EU countries are treated in the same way as home students from that particular country. That means that they pay the same fees as those for home students.

While England's tuition fees are now the highest in Europe, many countries charge no tuition fees to full-time EU students, including:

- Austria
- Cyprus (bachelor's degrees)
- Denmark
- Finland
- Germany

- Malta (bachelor's degrees)
- Norway
- Sweden.

Tuition fee loans may also be available to EU students, in the countries where they are offered to home students. There is no requirement to offer maintenance grants and loans to EU students, although some countries choose to do so. Your university should be able to tell you more about the possibility of a loan or grant and any conditions you might need to meet.

The Netherlands is one of the few countries offering loans to EU students, although you will need to be in work and under the age of 30. For more details, see the country profile for the Netherlands on page 156. Changes to the rules in Denmark means that EU students who work 10 to 12 hours per week may now be eligible for grants and loans. For more information on studying in Denmark, see page 128. Recent news coming out of Bulgaria suggests that EU students aged under 35 are eligible to apply for tuition fee loans. To find out more, use some of the websites listed in the European country profiles or get in touch with staff in the international office of your chosen university.

There are public and private universities across the EU and EEA. Public universities are more likely to have a standardised system of tuition fees. In France, for example, courses at public universities tend to cost the same, regardless of subject or institution. In other countries, different courses or universities can charge varying amounts. Private institutions will charge a broader range of fees, often based on what they believe the market (i.e. the student) is prepared to pay. On the other hand, private institutions may well have additional opportunities for scholarships and favourable financial support, so it is worth investigating further.

Cultural differences

Although you may be familiar with some of the European countries on the UK's doorstep, there will still be cultural differences to come to terms with. Different countries and their inhabitants have their own distinctive characteristics that you will need to get used to if you are to adjust properly. Although the language barrier may not impact on your ability to study (when courses are taught in English), it can add to your isolation outside the university environment. Taking advantage of language classes can be an important factor when trying to settle in.

In some countries, many students stay in their local area and part-time study is common, while elsewhere students traditionally go to university when they are older; all this will impact on your university experience, so it is important to look into this before you decide on your venue for study.

> **"** It's a wonderfully chilled and relaxed lifestyle, the people are friendly and their English is of great quality. They have many celebrations at points of the year where one can become a part of their culture and tradition. **"**
>
> *Simran Gill, Fontys University of Applied Sciences,*
> *the Netherlands*

Talk to your university's international office or try to make contact with other UK students in preparation for the cultural differences you will face.

Working while studying

The opportunities to work will vary from country to country, often based on the number of local job opportunities for those with skills in English. In some countries, your opportunities will be limited so, to be on the safe side, you should plan your finances with the expectation that you will not find work.

If you need to work to get access to student grants and loans, as in the Netherlands, it may be worth moving to your new country a little earlier to begin the search. Alternatively, you can search for job opportunities through the European Job Mobility Portal (EURES) at www.ec.europa.eu/eures/home.jsp?lang=en. Your university may also have job shops advertising student-job vacancies.

If you hope to work in Europe, either during or after your studies, it may be useful to prepare a Europass CV, which comprises a standard CV template used widely across Europe; it should make your educational background and work experience more easily understood. Find out more at www.europass.cedefop.europa.eu.

> ❝ I have a job at the university proofreading English and posting on the university's Facebook page in English. If you're a native English speaker, it's not too hard to get a part-time job or two. Your first port of call could always be the university in seeking work. ❞
>
> *Hannah Burrows, University of Southern Denmark*

Staying on after study

As a free mover in Europe, staying on after study should not be restricted by legislation, although it may be limited by local opportunities. Competence in the local language, economic issues and local job opportunities may determine whether you choose to stay on for further study or work. Even if they don't remain in their university town or country, most students talk about the realisation that there is a whole world of opportunities out there for them.

> **❝** I'd like to travel the world. I don't want to be fixed. I want to see the world and make a difference. I won't be going back to the UK, that's for sure. Being abroad has caught on like a bug. **❞**
>
> *Rebecca Jackson, Stenden University of Applied Sciences, the Netherlands*

Country-specific information

Note

A number of European countries are very limited in the undergraduate courses they offer taught in English at public institutions. The list includes Austria, Belgium, France, Iceland, Italy and Norway. However, private providers and international universities in these countries do offer a range of undergraduate degrees taught in English; they will be more expensive than the public institutions, but might still end up being cheaper than the UK options due to a more generous package of scholarships or financial support.

Belgium

There are 358 UK students enrolled in higher education in Belgium, according to OECD, Education at a Glance 2014.

Higher education in Belgium

The Flemish and French communities each have their own education system. Most higher-education opportunities in Belgium require Flemish- or French-language skills, but there are some courses taught in English. These are more often at postgraduate level, with quite limited options for undergraduate study.

> **❝** I decided to study in Belgium due to the opportunities to intern in Brussels alongside studying. KU Leuven fitted the bill perfectly; it has the best reputation both in Belgium and within EU institutions. **❞**
>
> *Tom Aitchison, KU Leuven, Belgium*

Applying

Application deadline dates vary although a number of institutions require applications by 1 June. Check the deadline with your chosen university before applying.

Costs

Tuition or registration fees range from around €600 (£443) per year. See the You could study . . . section below for examples. The cost of living in Belgium is comparable to that in France and the Netherlands, which makes it slightly less expensive than the UK. It is ranked at number 15 out of 119 countries on the Numbeo 2015 Cost of Living Index at www.numbeo.com.

> **❝** The cost was marginal in comparison to the UK: €2,800 (£2,070) for an Advanced Master's; €610.60 (£451) for Initial Master's. Most master's degrees at Russell Group Universities in the UK cost £7,000 plus. **❞**
>
> *Tom Aitchison, KU Leuven, Belgium*

Four of Belgium's universities can be found in the Times
Higher Education World University Rankings Top 200 for
2014–2015.

You could study . . .

Business Administration BA
KU Leuven, Brussels campus
Three years
Apply by 1 June
Annual fees €610 (£451)
Monthly living costs €750 (£554)

MSc Chemical and Materials Engineering
Vrije Universiteit Brussel (VUB)
Two years
Apply by 1 June
Annual fees €837 (£618)
Monthly living costs €900 (£665)

Useful websites
www.highereducation.be (Flemish community)
www.studyinbelgium.be (French community)

Also worth considering . . .

Luxembourg could provide an alternative venue to Belgium,
although any opportunities taught in English are likely to
require additional skills in French, German or Luxembourgish.
The only university is the University of Luxembourg (wwwen.
uni.lu), although there are a couple of international campuses
there too. Find out more at ENIC-NARIC's Luxembourg page,
www.enic-naric.net/luxembourg.aspx.

Czech Republic

The Czech Republic has a long tradition of higher education and is home to the oldest university in central Europe. It offers a range of courses in English, and low living costs. According to OECD, Education at a Glance 2014, 435 UK students are already studying in the Czech Republic.

Higher education in the Czech Republic

Courses in the Czech Republic are based at public universities and private colleges, some of which are international. They run a two-semester system, with courses starting in October or February.

Undergraduate studies tend to take three to four years, with master's degrees taking two to three years, and doctorates from three years.

There are opportunities to study for competitive courses like medicine, dentistry and veterinary science in the Czech Republic and in other countries in eastern Europe.

Applying

Applications are made directly to your chosen university, before a deadline often in late February or March. Additional requirements might include academic transcripts and certificates, a letter of motivation, an admissions test and interview. Your university's international office will advise further on all aspects of the application process.

You can search for courses taught in English through Education CZ (www.education.cz).

Costs

Although courses taught in Czech are free, you will be charged tuition fees for courses taught in English. The universities set their own tuition fees for such courses and there is no maximum limit.

Fees usually start at around €2,000 (£1,478) but can be as much as €15,000 (£11,086) for a degree in medicine or dentistry. Scholarships may be available; you can find out more at the Ministry of Education, Youth and Sports (www.msmt.cz) or from your university.

For its cost of living in 2015, the Czech Republic is ranked 83 out of 119 countries according to Numbeo (www.numbeo.com), which is considerably lower than western Europe and the Nordic countries. Study in the Czech Republic (www.studyin.cz) suggests allowing for living costs of around US$350–US$750 (£227–£487) per month.

You could study . . .

BSc Economics and Finance
Charles University, Prague
Three years
Apply by 30 April
Annual fees €6,000 (£4,435)
Monthly living costs CZK8,500 (£228)

MSc Electrical Engineering
VSB – Technical University of Ostrava
Two years
Apply by 30 April
Annual fees €4,000 (£2,956)
Monthly living costs CZK6,000–8,000 (£161–£215)

PhD Architecture and Urban Design
Brno University of Technology
Four years
Apply by 31 March
Annual fees €7,000 (£5,174)
Monthly living costs €250–€300 (£185–£222)

Useful websites

www.studyin.cz

www.education.cz

Also worth considering . . .

If you're interested in opportunities in eastern Europe, have you considered Bulgaria, Croatia, Hungary, Poland, Romania, Slovakia or Slovenia? Find out more at:

- ENIC-NARIC country page for Bulgaria, www.enic-naric.net/bulgaria.aspx
- Study in Croatia, www.studyincroatia.hr
- Study Hungary, www.studyhungary.hu
- Study in Poland, www.studyinpoland.pl
- ENIC-NARIC country page for Romania, www.enic-naric.net/romania.aspx
- Study in Slovakia, www.studyin.sk
- Slovenia, www.slovenia.si/en/study.

Denmark

According to annual figures from OECD Education at a Glance 2014, 680 UK students have already made the move to study in Denmark. You will find that education in Denmark centres on problem-based learning, developing your ability to present creative solutions to complex problems. The country has a strong tradition of public universities and, best of all, there are no tuition fees. At PhD level, there are even fully funded, salaried opportunities in English.

> **66** The university I chose is the biggest in Denmark, and the course gave me the best opportunity of all of the ones I looked at. It's entirely in English and I study a full-time two year programme to get a broad base of topics. I get the opportunity to do internships and study abroad as part of the programme. I can have a part-time English-speaking student job alongside studying. The university offers accommodation for the full length of my degree, all of my teachers are recognised experts on America, and, best of all, there were no tuition fees whatsoever. **99**
>
> *Hannah Burrows, University of Southern Denmark*

Higher education in Denmark

Denmark offers over 500 higher-education programmes taught in English. You can study at research universities (*universitet*) at undergraduate and postgraduate level; it takes at least three years to complete a bachelor's degree, two years for a master's, and three or four for a doctorate. Programmes at university colleges (*professionshøjskole*) are more professional in nature, leading to three-year to four-year professional undergraduate degrees in areas like engineering, teaching or business. Academies of professional higher education (*erhvervsakademier*) offer degrees in partnership with universities and two-year academy professional degrees (AP); an AP can be topped up to a professional bachelor's degree with further study.

The academic year runs from September to June, with the possibility of February intake too. Some courses are competitive and have additional requirements beyond the completion of A level-standard qualifications.

All courses in Denmark are assessed by oral or written exams.

> **❝** The teaching style is more like seminars than lectures, with a discussion by all students and teacher together. You have a lot of group work in class, and sometimes homework can be preparing a Powerpoint presentation with two other students. **❞**
>
> *Hannah Burrows, University of Southern Denmark*

Applying

At undergraduate level, applications can be made through the Danish Co-ordinated Application System (KOT) at www.optagelse. dk/admission/index.html. Danish students can apply online but UK students will need to send some paperwork by post. Applications can also be obtained from your chosen institution. Forms are available around two months before the application deadline.

Through KOT, you can choose up to eight courses and can opt for a quota 1 or quota 2 application; the option you choose depends on the qualification you are applying with – your chosen university will advise you as to which one is most suitable. Applications for undergraduate courses starting in August and September open on 1 February and close on 15 March.

Students applying through KOT also have the option to be put on standby: this means being added to a waiting list if you are not admitted initially. If you get a standby offer, you may be contacted about a place as late as two weeks into the semester; if you get a standby offer that doesn't become a study place, you will be guaranteed a place for the following year.

Direct application is required at postgraduate level, with deadlines varying; your chosen university will be able to advise you further.

Costs

Danish students are eligible for State Educational Support (SU) in the form of a grant up to DKK5,903 (£585) per month and access to loans of DKK3,020 (£299) per month. Under a recent EU court ruling, students from other EU countries should qualify for this support as long as they are working 10 to 12 hours per week. For further explanation, see the Ministry of Education website, www.su.dk/English/Sider/default.aspx. Some scholarships may be available. See Study in Denmark (www.studyindenmark.dk) for details.

Denmark is an expensive country to live in. It comes in at number five in the cost-of-living rankings 2015 (www.numbeo.com), but with no fees and with wages of around £13 per hour for students, it is still possible to have a reasonable standard of living. Students with no Danish language may be able to find jobs in English-speaking bars and cafés, for example.

The Technical University of Denmark (ranked 121), Aarhus University (ranked 153) and University of Copenhagen (160) are all in the Times Higher Education World University Rankings Top 200 for 2014–2015. UK universities with comparable rankings are University of Sheffield, University of Birmingham and University of Liverpool.

You could study . . .

AP Service, Hospitality and Tourism Management
Copenhagen Business Academy
Two years
Apply by 15 March
Tuition fees DKK0
Annual living costs DKK120,500 (£11,932)

BEng Global Management and Manufacturing
University of Southern Denmark, Odense
Three and a half years
Apply by 15 March
Tuition fees DKK0
Monthly living costs DKK4,400–DKK7,000 (£436–£693)

MA Film and Media Studies
University of Copenhagen
Two years
Apply by 15 January
Tuition fees DKK0
Monthly living costs DKK7,000–DKK9,000 (£693–£891)

Useful websites
www.studyindenmark.dk

Estonia

Estonia offers good value for money and a vibrant student life. As many as 90% of international students say that Estonia is a good place to study (International Student Barometer™ 2011) but, so far, there aren't many UK students based there.

Higher education in Estonia

The country is keen to attract international students and is expanding its courses taught in English; it currently offers more than 100 recognised degrees taught in English. These programmes are accredited and are available at the following institutions:

- Estonian Academy of Arts: www.artun.ee
- Estonian Academy of Music and Theatre: www.ema.edu.ee
- Estonian University of Life Sciences: www.emu.ee
- Tallinn University: www.tlu.ee
- Tallinn University of Technology: www.ttu.ee/en

- University of Tartu: www.ut.ee
- Estonian Business School: www.ebs.ee.
- Estonian School of Hotel and Tourism Management: http://estonianhotelschool.com
- Estonian Entrepreneurship University of Applied Sciences: www.euas.eu

Other higher-education institutions may offer alternative options taught in English, including modules for exchange students or short courses.

Education in Estonia takes place in public universities, private universities and professional higher-education institutions. The academic year starts in September and is divided into two semesters. Generally, you would be looking at a three-year academic bachelor's degree, a one-year to two-year master's qualification, and a three-year to four-year doctorate. Programmes in medicine, dentistry, pharmacy, veterinary science, architecture and civil engineering take five to six years.

All courses include exams which take place at the end of each semester. Grades are standardised, ranging from A (or 5) to E (or 1). Grade F (or 0) means that the assessment has not been passed.

Applying

You can search and apply for many courses online through Dream Apply (https://estonia.dreamapply.com). Deadline dates are set by the individual institutions and range from May to August for courses starting in September. Some doctorates are open to applications all year round.

Costs

According to Study in Estonia, fees for bachelor's and master's degrees range from €1,660 to €7,500 (£1,227 to £5,543) per year.

Medicine, law, business administration, and social sciences are often more expensive. PhD students should not have to pay fees.

Estonia is one of the countries offering some form of financial support to EU students. Since 2013–2014, the government has offered a need-based study allowance if a student's average monthly income is below €280 (£207) per family member. Students could be entitled to an allowance of between €75 and €220 (£55 and £163) per month.

Some scholarships are available, primarily for postgraduate study; ask your university for more information.

Livings costs in Estonia are reasonable. On average, you should allow €300–€500 (£222–£370) per month for living costs. Expect to pay from €100 (£74) per month for a room in a dormitory or up to €450 (£333) for a private flat. Estonia is ranked at number 45 out of 119 countries on the cost-of-living rankings for 2014; this is considerably lower than the UK and much of western Europe.

You could study . . .

Bachelor of Liberal Arts in Humanities
Tallinn University
Three years
Direct application by 1 July
Annual fees €3,000 (£2,217)
Monthly living costs excluding accommodation €300–€500 (£222–£370)

MSc Financial Mathematics
University of Tartu
One year
Direct application by 16 April
Annual fees €3,200 (£2,365)
Monthly living costs €550 (£407)

PhD Zoology and Hydrobiology

University of Tartu

Four years

Direct application by 3 June (contact potential supervisors in advance)

Annual fees €0

Monthly living costs €550 (£407)

Useful websites

www.studyinestonia.ee

Also worth considering . . .

If you're interested in opportunities in the Baltic states, have you considered Latvia and Lithuania? Find out more at Study in Latvia, www.studyinlatvia.lv and Study in Lithuania, www.lietuva.lt/en/education_sience/study_lithuania.

Finland

Finland is considered to be a safe and forward-looking nation with a high-quality education system. Temperatures can range from +30°C to –20°C and the sun never sets in parts of the country in June and early July. The academic year runs from August to the end of May; it is split into two semesters, August to December, and January to May. Most students start in August, with limited opportunities to join in January.

The latest figures from OECD Education at a Glance 2014 show us that 218 UK students were studying in Finland at the last count.

Higher education in Finland

Higher education in Finland takes places in research-based universities or vocationally focused polytechnics (or Universities of Applied Sciences). In the universities, few programmes are taught in English at undergraduate level, although master's and doctoral degrees are more widely available. It is the opposite in the polytechnics, where there are plenty of programmes taught in English at undergraduate level, with a smaller number of UAS master's programmes. (Doctoral qualifications are not available in the polytechnics, only in the universities.) To access a UAS master's programme, you will need to have had three years of relevant experience, in addition to any academic requirements. To search for programmes, go to the Study in Finland database at www.studyinfinland.fi/study_options/study_programmes_ database.

The degrees vary in length as follows:

Universities

- Bachelor's degree: three years
- Master's degree: two years
- Doctoral degree: four years

Polytechnic/university of applied sciences

- Bachelor's degree: three-and-a-half to four-and-a-half years
- Master's degree: one to one-and-a-half years (after at least three years of relevant experience)
- Doctoral degrees: not available

Applying

Applications tend to be online, although the application process and timescale are split between the universities and polytechnics.

At universities, applications to undergraduate and master's programmes can be made direct or via www.studyinfo.fi; ask your university which way to proceed. In most cases, you should apply for bachelor's and master's degrees between November and January. Doctoral programmes require direct application; the application timescale varies between institutions: some accept applications at any time, while others have specific timescales in which to apply. Speak to the international office or the relevant faculty at your chosen university.

At polytechnics, undergraduate applications should be made in January via www.studyinfo.fi. For a UAS master's degree, you should apply direct to the polytechnic or via www.studyinfo.fi. at the time they specify, usually around February or March; you can find out more on your chosen institution's website.

As the academic year begins in August shortly after A level results come out, there is normally insufficient time to confirm a place, so applicants might need to consider a gap year.

Undergraduate admissions procedures normally require an entrance test. This tends to be a written test, but may be an audition or portfolio for certain art, drama or music programmes. Most university tests are taken in Finland, but some polytechnic entrance tests can be taken outside the country. Make sure that you prepare fully, following any instructions provided by the institution.

> **❝** If you get your school grades and meet the admissions criteria, they put you through to the entrance exam, which includes an English exam. The next step is a group aptitude test and then an interview. This definitely ensures that all the students are serious about studying at this university. **❞**
>
> *Fiona Higgins, HAAGA-HELIA, University*
> *of Applied Sciences, Finland*

Costs

Higher education in Finland is free to EU students at all levels of higher education. There is no entitlement to grants or loans.

Overall, Finland is slightly more expensive than the UK, coming 13th (to the UK's 10th) in the cost-of-living rankings for 2015 (www.numbeo.com). It comes in lower than Norway, Denmark, Ireland and Australia. The average monthly living costs are between €700 and €900 (£517 and £665); expect to pay more in Helsinki than in smaller towns and cities. Student housing is reasonably priced; your university will support you in finding accommodation. As an EU citizen, you have the right to work in Finland, although language issues and a fairly heavy workload at university mean that this is unlikely.

> **❝** The housing is very cheap (cheaper than the UK) and relatively decent. The only thing that costs a lot is the food and the alcohol, but as long as you are aware of money, then it should work out! **❞**
>
> *Fiona Higgins, HAAGA-HELIA,*
> *University of Applied Sciences, Finland*

Most scholarships are for doctoral study or research, although institutions may have limited scholarships for students on other levels of study. Speak to your institution about this possibility. For more details, see the 'Scholarships' section at Study in Finland, www.studyinfinland.fi/tuition_and_scholarships/other_ possibilities.

You could study . . .

Bachelor of Hotel, Restaurant and Tourism Management
Saimaa University of Applied Sciences, Imatra
Three and a half years
Apply by 12 February
Tuition fees €0
Monthly living costs €700 (£517)

MSc Software Development
University of Tampere
Two years
Apply by 30 January
Tuition fees €0
Monthly living costs €700–€900 (£517–£665)

PhD in Marketing
Hanken School of Economics, Helsinki
Four years
Apply by 27 March for autumn start, 2 October for January start
Tuition fees €0
Monthly living costs up to €900 (£665)

Useful websites
www.studyinfinland.fi

Also worth considering . . .

If you're interested in the Nordic countries, perhaps you would be interested in studying in Iceland. To find out more, go to Study in Iceland at www.studyiniceland.is and the ENIC-NARIC country page for Iceland at www.enic-naric.net/iceland.aspx.

France

France is the UK's closest continental neighbour, offering good-quality education with a strong international reputation. According to the UNESCO Institute for Statistics, the country attracts 7.7% of all international students at university level. On the downside, it has limited English-medium options at undergraduate level in its public universities. This may well change, as the rules preventing teaching in English at public universities have been relaxed. According to OECD Education at a Glance 2014, 3,186 UK students are studying in France.

France has seven universities in the Times Higher Education World University Rankings Top 200 Universities 2014–2015.

Higher education in France

Higher education takes place in universities, grandes écoles and institutes of technology. The grandes écoles focus on science, engineering and business courses, offering some of their programmes in English. They are the most prestigious and selective institutions. They charge higher fees and require a competitive exam for entry, which students may spend two years working towards (after achieving A level-standard qualifications).

There may be some opportunities for the best international students at these institutions, perhaps after initial study at another university. You are advised to contact them to discuss their requirements, but you are likely to need proficiency in the French language.

The academic year starts in September or October and ends in May or June, much as in the UK.

> **❝** The class size is around 30–40 students, and there is an emphasis on group work. Furthermore, the professors are always willing to help students individually, and often give up their spare time in order to ensure that each student is on the same level. **❞**
>
> *Alican Spafford, Rouen Business School, France*

Applying

Applications for courses taught in English should be made through the international office of your chosen institution. There is a centralised application process known as APB or Admission post-bac for courses taught in French. You can normally make direct applications from around November. Application deadline dates vary between spring and summer, but you should apply as early as you are able. Some institutions have a rolling programme of application and recruitment, which goes on throughout the year.

In addition to your application form and application fee, you may need to include some of the following documents:

- academic transcript
- certificates
- personal statement, to include motivation for studying and future career goals

- letters of recommendation (normally two)
- research proposal (for postgraduate research)
- copy of passport.

The master's degree you choose depends on your future plans; choose a professional master's degree as a route to employment, and a research master's degree as a route to a doctorate.

Costs

France spends an average €10,000 (£7,391) per student per year on higher education. One result of this is the low price for degrees from public universities, which are generally under €500 (£370) per year for undergraduate and postgraduate study. Fees at public universities are set by law, while private institutions are more expensive, ranging from €3,000 to €10,000 (£2,217 to £7,391) or more per year.

The fees listed below are those set for 2014–2015.

- Bachelor's degree or licence: three years, annual tuition fees of €189.10 (£140).
- Master's degree: two years, annual tuition fees of €261.10 (£193).
- Doctoral degree or doctorate: three years, annual tuition fees of €396.10 (£293).

France is a fairly expensive place to live, ranked number 14 of 119 countries in the cost-of-living index (www.numbeo.com), a few places below the UK. CNOUS, the National Centre for University and Student Welfare, suggests that students would need around €700–€850 (£517–£628) per month for living costs. Costs in Paris are considerably higher. You'll find lots of useful information on student costs, and student life in general at www.cnous.fr.

Grants may be available to some international students through the French Ministry of Foreign and European Affairs. Entente Cordiale scholarships are awarded for postgraduate-level study. Information on these and other scholarships can be found at CampusBourses (www.campusfrance.org/fria/bourse), while CNOUS (www.cnous.fr) has more information on the system of grants and loans. Note that application deadlines for funding may fall earlier than course application deadlines.

You could study . . .

BA in Arts with third year abroad
College Universitaire de Sciences Po, Reims (private)
Apply before 5 May
Three years
Annual fees up to €10,040 (£7,421), depending on family income
Monthly living costs from €580 (£429)

MSc in Public Health
EHESP School of Public Health, Rennes
Apply by 27 February
Two years
Annual fees €256 (£189)
Monthly living costs approximately €800 (£591)

PhD Neutronics
National Institute of Nuclear Sciences and Engineering (INSTN), Gif-sur-Yvette
Apply by 11 March
Three years
Annual fees €0
Monthly living costs not provided, thesis allowances available

Useful websites
www.campusfrance.org/en

Germany

Germany offers a world-class education with no tuition fees in a country with the largest economy in Europe. 2,162 UK students already study there (OECD Education at a Glance 2014).

This year, Germany finds itself in third place in the Times Higher Education World University Rankings 2014–2015, with 12 of its universities featuring in the top 200. It comes behind USA and the UK, but has just pushed the Netherlands into fourth place.

Higher education in Germany

In Germany, higher education is run by each of the 16 states, rather than by one central Ministry of Education. You can choose between universities, universities of applied sciences and specialist colleges of art, film or music. Universities offer the more academic options up to doctoral level, with universities of applied sciences taking a more practical approach, but only to master's level. Colleges of art, film and music offer creative or design-based courses and often have additional entry requirements to determine artistic skill or musical aptitude.

What is *numerus clausus*? This phrase relates to courses that have far more applications than there are places (medicine, dentistry, veterinary medicine and pharmacology, for example); some courses have a nationwide *numerus clausus*, while other courses may be restricted only at a particular university. If your chosen course is classed as *numerus clausus*, pay careful attention to any additional entry requirements and check how they will decide who will gain a place.

Most institutions are publicly funded, with a smaller number financed by the Church or privately funded. Most German students study at the public institutions; they are cheaper and the standard of education is comparable, although they can suffer from overcrowding. At HochschulKompass (www.hochschulkompass.de) you can search for institutions by the way they are funded or by the category of institution.

The academic year officially begins in September, with classes starting in September or October. *Wintersemester* teaching runs until mid-February or March, while *Sommersemester* commences in March or April and ends in late July. The semester dates vary slightly between universities and universities of applied science.

If you want to study in Germany, you'll need a *Hochschulzugangsberechtigung* or university entrance qualification. You can check whether your qualifications are comparable at the German Academic Exchange Service (DAAD) online admission database www.daad.de.

Some German universities prefer students to have studied maths at A level, even for courses without mathematical content. A language A level, not necessarily German, is also a common requirement.

Applying

Application processes vary between different universities and even between different courses at the same institution. Some will opt for a central application service, like those listed below, while others require direct application. The best advice is to check with the international office at your university.

Over 100 universities are members of uni-assist (www.uni-assist.de/index_en.html), the university application service for international students, most often used when applicants have qualifications from outside Germany.

Applications for competitive options like medicine, dentistry, veterinary medicine and pharmacy tend to be made through the Foundation for Higher Education Admission at www. hochschulstart.de. You may need to translate this website through a service like Google Translate (www.translate.google.co.uk) as it isn't available in English.

Regardless of the system you use, you may be charged a fee for processing and you may need to provide additional information or evidence, including:

- certificates of qualifications achieved (your university will tell you how to get an authenticated copy)
- CV
- essay
- academic reference
- educational transcript
- SAT or ACT (American College Test) scores (see College Board for further details, www.sat.collegeboard.org/ home)
- research proposal.

Most application processes are open between October and June or July (for an autumn start), although you should check individual deadline dates and apply in good time.

Costs

Fees for undergraduate-level study at public institutions were phased out completely in 2014. However, higher-education institutions across the country make a charge for semester contributions; this covers certain administration charges and should entitle you to student discounts and free public transport. The cost varies between institutions; you should budget for around €250 (£185) per semester.

Where fees are charged for postgraduate study, they range from around €650 (£480) to as much as €10,000 (£7,391) per semester. You can expect to pay higher fees at private universities and colleges, at both undergraduate and postgraduate level, in some cases as much as €30,000 (£22,173) per year.

If you're lucky enough to get a scholarship, it is unlikely to cover all costs. Scholarships are particularly limited for undergraduate study. Search on the DAAD Scholarship Database and ask your university about their opportunities, www.daad.de/deutschland/en.

Living costs vary depending on where you study and the type of lifestyle you enjoy. According to the Study in Germany website, students should allow around €670 (£495) per month. Cities like Chemnitz, Dresden and Jena come out cheapest, with Munich, Hamburg, Cologne and Frankfurt the most expensive cities.

Germany is ranked number 25 of 119 countries on a 2015 cost-of-living ranking (www.numbeo.com), so living there should be not only cheaper than the UK, but also cheaper than New Zealand, the Netherlands and Singapore.

You could study . . .

BA Aviation Management
Worms University of Applied Sciences
Three years
Direct application by 15 January (for March entry)
Tuition fees €0
Monthly living costs €800 (£591)

Master's degree in Advanced Construction and Building Technology

Technical University of Munich

Two years

Direct application by 31 May

Tuition fees €0

Monthly living costs €830 (£613) in Munich

PhD Political Science

Graduate School of Economics and Social Sciences, University of Mannheim

Three years

Direct application by 15 March

Tuition fees €0

Monthly living costs €600–€700 (£443–£517)

Useful websites

www.study-in.de/en

Also worth considering . . .

Alternatives to Germany might include Austria or Liechtenstein. Discover education in Austria at www.studyinaustria.at/study_in_austria. You can research opportunities in Liechtenstein through ENIC-NARIC, www.enic-naric.net/liechtenstein.aspx.

Republic of Ireland

The Republic of Ireland is close to home and English-speaking, with a higher-education system that has much in common with the UK system. It is therefore a popular choice among UK students, with 5,068 UK students based there at the last count (OECD Education at a Glance 2014).

Higher education in Republic of Ireland

Degrees can be awarded by universities and by a number of institutes of technology. Other higher-education institutions exist, where qualifications are awarded through HETAC, the Higher Education and Training Awards Council (www.hetac.ie). A number of the higher-education institutions in Ireland are private. For a list, see the Education in Ireland website, www.educationinireland.com/en/Where-can-I-study-/View-all-Private-Higher-Education-Institutions.

For general information on education in Ireland, go to the Irish Council for International Students website, www.icosirl.ie.

One Irish university appears on the Times Higher Education World University Rankings Top 200 2014–2015. Trinity College Dublin is ranked number 138 (just below Birkbeck University of London and Brunel University of London).

The qualifications on offer differ slightly from those in England, Wales and Northern Ireland in that a three-year ordinary degree is available, as well as a three-year or four-year honours degree (Scotland offers a similar choice). The grading system (first, upper second, lower second and so on) echoes the UK. Taught and research master's degrees should take one to two years, with doctorates taking a minimum of three years' research.

You can search for undergraduate and postgraduate courses through the Qualifax Course Finder (www.qualifax.ie). Postgraduate options can be found through Postgrad Ireland (www.postgradireland.com).

Entry requirements

The A level requirements for most degrees can make Irish universities a challenge to enter. This contrasts with many other European countries where the completion of A level-standard qualifications is sufficient and specific grades aren't always necessary. Irish universities tend to be looking for academic subjects that echo those taken at school in Ireland. If you are applying with different qualifications, you should speak to the university's international office or admissions office in advance; they may need to evaluate your qualifications before you apply.

Most degree-level programmes ask for three Cs at A level, or equivalent, as a minimum requirement. At universities and associated colleges, your best four A levels (or three, plus an AS in a different subject) will be considered up to a maximum of 600 points. In the scoring system for A levels, grade A* at A level is worth 150 points, and grade E is worth 40. (For full details, see the Central Applications Office website at www.cao.ie/index.php?page=scoring&s=gce.) Some institutions will consider different combinations of A level and AS level grades, so may be accessible for those without four A levels. For the more competitive courses, like medicine, the need for particularly high grades can make four A levels a necessity.

Entry to medicine

For entry to medicine, applicants must have at least 480 points (which can be obtained from four Bs at A level, for example), plus any minimum requirements from their university. Both exam results and HPAT scores will be considered when offering a place. See Undergraduate Entry to Medicine brochure for more details, (www2.cao.ie/downloads/documents/UGMedEntry2015.pdf).

The Health Professions Admission Test (HPAT, www.hpat-ireland.acer.edu.au) is required for undergraduate entry to medicine, while the Graduate Medical School Admissions Test (GAMSAT, www.gamsat.acer.edu.au/gamsat-ireland) is needed for applications to postgraduate medicine. Application dates are often early and examination dates may be restricted to a single day.

Applying

While the academic year is in line with the UK, running from September to June, the application system has its differences. Undergraduate applications are based on actual grades (and an admissions test, in some cases) and little else, so offers aren't made until results come out.

You can apply online or on paper from 5 November through the Central Applications Office (CAO) at www.cao.ie. Applications should be made by 1 February or earlier, particularly for restricted-entry courses, although there is a late closing date for other courses of 1 May. In most cases, there is no need for references or a personal statement. A fee is charged for processing.

Postgraduate applications

Postgraduate applications can be made direct to your chosen university, often via the international office. Some institutions use the Postgraduate Applications Centre (PAC) at www.pac.ie. Closing dates vary, even within a single institution. In most cases, a minimum of a 2:2 grade in an undergraduate honours degree is required for a master's degree.

In addition to the application form and fee, you may need to include an academic transcript, references, a CV, a research proposal (where relevant) and a statement of interest, explaining your motivation, commitment and what you hope to achieve.

Costs

UK students on their first full-time undergraduate degree should not have to pay tuition fees. However, you will be required to pay a student contribution or registration fee of a maximum €2,750 (£2,033) in 2014/2015. This will increase to €3,000 (£2,217) in 2015/2016.

According to Postgrad Ireland, you can expect postgraduate fees of over €4,000 (£2,956) for research degrees, with taught programmes ranging from under €4,000 (£2,956) to as much as €29,500 (£21,803) for an MBA.

At number 11 out of 119 countries on a 2015 cost-of-living ranking, Ireland falls directly below the UK (see www.numbeo.com for more details). Education in Ireland estimates that, on average a student can expect to spend between €5,000 and €11,000 (£3,695 and £8,130) per year; of course, this will depend on where you live and the lifestyle you choose. Dublin is the most expensive place to live, with the Irish Council for International Students reporting living costs of around €10,000 (£7,390) to €15,000 (£11,086) per year.

You could study . . .

BArch in Architecture
University of Limerick
Five years
Apply through CAO by 1 February
Registration fee €2,750 (£2,033)
Monthly living costs €1,000 (£739)

MA Celtic Civilisation

University College Cork

One year

Apply by 18 November

Annual fees €6,000 (£4,435)

Monthly living costs €1,145–€1,495 (£846–£1,105)

PhD Agriculture and Food Science

University College Dublin

Three years

No application deadline date

Annual fees €6,300 (£4,656)

Monthly living costs from €1,050 (£776)

Useful websites

www.educationireland.ie

Italy

Few public universities in Italy teach their courses in English. Even so, the latest figures show us that 259 UK students are studying in the country (OECD Education at a Glance 2014). Italy also remains a popular destination for students on Erasmus exchanges.

Higher education in Italy

The majority of universities in Italy are state-funded, although there is a range of alternative provision including non-state universities, universities for foreigners (focusing on Italian language, literature and culture), specialist postgraduate schools, and telematic (or distance learning) universities. Most programmes are taught in Italian; English-medium opportunities in Italy are most often found at private universities and colleges.

There are a number of options to study medicine in Italy, taught in English and often at a cost of below €3,800 per year:

- University of Bari: www.uniba.it/offerta-formativa/english-medical-curriculum
- University of Milan: www.mimed.it/unimi.shtml
- University of Pavia: http://nfs.unipv.it/medicinecourse/school/school.html
- Sapienza University of Rome: http://en.uniroma1.it/structures/faculties–0/medicine-and-dentistry
- Tor Vergata University of Rome: http://med.uniroma2.it/node/4114
- Second University of Naples: www.medicina.unina2.it

Competition can be intense and you will need to learn Italian to cope with patient contact as the course progresses. The IMAT test is often a key part of the selection process; you can find out more at Admissions Testing Service (www.admissionstestingservice.org).

> **66** All the teaching is done through large lectures (130 students per class) but the professors do have office hours and are reachable by email. There are no seminars and classes aren't compulsory: a big bonus. **99**
>
> *James Wheeler, Bocconi University, Italy*

The academic year runs from September or October until July. The qualifications on offer are a three-year *laurea* which is the Italian bachelor's degree, the two-year *laurea specialistica* which is comparable to a master's degree, while the *dottore magistrale* is comparable to a doctorate. Much of the assessment in Italian higher education is exam-based.

> The Politecnico di Milano now delivers most of its undergraduate and postgraduate degree courses in English.

Applying

Provided that you meet the general entry requirements for higher education in the UK and have completed 12 years of education, you can be considered for undergraduate study in Italy. If you have a bachelor's degree, you can be considered for a master's degree, and if you have a master's degree, you can consider applying for a doctorate. You should apply direct to individual institutions, which may set their own additional entry requirements. You can discuss the process and timescale with your university's international office before you apply.

Costs

Fees are set by the individual institutions. You should expect to pay up to €1,000 (£739) per year for undergraduate study in the public institutions, although some institutions will charge more for courses taught entirely in English. Fees at private institutions are higher again, although these might still end up costing less than many of the courses in the UK, particularly as fees tend to be reduced for those with low family income. Postgraduate fees start at around €700 to €800 (£517 to £591) per year.

EU students should be entitled to the same student financial support as Italian students. This includes student loans and housing assistance. You'll find out more at your chosen university's *Diritto allo studio universitario* or DSU. For living costs, Italy comes out a little cheaper than the UK. It is ranked 19th (to the UK's 10th) in the cost-of-living rankings for 2015 at www.numbeo.com.

You could study . . .

Laurea (Bachelor's) degree in Computer Engineering
Politecnico di Torino, Turin
Three years
Apply by 31 July
Annual fees €2,529 (£1,869)
Monthly living costs €600–€800 (£443–£591)

Master's degree in Economics and Political Science

University of Milan, Milan

Two years

Apply between April and September (competitive application)

Annual fees €2,755 (£2,036)

Monthly living costs of up to €1,000 (£739)

PhD Modern Languages, Cultures, Societies and Linguistics

Ca' Foscari University of Venice

Three years

Apply by 29 May

Annual fees €1,011 (£747)

Monthly living costs from €750 (£554)

Useful websites

www.study-in-italy.it

Also worth considering . . .

If you're looking for higher education near Italy, then how about Malta? There are no tuition fees (even for medical courses) and the island attracts a number of UK students every year. Find out more at the ENIC–NARIC country page for Malta: www.enic-naric.net/malta.aspx. Malta only has one university; the website for the University of Malta is at www. um.edu.mt.

Greece could also provide an alternative to Italy, although few international students choose Greece for their studies. You can find out more at the Greek Ministry of Education (www. minedu.gov.gr).

The Netherlands

Interest in the Netherlands as a study venue has been growing steadily, with its cheaper fees and hundreds of programmes taught entirely in English. Dutch universities are keen to attract international students and have been actively recruiting in the UK by visiting schools and attending education fairs. According to the latest figures, some 1,209 UK students are studying in the Netherlands. That's an increase of 205 students since last year, with the universities also reporting an increase in applications.

The Netherlands has an impressive 11 universities in the Times Higher Education World University Rankings Top 200 2014–2015. The country finds itself in fourth position, after the US, UK and now Germany, for the number of institutions in the top 200.

Higher education in the Netherlands

The style of teaching in the Netherlands is interactive and student-centred, with tutorials and seminars taking place in smaller groups than you would expect in many UK institutions. The academic year runs from early September to late June.

You can opt to study at a research-based university (WO) or a University of Applied Sciences (HBO), which offers more vocational options. An academic or research-oriented bachelor's degree (WO) takes three years, while the applied alternative (HBO) would take four years, with the chance of a work placement and often a study-abroad opportunity. Associate degrees take two years, with the option to move on to an applied bachelor's degree.

If you are not ready to specialise in a single subject, a number of institutions in the Netherlands offer liberal arts programmes where you can opt from a number of subject options before deciding on a final major subject.

> 66 We're taught in a classroom. There are no lectures.
> The classes are very practical and laid back. I find
> the teaching style very personal as there are only up to
> 30 people in a class. We're really aided and guided. 99
>
> *Rebecca Jackson, Stenden University*
> *of Applied Sciences, the Netherlands*

At master's level, you again have the choice of either a research-based degree (WO) or the applied route (HBO), both of which take one to two years. In contrast, doctorates are only available through the research universities (WO).

To find a course, you can browse the NUFFIC database at http://ispacsearch.nuffic.nl or use Study in Holland's database at www.studyinholland.co.uk/what_to_study.html.

> 66 I had to get used to a more concise way of writing,
> but it was more the workload that presented the
> real challenge for me. I did far more in my first few months
> in comparison to my friends at UK-based universities.
> I guess you are eased into it in the beginning but by the
> second month you are expected to be up to speed. Now that
> I'm in the second year, I would say that the course has now
> become more focused, whereas last year it was rather
> generalised. 99
>
> *Simran Gill, Fontys University of Applied Sciences, the*
> *Netherlands*

Applying

In most cases, two or three A levels, or equivalent, should be sufficient to meet the requirements for most bachelor's degrees. If you studied an alternative qualification, you should discuss it with your chosen university. At postgraduate level, you will need a bachelor's degree to progress to a master's. It is likely that any offer you receive will require you to pass your courses, rather than achieve specific grades. Although getting a place at university may seem easier than in the UK, the university will need you to prove your capability in the first year. Students who can't cope academically will be asked to leave the course.

In some popular subjects like medicine or law, places may be restricted through a scheme known as *numerus fixus*. For these courses, the allocation of places is decided through a slightly complicated lottery system, which can vary according to the requirements of the university. According to studyinholland. co.uk, if you're applying to courses like medicine, psychology, economics, physiotherapy or law then you may be affected by *numerus fixus*. Talk to your chosen institution to gain an understanding of how to give yourself the best chance of success.

As A level results are published after the qualification confirmation deadline for Dutch institutions, you should be asked to complete a late submission form. Your university will be able to tell you how and when to complete this.

Studielink

You can apply to public institutions at undergraduate and postgraduate level through Studielink (http://info.studielink. nl/en/studenten/Pages/Default.aspx) from September or October onwards. You can choose up to four options, including one *numerus fixus* course. Requirements for supporting documentation vary, but could include:

- certificates
- academic transcript
- personal statement or letter of motivation indicating why you are applying
- copy of passport
- CV
- two letters of recommendation
- research proposal (where relevant).

For some postgraduate study, an admissions test like GRE (www.ets.org/gre) or Graduate Management Admission Test (GMAT; visit www.mba.com) will be needed. In all cases, your institution will be able to tell you whether they require application through Studielink and any supporting information they need.

Most courses have an application deadline of mid-May, although *numerus fixus* courses require an earlier application. You can find a helpful guide to Studielink at the Study in Holland website, www.studyinholland.co.uk/studielink.html. Some courses will require a direct application instead.

The application process at university colleges differs, in that it requires an earlier application that should be made direct; another key difference is that students are invited to an interview.

> **❝** I had to write a personal statement and an essay. I was out of Europe when I applied so they did the interview over Skype. They were also fine with me scanning and emailing a lot of the documents, which was a huge help. **❞**
>
> *Shanna Hanbury, Amsterdam University College,*
> *the Netherlands*

Costs

In the public universities, the annual fees were set at €1,906 (£1,409) for 2014–2015 at undergraduate level, and something similar at postgraduate level; the fees have been agreed at €1,951 (£1,442) for 2015–2016. This can be paid upfront or through an instalment system. Fees at university colleges are usually higher.

EU undergraduate and postgraduate students can apply for a loan from the Dutch government of just over €1,000 (£739) per month to put towards living costs and tuition fees. This is open to EU students under the age of 30 at the start of the course who are working for at least 56 hours per month. Previously, this was offered as a grant, but this changed in September 2015.

You can find out more about student finance at DUO-IB-Groep (Department of Education), www.duo.nl/particulieren/international_Student/Student_finance/how_does_it_work.asp.

Scholarships are also available. You can search for a scholarship through NUFFIC's Grantfinder at www.studyinholland.nl/scholarships.

At number 16 out of 119 countries on the 2015 Numbeo (www.numbeo.com) cost-of-living ranking, the Netherlands is not particularly cheap, but you should find slightly better value for money than in the UK. You should budget for between €800 and €1100 (£591 and £813) per month, according to www.studyinholland.nl.

> **❝** Living costs are relatively cheap. There are low price supermarkets which offer a wide variety of products at good prices. Food is pretty much the same here as it is in the UK. Supermarkets are tremendously accessible; I live above one. I'd recommend setting a budget and making food in bulk, if necessary. Going out to party is not too expensive, as drinks are cheap in Venlo and I rarely spend over €80 (£59) a week. **❞**
>
> *Simran Gill, Fontys University of Applied Sciences,*
> *the Netherlands*

You could study . . .

BSc Psychology
Leiden University
Three years
Apply by 15 May
Annual fees €1,951 (£1,442)
Monthly living costs €850–€1,400 (£628–£1,035)

Master's degree in Human Geography
Radboud University Nijmegen
One year
Apply by 1 May
Annual fees €1,951 (£1,442)
Annual living costs of up to €10,000 (£7,391)

MA Arts and Culture
University of Amsterdam
One year
Apply by 15 December (later deadlines also available)
Annual fees €1,951 (£1,442)
Monthly living costs €850–€1,400 (£628–£1,035)

Useful websites

www.studyinholland.nl

Norway

With around 19,000 students from overseas, approximately
346 students from the UK and no fees at public universities,
how about studying in Norway? It offers many postgraduate
courses in English, although only a handful at bachelor's-degree
level. Norway has high costs but one of the best standards of
living in the world; it has been ranked top by the UN four
times. It can be cold, but you will discover a great outdoor
lifestyle.

> ❝ Within the first month of arriving here, I'd been on
> fishing trips, hiking trips, whizzing around in a
> little rib boat on the Saltstraumen, swimming in some of the
> most beautiful lakes which are a 15-minute walk from the
> university, and even met the Norwegian Prime Minister. It's
> been quite something! ❞
>
> *Megan Doxford, University of Nordland, Norway*

Higher education in Norway

Higher education takes place at universities, specialised university
institutions, university colleges or national colleges of the arts.
Universities have a research focus, while university colleges focus
on professional studies. It is possible to gain a master's degree and
sometimes even a doctorate at a university college. Most higher-
education institutions in Norway are state-funded, although
there are some private university colleges. In Norway, you
would generally study a three-year bachelor's degree, a two-year

master's, and a three-year doctorate. The academic year runs from mid-August to mid-June.

It is common for students in Norway to take time out to work or travel before university, so they may be a little older.

You can search for study opportunities through Study in Norway at www.studyinnorway.no.

Applying

According to the GSU list (the list of minimum requirements for admission to Norwegian higher education), you will need five subjects in total, including two A levels; you could make up the other three subjects from GCSEs. From 2016–2017, three A levels may be required. Students from Scotland will need to pass five Highers or Advanced Highers. Some subjects will have additional requirements. You can find the GSU list at the Norwegian Agency for Quality Assurance in HE (NOKUT) website, www.nokut.no/en/facts-and-statistics/surveys-and-databases/gsu-list. Successful completion of a bachelor's degree is needed to progress to master's level.

You should apply direct to your chosen institution sometime between December and March for courses starting in August. Application deadlines vary, but your institution will be able to advise on specific deadline dates, as well as any supplementary information needed. This could include:

- academic transcript
- copies of certificates, for qualifications already gained
- CV
- research proposal, where necessary.

> ❝ The application process was very simple and relatively hassle-free. Everything was done online and they only required a few documents such as my undergraduate transcripts, my CV and some essays I was required to write to apply for a scholarship. A GMAT score was also required. ❞
>
> *John Magee, BI Norwegian Business School, Norway*

Costs

Whether you are studying at undergraduate level or for a master's degree or a PhD, you are unlikely to have to pay fees at a state-funded university or university college. There is a small semester fee of NOK300–NOK600 (£26–£52), which gives you a student discount card along with membership of student welfare associations, access to campus health services, sports facilities and so on. Private institutions charge fees, although these should still be lower than those charged by universities in the UK, perhaps with the exception of some MBAs.

There are some scholarships available for study in Norway. See the Study in Norway website for details.

Living costs in Norway are high; in fact, it ranks number two out of 119 countries in a 2015 cost-of-living index, see www.numbeo. com. You should expect to have at the very least NOK8,900 (£768) per month for living expenses.

> 66 The price of living is very high, so the Norwegian government requests you have ample funds for the year ahead. You have to have NOK90,000 (£7,769) in a Norwegian bank account in order to be accepted. This is the amount of money needed to survive a year at university out here. It is possible to get work, which helps an awful lot financially, especially as the minimum wage is a lot higher than in the UK. 99
>
> *Megan Doxford, University of Nordland, Norway*

You could study . . .

BSc Biology
University of Nordland, Bodø
Three years
Apply by 1 April
Tuition fees NOK0
Monthly living expenses NOK9,785 (£845)

Master's degree in Contemporary Art
University of Tromsø
Two years
Apply by 1 March
Tuition fees NOK0
Monthly living expenses NOK9,785 (£845)

PhD Marketing
BI Norwegian Business School
Four years
Various application deadlines
Tuition fees NOK0
Monthly living expenses NOK9,250 (£798)

Useful websites

www.studyinnorway.no

Spain

Although the option to study in Spain on an exchange programme is a popular one for UK students, with 1,115 university students based there according to latest figures, opportunities for a full degree are limited. Most options at public institutions are taught in Spanish though there are opportunities in private institutions, which make up around a third of the higher-education institutions in Spain. The number of courses taught in English is on the increase as a direct result of the Spanish government's interest in recruiting more international students, with plans for one in ten students to be from overseas by 2015.

Higher education in Spain

You can find information on studying in Spain and search for courses at Study in Spain (www.studyinspain.info/). To search for courses taught in English, try Study Portals (www.studyportals. eu), EUNICAS (www.eunicas.co.uk) and A Star Future (www. astarfuture.co.uk).

Undergraduate degrees take three to four years, master's degrees last one or two years, while doctorates take from three to four years. Some of the private universities offer accelerated programmes to reduce the length of study. The academic year runs from October to June.

> ❝ It is a young university that is keen to keep growing with student participation; I was excited to influence and to be part of a new and growing institution. ❞
>
> *Tudor Etchells, IE University, Spain*

Applying

Application deadlines tend to fall in May or June for October start courses, but it is worth applying well in advance of this date as there are often more applicants than places. Some courses also offer a February intake.

As long as you have the general qualifications to access higher education (HE) in the UK, you should meet the general requirements for HE in Spain. Talk direct to your chosen university about their application procedures. You will need to register with UNED at www.uned.es for evaluation of your qualifications or *credencial de acceso*.

Completion of a bachelor's degree in the UK or the European Higher Education Area will satisfy the general requirements of a master's degree. Sixty ECTS credits are required to progress to research at doctoral level.

> **❝** The university application process explored your whole range of interest and motivations. It was personal and comprehensive, wanting to derive the best aspects from their applicants. **❞**
>
> *Esme Alexander, IE University, Spain*

Costs

A bachelor's degree or *grado* at a public university costs from around €850 (£628) per year, with some institutions charging three times this amount. At private universities, fees start at around €7,000 (£5,174), but can be considerably higher than this, although these institutions often have generous schemes of financial support.

Master's (*máster*) and doctoral (*doctorado*) degrees are paid for per credit, with the annual cost of a master's course ranging from €1,000 (£739) and with some public institutions charging up to €6,000 (£4,435). Private institutions set their own fees, but these must still fall within government limits.

Some scholarships are available and can be found through the Study in Spain website at www.studyinspain.info/en/reportajes/ propuestas/How-to-obtain-a-grant-to-study-in-Spain. You can also ask the international office of your chosen university.

Living costs are lower than in a number of the European countries mentioned in this chapter. Spain is ranked number 39 out of 119 countries in a cost-of-living survey for 2015 (see www. numbeo.com), comparing favourably to the UK at number 10. Prices in the major cities, like Madrid or Barcelona, can be much higher.

You could study . . .

Bachelor's degree in Energy Engineering
Leganes campus, University Carlos III de Madrid
Four years
Apply by 30 June
Annual fees €1,860 (£1,375)
Monthly living costs €500–€600 (£370–£443)

Master's degree in European Integration
Universitat Autònoma de Barcelona
Apply by 12 October
Annual fees €2,760 (£2,040)
Monthly living costs €700–€1,000 (£517–£739)

PhD Mental Health: Genetics and Environment

University Rovira I Virgili, Tarragona

Three years

Apply by 1 March

Fees per module €536 (£396)

Monthly living costs €550 (£407)

Useful websites

www.universidad.es/en

www.studyinspain.info/?/=en

Also worth considering . . .

Interested in studying in Portugal? Nearly all courses are in Portuguese, but you can find out more at www. studyinportugal.edu.pt.or DGES (General Directorate for Higher Education) at www.dges.mctes.pt/DGES.

Sweden

As many as 30,000 international students currently choose Sweden for their studies and 647 of them are from the UK. With a strong focus on innovation and a forward-thinking, student-centred academic environment, Swedish higher education has much to offer.

Five Swedish institutions are in the Times Higher Education World University Rankings Top 200 2014–2015.

Higher education in Sweden

The academic year runs from late August to early June and is divided into two semesters. Three-year bachelor's degrees or *kandidatexamen* are the norm. A master's degree or *masterexamen* will take one to two years, while doctoral research or *doktorsexamen* takes at least four years.

Higher education takes place in universities and university colleges, with universities the only institutions with the automatic right to issue doctoral degrees. Local collaboration is widespread, so many institutions offer options reflecting the needs of local industries and businesses.

You can search for study options at www.universityadmissions.se.

The name of the institution will not always reveal whether it is a university or university college; most university colleges will call themselves universities, while some universities are called *högskola* (or university college) in Swedish. Degrees awarded by both types of institution are equivalent to one another.

Applying

Any qualification that gives you access to HE in the UK should do the same for undergraduate studies in Sweden. Individual institutions then set their own procedures for selecting applicants; this might include grades, assessment of samples of work, interviews, admissions tests or work experience. Your institution's international office will be able to advise further about any special requirements.

For bachelor's and master's degrees, applications are made online through University Admissions at www.universityadmissions. se. Deadlines are generally mid-January for August start and mid-August for any courses starting in spring. At doctoral level, applications are made direct to the institution and often to the specific department, accompanied by copies of certificates, academic transcripts and letters of recommendation. Check any deadline dates with your academic department.

As the Swedish academic year begins in August, shortly after A level results come out, there may be insufficient time to confirm a place for the same academic year; applicants might need to consider a gap year.

Costs

In most cases, university courses in Sweden are free of tuition charges, although student-union membership fees are payable at SEK50–350 (£4–£27) per semester. A range of scholarships are available at Study in Sweden (www.studyinsweden.se/Scholarships). Ask your institution about any scholarships that they administer.

An average monthly budget for a student is around SEK7,300 (£566). Sweden is ranked number 17 out of 119 countries in Numbeo's 2015 cost-of-living table at www.numbeo.com, which makes it cheaper than the UK, Denmark and Australia.

You could study . . .

BA in Fine Art
Lund University, Malmö
Three years
Apply via www.universityadmissions.se by 2 March
Tuition fees SEK0
Monthly living costs SEK7,500 (£581)

Master's degree in Bioentrepreneurship
Karolinska Institute, Stockholm
Two years
Apply via www.universityadmissions.se by 15 January
Tuition fees SEK0
Monthly living costs from SEK8,750 (£678)

Useful websites

www.studyinsweden.se

Switzerland

If you choose Switzerland for your studies, you'll be in good company: Albert Einstein studied and carried out research at the country's universities at the turn of the last century. More recently, 642 UK students have chosen Switzerland as the venue for their higher education. Switzerland offers world-class programmes in science and technology, but it is also a good country for budding linguists. There are four national languages: German, French, Italian and Romansh.

An impressive seven Swiss institutions feature in the Times Higher Education World University Rankings Top 200 for 2014–2015.

Higher education in Switzerland

The academic year runs from September to June and is split into two semesters. A bachelor's degree tends to take three years to complete. A master's degree will take one-and-a-half to two years, while doctoral research takes from three to five years.

Higher education takes place in universities, federal institutes of technology and universities of applied sciences. If you're looking for traditional, research-based learning you'll find it at the universities. The two federal institutes of technology are world-class centres of education and research in technology and the sciences. The universities and federal institutes of technology offer education up to doctoral level.

The universities of applied sciences focus on technical or vocational learning; many of these institutions include some form of work experience. You may well have heard of the Swiss hotel management schools. They are known all over the world, although you will pay a premium in tuition fees for their quality and prestige.

You can find links to the Swiss institutions at Swiss University, www.studyinginswitzerland.ch.

Applying

Entry to a Bachelor's degree in Switzerland is possible with A levels or equivalent qualifications. There is a competitive entry process known as *numerus clausus* for some courses including medicine, dentistry and veterinary medicine. Entry to a master's degree or PhD is possible after a bachelor's degree or master's degree respectively.

Applications should be made direct to your chosen institution, with deadlines generally set around April.

No A level or equivalent qualification in Maths? You might struggle to get into a public university without this, even for unrelated courses. The private universities might be a bit more flexible. In addition, at some institutions, you'll be required to sit an entrance exam.

Costs

For undergraduate-level study at a public institution, tuition fees start at around €700 (£517) rising to around €4,000 (£2,956). You can expect to pay considerably more in private institutions, including the schools of hotel management.

Universities can provide details of any scholarships they offer. Swiss University provides some information on application processes for funding at www.studyinginswitzerland.ch/grants-scholarship-fees.htm

Switzerland is not a cheap country to live in. In fact, it appears at the very top of Numbeo's (www.numbeo.com) 2015 cost-of-living table. The Swiss University website estimates living expenses between CHF18,000 (£12,461) and CHF28,000 (£19,384) per year.

You could study . . .

BA Multilingual Communication

University of Geneva

Three years

Apply to university by 30 April (entrance exam required)

Annual tuition fees €700 (£517)

Monthly living costs CHF1,400–CHF1,900 (£969–£1,315)

MSc Geology

University of Lausanne

Two years

Apply to university by 30 April

Annual tuition fees CHF1,160 (£803)

Monthly living costs from CHF1,950 (£1,350)

Useful websites

www.studyinginswitzerland.ch

Pros and cons of study in Europe

Pros

- Relatively close to home.
- Often cheaper for tuition fees than much of the UK.
- No visa restrictions.
- Able to work and to stay on after study.

Cons

- Language issues.
- Some countries have high costs of living.
- Pressure to do well in first year to remain on the course.

Student story
Tom Aitchison, KU Leuven, Belgium

Tom Aitchison was no stranger to international study when he started to consider where he would take his master's degree. 'I previously studied abroad as part of my undergraduate degree in Washington, DC and it opened my eyes to the possibilities and ease of moving abroad.' Tom now finds himself in the unusual position of being able to compare university education in the UK, US and Belgium, after choosing an Advanced Master's degree in European Politics and Policies at KU Leuven.

'I decided to study in Belgium due to the opportunities to intern in Brussels alongside studying. KU Leuven fitted the bill perfectly: it has the best reputation both in Belgium and within EU institutions. There are very few graduate schemes for politically-minded students and therefore you are most likely going to be applying for jobs against people who have experience. In this market, a master's alone is not enough and therefore interning, and gaining work experience alongside, allows you to develop your CV.

'In the UK, politically-focused experience is generally in London where the cost of living is significantly higher. Belgium offered a world-renowned university at the heart of Europe for a fraction of the tuition price at American and British institutions. The proximity to Brussels meant that classes regularly utilise EU professionals as guest lecturers or actual course tutors. This was also something that was a particular advantage of studying in DC where you were able to engage with actual practitioners in your field of study. The opportunity to develop language skills was also particularly appealing.

'Due to the small class size there is great support for your academic studies. Especially when studying a selective course like an advanced master's, tutors are extremely keen to help you. Tutors are always willing to discuss, help you prepare your dissertation and also offer careers advice.'

Another benefit that Tom has experienced is increased flexibility in setting his own timetable. 'Modules have already been scheduled when you select them, so any clashes are your own fault, but the main advantage is that you can skew your timetable to favour the beginning of the week, or afternoons, or a particular semester. This is particularly useful to know if you are working or interning alongside studying, as you can plan your timetable around work. My experience in the UK is that you pick your modules based only on the topics and you don't find out your timetable until September which could limit your ability to work outside of study.'

Tom considered four main factors when deciding where to study: reputation, location, cost and course. 'KU Leuven ranks in the top 13 in Europe and top four on the continent (THE World Rankings 2013–2014). Speaking to EU professionals in Brussels it is clear to see that many have studied at KU Leuven, most prominently the President of the European Council, Herman Van Rompuy. The location, as mentioned, was ideal for career development. The cost was marginal in comparison to the UK: €2,800 (£2,069) for an advanced master's; €610.60 (£451) for an initial master's. Finally, the course at the institution was part of the EMPA (European Masters of Public Administration) structure, enabling me to possibly move to another university in the EMPA network for my second semester. Being accredited by EMPA also meant the course itself would be very academically rigorous and highly regarded. The course is also selective, meaning that you study as part of a small, close-knit class.'

'I applied to a variety of universities across Europe and the application process seems a lot more relaxed than the UK, with deadlines being far later. Moreover, many Benelux (Belgium, the Netherlands and Luxembourg) universities do not require deposits on accepting a place and therefore it allows you to finish your undergraduate studies before spending money on something you will not begin for a further six months. In Belgium, they are not selective about undergraduate admissions and initial master's admissions, but they can be with advanced master's. Therefore the application process regularly asks for transcripts, motivational letters, a writing sample, TOEFL or IELTS scores (English language tests) and ideas for research upon entry to the programme.'

Tom has had to adjust to two different countries over the past few years, so he understands many of the challenges of settling in. 'Moving abroad for the first time is not easy; it can take some time to properly settle. Stick with it. The values and memories that studying abroad gives you are always worth it and it equips you with skills to do it again or adapt to similar alien situations in the future.'

Tom's top tips

Sources of information
'Expat websites can be extremely helpful in finding your way around cities and how things work. As official country websites sometimes overlook minor details, which as a UK student you actually need, expat sites are particularly helpful.'

Housing
'The university provided a database for housing and the opportunity to apply for halls. Whilst halls primarily go to undergraduates, there is always a chance for postgraduate students. Housing in Leuven is a mixture of studios, rooms and shared apartments. The database is made up of registered landlords who sign up to a university-drafted contract, giving you full support if anything was to go wrong.

'If you can visit, go. It is always best to see it in person. Always begin by checking what their stance is with regards to guarantors. In America, many private apartments require guarantors with American bank accounts and certain levels of income, which you will be unlikely to have. You need to check if your visa can count as a guarantor. And try and get bills included, it is more common abroad than in the UK and it avoids utility company hassle.'

Food
'Finding British items such as PG Tips can be a welcome sight, but finding new favourites is equally rewarding.'

Living costs

'Remember that start-up costs are a lot. Whether it is desk lamps or mattresses, it soon spirals. Your first month's living costs will likely be twice as high as a normal month.'

Financial support for study

'Save up as much of your maintenance loan in your final year in the UK as you can. It is the best loan you will ever get! Allow two months if you're applying for a Professional and Career Development Loan as they can take some time.'

Working while studying

'Do it! Either you will be working to fund your studies and then it is necessary, or you are doing it for experience, and then it will give you the practical insight no academic course can.'

Making friends

'Whatever clubs and societies you are part of back home, they will be available abroad. Join them for the chance to meet like-minded people.'

Travel and transport

'Price comparison sites such as Skyscanner (www.skyscanner.net) allow you to view the cheapest days to travel each month. Unless you have a rewards card with an airline, there is no point sticking with one. Look out for airlines which offer student tickets, such as Brussels Airlines.

'Booking flights and trains in advance is the best way to cut the cost of travel. If you are bringing a lot of luggage, it may be worth looking at companies such as sendmybag.com. It ships luggage ahead of your arrival.'

For Tom, this next year will be an important year as he decides on his future direction. 'I hope to work for the EU in some capacity or in the field of international relations. This year will definitely define what my eventual career will be.'

And throughout Tom's experiences, the best and most important aspects of studying abroad have been the people. 'You can make some of your best friends being overseas, especially if they are non-natives like yourself. Even when they are not your friends, they may be a contact that can help you in your career.

'Studying abroad can help you in a career and socially, and it's the people that you meet that help create those opportunities.'

KU Leuven (www.kuleuven.be/english) is a Dutch-language university in Flanders, Belgium offering undergraduate and postgraduate opportunities taught in English. It appears at number 55 on the Times Higher Education World University Rankings Top 200 2014–2015 (the highest ranking Belgian university), just below the University of Manchester.

IE university
REDEFINING UNIQUENESS

YOU'VE
GOT
IT

At IE University we enable you to discover your full potential and enhance your unique value in an international environment that will broaden your horizons and connect you to the world. Our campuses in Madrid and Segovia, Spain, offer bachelor degrees in English that integrate a broad range of teaching approaches and personalized options that allow you to shape your own education according to your professional aspirations. At IE University you will develop the outlook and skills you need to map your own path to success on a global scale.

BACHELOR IN BUSINESS ADMINISTRATION (BBA)	BACHELOR IN PSYCHOLOGY
BACHELOR IN INTERNATIONAL RELATIONS	BACHELOR IN ARCHITECTURE
	DUAL DEGREE BBA + BACHELOR OF LAWS
DUAL DEGREE BBA + BACHELOR IN INTERNATIONAL RELATIONS	DUAL DEGREE BACHELOR OF LAWS AND LEGAL PRACTICE COURSE
BACHELOR OF LAWS (LL.B.)	DUAL BACHELOR DEGREE OF LAWS AND INTERNATIONAL RELATIONS
BACHELOR IN COMMUNICATION	

CAMPUS MADRID/SEGOVIA. SPAIN | TEL. +44 (0)2037272614 | UK@IE.EDU

WWW.IE.EDU/UNIVERSITY

NHH
NORWEGIAN SCHOOL OF ECONOMICS

DO YOU WISH FOR A BUSINESS EDUCATION THAT:

- is top ranked in the world?
- emphasizes a practical approach, internationalism, ethical awareness and social responsibility?
- in a worldwide perspective, probably has the best integration with industry?
- prepares you for an international management position?

Then CEMS Master's in International Management (CEMS MIM) is the perfect choice for you.

Combine CEMS MIM with any of the six master programmes at NHH;
- Economics
- Energy, Natural Resources and the Environment
- Finance
- International Business
- Marketing and Brand Management
- Strategic Management

NHH is also offering international students:
- No tuition fees (state funded)
- Guaranteed accommodation
- Granted work permission

WWW.NHH.NO

HAN University of Applied Sciences: Profile

Inspiring environment. Innovative and skilled professional staff. International student body. At HAN University of Applied Sciences, we make it our business to offer higher education of an outstanding quality to students across the globe.

HAN University of Applied Sciences is one of the largest providers of education in the Netherlands, with more than 30,000 students and almost 2,500 staff members spread over two campuses. With more than 3,000 international students, HAN excels at putting theory into practice in an international context throughout all 4 years of undergraduate study. Spread over the cities of Arnhem and Nijmegen close to the German border, HAN has modern buildings, state-of-the art multimedia centres, world-class laboratories and wireless internet access.

By following a Bachelor course at HAN University of Applied Sciences, students obtain a degree that will be an asset to any employee anywhere in the world. Fully accredited by the Dutch Ministry of Education and internationally recognised, the HAN Bachelor diploma is the starting point of graduates' successful careers and further studies in international postgraduate programmes.

The HAN Bachelor's degree delivers its graduates high-powered credentials and marketable skills upon entering the global career market. It is our goal to prepare each of our students to meet the unique challenges found in today's working world. At HAN we ensure that our lectures and projects leave room for personal attention and student development.

Our students benefit from the experience and knowledge of foreign lecturers and international companies. Independence is stimulated and initiative rewarded by providing students with the opportunity to spend part of their education in more than one country. Students attend lectures in the Netherlands, do their work placement abroad, study at partner universities anywhere in the world and do their graduation assignment for an international company.

To maximise the learning process, classes are held only in English and in small groups of maximum 30 students, facilitating individual contact with teachers and fellow students. At HAN, personal development is just as important as professional education, therefore student guidance is offered throughout all 4 years of study. Joining the international student body means merging education with social networks. In the dynamic HAN community students are the heart of a multitude of activities: city trips, parties, thematic weeks, etc.

The Faculty of Engineering and Arnhem Business School, two renowned institutes within HAN University of Applied Sciences, provide international courses in three different fields.

Bachelor courses taught in English:

- Automotive Engineering
- Communication
- Finance and Control
- International Business and Management Studies
- Logistics Management (Economics)
- Life Sciences

More information about course content and admission requirements can be found on www.han.nl/english

THE WORLD IS YOURS...GO INTERNATIONAL!

HAN University of Applied Sciences: Case Study

This world is at a constant state of change, evolving and changing towards a brighter future. Increased internationalism and the feeling of a smaller world is one important aspect of the future of the planet. HAN University of Applied Sciences is already a part of this international future. It's a place where you'll find people from all across the globe; from Australia to Canada and everywhere in-between! The differences in cultures can be interesting, entertaining or scary, but will always manage to enlighten you further and better your perspective of the world.

A well balanced course gives you both academic and practical skills essential to excelling in a professional environment. The learning environment itself is also great; with small class sizes and flexible teachers willing to spend extra time if you need the extra help. Smaller groups are also created for the purpose of set group projects, which teach you great teamwork and leadership skills as you rotate through different assignments in the group.

Not only is the class internationally focused, but so is this course itself; with opportunities to do 6 months study abroad, along with 6 months internship abroad during your final two years, which make for great life and professional experiences. These international experiences, along with the practically focused parts of the course are certain to make you more appealing and interesting towards prospective employers; it definitely gives you some good stories to tell!

By Ben Pyman (3rd year Bachelor of Automotive Engineering, British student, currently doing his internship at Fontys in Helmond, near the Belgium border).

Amsterdam University College: Profile

Looking for a challenging, international learning experience? Study Liberal Arts & Sciences at Amsterdam University College!

Amsterdam University College offers a liberal arts and sciences programme, leading to a joint Bachelor (Honours) degree from the University of Amsterdam and VU University Amsterdam.

You can major in the sciences, social sciences or humanities. Discussions start from 'big questions' in science and society and lead to in-depth study in a wide range of disciplines. AUC enrols up to 50% science majors, offering them a thorough in-depth training in disciplinary sciences such as physics, biology, informatics, earth and environmental sciences and (bio) medicine, but also requiring immersion in other fields of study.

AUC offers a wide range of study abroad opportunities and all AUC students undertake community service or an internship.

As a residential and selective honours college, AUC attracts students from all over the world. AUC students live and study together on our modern international campus, located in Amsterdam Science Park, creating a true intercultural and social learning experience.

Why AUC?

- Programme taught entirely in English
- Majors in sciences, social sciences or humanities
- Strong offering in the sciences (physics, biology, earth- and environmental sciences & (bio)medicine)

- Joint (honours) degree from University of Amsterdam and VU University Amsterdam
- Small class size
- Modern campus with state-of-the-art facilities
- Students live on-campus; guaranteed accommodation in Amsterdam
- International community
- Opportunity to study one semester abroad at AUC, UvA and VU partner universities
- Scholarship opportunities

The AUC Scholarship Fund offers financial assistance to outstanding AUC students with financial need. Would you like to know more or get to know us? Visit the AUC website: www.auc.nl

Spring application deadline, for a February 2016 start:
Deadline: 1 November 2015

Autumn application deadline, for a September 2016 start:
Early bird deadline: 1 December 2015
Regular deadline: 1 February 2016

Amsterdam University College: Case study

Thao Lam
Vietnam
Class of 2016

'The moment I got accepted to AUC I knew that this was definitely the place. Liberal arts education, Amsterdam, excellence and diversity – signed, sealed, delivered, I'm all yours AUC!

Indeed, my first year at AUC was extraordinary: eye-opening perspectives gained, exotic lands ventured to and precious friendships made. Above all, I most certainly value the personal interactions with many inspiring faculty members whom I was so privileged to be taken under. And after all, it proved that I made the perfect choice!

Right now I am a science major with focus on Environmental Science and potentially a minor in International Relations. At first glance, the two disciplines may sound unrelated – however, I believe they would best prepare me to deal with complex, multi-faceted environmental issues. As for the future – as unpredictable as it could be – I hope to pursue a Master in Eco-Toxicology and eventually seek to find solutions to prevalent pollution problems not only in my home country but also many other parts of the world.

Nevertheless, all the wonderful things above would not have happened to me without the support from the AUC Scholarship Fund. It is truly an honour and a responsibility to undertake, and I am forever grateful for the life-changing experiences it enables me.'

Claire Bourdin
Exchange student at AUC
McGill University, Canada

'AUC is a tight-knit community with its sights constantly placed on bigger and brighter things – whether it's a new guest lecture or a new theatre production, there are always things to do and always ways of feeling involved.'

Alumniportal
Deutschland:
Profile

Alumniportal Deutschland is a social online network, which sees itself as a service for all Germany-alumni as well as for companies, networks, organisations and institutes of higher education. A unique combination of topical and emotional services with a connection to Germany and an online community opens entirely new opportunities for maintaining contacts and networks. Career opportunities, language services and both on- and offline events complement the online community.

'Germany-alumni' are people from all over the world who have studied, researched, worked or completed a course of advanced training in Germany. We also welcome those who have attended programmes of training or advanced training abroad with the support of a German organisation. Alumniportal supports your efforts to secure, expand and apply the skills and qualifications you have obtained. It also promotes the establishment of international networks among interesting protagonists from the fields of economy, society, culture, science and research.

Furthermore, Alumniportal Deutschland enables companies, networks, organisations and institutes of higher education to publicise their own services and to profit from the unique expertise of Germany-alumni.

The portal is financed by several federal German ministries and is a joint project of Alexander von Humboldt-Foundation (AvH), German Academic Exchange Service (DAAD) and Goethe-Institut, under the overall direction of Deutsche Gesellschaft für Internationale Zusammenarbeit (GIZ).

On Alumniportal Deutschland, **Germany-alumni** can

- Keep in touch with Germany
- Establish new contacts and maintain existing ones
- Take part in topical discussions, contribute their knowledge and ideas and profit by the experience of others

- Establish contacts with organisations and companies
- Find job vacancies and assignments and present themselves in a professional profile
- Get information from funding organisations
- Practise their German language skills
- Research events and advanced training programmes
- Stay informed on current issues

Companies and organisations can:

- Find qualified employees, experts and contact persons
- Publish assignments and job vacancies or view professional profiles
- Promote events

Institutes of higher education and foundations can:

- Recover their alumni
- Maintain contact with their international alumni
- Present themselves and their alumni networks
- Promote their degree and scholarship programmes

Simply register and join the community. Registration is free of charge.

www.alumniportal-deutschland.org

HAS University of Applied Sciences: Profile

Green and growth: our two favourite words. HAS University of Applied Sciences offers three Bachelor's programmes taught in English. They will show you the way in the world of food, horticulture and agribusiness.

International Food & Agribusiness

Sustainable international business, that's what International Food & Agribusiness is all about. That means doing international business with respect for people and planet. Are you open-minded and interested in other cultures and the world around you? Are you motivated, creative, and have a knack for business? Then this is the right study programme for you!

Horticulture & Business Management

Dutch flowers, vegetables and potatoes are world famous and exported all over the globe. With our vast knowledge of horticulture and agriculture, built over centuries of experience, there is no doubt about it: the Netherlands is the country to be if you want to study horticulture.

International Farm Management

Animals and plants, seven billion citizens need them every day. To provide in the needs of this massive number of people, agriculture has to grow along with the population. The Netherlands has a leading role in the field of horticulture, animal husbandry and arable farming. International Farm Management provides you with the opportunity to be part of this innovative, complex, and exciting world.

Read more about HAS University of Applied Sciences at www.hasinternational.nl

HAS University of Applied Sciences: Case Study

Horticulture & Business Management

Liene (22) from Latvia: 'At HAS nobody holds your hand'

'Living an international life is important to me, so I liked the idea of going abroad for my education. To widen my chances of getting an international job. At HAS you get stimulated to be an independent thinker. The project work is really important. Nobody holds your hand, you just go for it. And that stimulates the creative and resourceful mind! All the excursions we get to make trigger your imagination. They make you realise the enormous variety of possible jobs in horticulture. Possibilities you would never have thought of yourself. In my course you learn about the biological aspects of growing things. But you also learn to look at what you grow as a lucrative product. As something you can put in the market, as a commercial possibility.'

International Food & Agribusiness

Max (23) from Germany: 'This study programme is the best option out there.'

'The most important thing about HAS is that you are not just a number in the system. The school has a very relaxed atmosphere and I really feel at home here. The main reason for me to choose International Food & Agribusiness is that it's so international. And because there is a lot that can be improved in the food industry. What I like most about my study programme is that our lecturers come from all kinds of different backgrounds. Some have worked for the European Union or the United Nations, others for NGOs or the private sector. It's great to learn from their experiences. I can only recommend anybody who is interested in food and sustainability to choose this study programme. I think it's the best option out there.'

Chapter 6
Studying in the USA

The USA is an increasingly attractive destination for UK students; last year, over 9,400 UK students went to the USA according to the UK-US Fulbright Commission. The majority opted for undergraduate-level study, followed by postgraduate education, with the rest on non-degree programmes or post-study work schemes.

More and more students seem to want to discover the appeal of the American higher-education system: a system with a choice of over 4,500 universities and a broader, more flexible approach to university studies. Quality of education in the USA is unsurpassed; 74 of the 200 universities featured in the Times Higher Education World University Rankings 2014–2015 are from the USA. Some students are turning down places at the leading universities in the UK to take advantage of the breadth and quality of education on offer stateside.

> The academic year in the USA runs from mid-August or early September to late May or early June.

The education system

In the States, the terms 'university' and 'college' are generally used interchangeably. However, community colleges are different; they can only offer two-year associate degrees, rather than four-year bachelor's degrees.

Choosing where to study

When deciding where to apply, you need to consider which type of institution is right for you.

- Public universities are funded by the state and tend to have more students and lower fees. International students will end up paying more than state residents.
- Private universities tend to be campus-based, with better facilities and fewer students. They are funded by private donations, grants and tuition fees. Fees are higher, but the same fees are charged for all. More scholarships tend to be available.
- Community colleges offer associate degrees over two years (see page 194), with the possibility of transferring to a university to top up to a full bachelor's degree. They are often cheaper and less competitive.

The Ivy League is made up of eight prestigious private universities and colleges in the north-east of the USA. It started out as a sports league, rather than any kind of elite group or ranking system. For this reason, many top universities from across the country are not in the Ivy League, including Berkeley, which is a public university, and Stanford, which is on the west coast.

Keep an eye out for the public Ivy League which includes the universities of Michigan and California; these institutions offer a quality education without such extortionate fees.

American degrees offer a much wider choice of subjects to study than you would expect in the UK. They are made up of a range of types of courses.

- Core (or general education), providing the compulsory foundation for university study. Students will often be required to select from a broad range of courses including sciences, history, maths, English composition and literature and so on.
- Major courses, your main subject area; choose from options like English, engineering or history.
- Minor courses, taken in a secondary subject or allowing you to specialise within your main subject area. You could minor in a foreign language or consider adding a computer-science minor to a maths major.
- Academic track, a group of courses focused on a specific topic within a major; a student majoring in computer science could select a track in computer systems, for example.

Some universities offer co-operative education programmes, made up of paid work experience, rather like a sandwich course in the UK. In other cases, unpaid internships may offer degree credit.

Finding a course

You can use College Board (undergraduate), www.collegeboard. org, or College Navigator (undergraduate and postgraduate), www.nces.ed.gov/collegenavigator, to search for courses at public, private or community colleges. EducationUSA features a list of other college or course search sites on its '5 steps to study' web page, www.educationusa.info/5_steps_to_study.

The US system means it is essential to find somewhere that is a great match for you and what you have to offer. With this in mind and with so many institutions to choose from, why not start by writing a list of essential and desirable criteria relating to your preferred US state, size of institution, funding, diversity or activities on offer; whatever really matters to you. Use the information to filter your search at College Board or Peterson's (www.petersons.com). If you're looking for a student perspective, you'll find some useful information at Princeton Review (www.princetonreview.com).

Transfers

It is possible to transfer between universities. Transfers would normally take place after freshman year (Year 1), but (since you need a minimum of two years at a university to graduate) any later than sophomore year (Year 2) could prove tricky.

> The Sutton Trust runs a US Summer School Programme to encourage talented young people from low-income backgrounds to consider university in the USA. You can find out more at www.us.suttontrust.com.

Associate degrees

Associate degrees like Associate of Arts (AA) or Associate of Science (AS) are two-year programmes of general studies along with foundation courses in a chosen subject (a major or field of concentration). The qualifications often relate to vocational areas like hospitality management or health sciences. The programme might include core and concentration courses, electives, practical work, fieldwork and supervised study.

They are broadly equivalent to the first year of UK undergraduate study. After completion, students may wish to transfer to a US bachelor's degree by completing an additional two years of study.

Students who are only applying with GCSE qualifications could apply for an associate degree. Certain vocational qualifications might be accepted by community colleges, but not by the more competitive universities.

American college year names

Year 1   Freshman Year
Year 2   Sophomore Year
Year 3   Junior Year
Year 4   Senior Year

Bachelor's degrees

Bachelor's degrees generally take four years to complete, although there are some five-year courses in architecture, sciences and engineering. A US bachelor's degree is comparable in level to a British bachelor's degree. Unlike in the UK, where you choose your subject before you apply, you can apply for an undecided major, and decide on your chosen subject at the end of sophomore (or second) year. This has more in common with the Scottish system of education than with the rest of the UK. Much of the first year, and some of the second year, is spent on a range of introductory courses. Some of this core curriculum will relate to subjects you may wish to make your main subject choice (or major). For example, if you are considering majoring in psychology, you might opt for maths and quantitative reasoning, and social and behavioural sciences as your core subjects.

> **66** I have had one-to-one support from the international student adviser who was fantastic in setting up my schedule and what I was going to study. **99**
> *Stuart Bramley, Scottsdale Community College, USA*

Entry requirements vary, but most would require a minimum of five GCSEs or National 5s at C or above, including maths and English. You would need to show that you are completing advanced-level study; the universities will be able to check your attainment from your academic transcript and any admissions tests you sit. Competitive universities will be looking for three A levels or equivalent. Less competitive universities may consider vocational qualifications, like a BTEC level 3 Extended Diploma, a vocational course broadly equivalent to three A levels. For more information on applying, see the following section.

Honours degrees

Gaining an honours degree in the USA tends to indicate that the student has defended an undergraduate thesis (or piece of original research) known in the UK as a dissertation. Confusingly, a degree with honours can also mean that someone has achieved with particular academic merit, although this is more usually known in the USA as *Cum laude* (with honour), *Magna cum laude* (with great honour) or *Summa cum laude* (with highest honour).

Graduate school

What we know as postgraduate education in the UK is described as graduate education or grad school in the USA. Master's degrees and PhDs gained in the USA are comparable to British master's degrees and PhDs. Certain subjects that you could start at undergraduate level in the UK can only be taken at graduate level in the USA; these include medicine and law. Pre-med and pre-law programmes are available at undergraduate level, although these programmes aren't a mandatory requirement for medical or law school.

Applying

The application process for undergraduate and postgraduate courses has some similarities to the UK system, although there is no admissions service like UCAS to coordinate applications. For the most part, applications are made direct to the chosen institution, although some universities use the Common Application for undergraduate programmes; see page 198 for more information.

As part of the application process, you will be required to send detailed academic records and official course information for qualifications you have completed. You may be required to submit your academic documents to an organisation that can convert your qualifications to a comparable level of study in the USA. Your university will give you further details of which organisation to use or, for a list of approved agencies, try the National Association of Credential Evaluation Services (NACES), www.naces.org.

Undergraduate applications

The timescale for applications is similar to that of UCAS, although there is a separate system if you are applying for a sports scholarship.

After Christmas in your first year at sixth form or college (Y13 in Northern Ireland or S5 in Scotland), you will need to start researching degree programmes and universities. It is suggested that you narrow down your choice to between three and seven universities, due to the time and costs involved.

The process of application is likely to include some or all of the following:

- application form
- admissions test scores
- a few essays (of around 500 to 750 words)
- transcript (details of your academic performance)
- two or three recommendations
- financial statement
- possibility of an interview.

You should expect to pay an application fee of around $50 to $100 (£32–£64) per university.

You will be applying to the university as a whole, so you will need to demonstrate why the university should consider you. Admissions staff will decide your fate, rather than academic staff from your chosen department. They will be looking at more than just success at A level; GCSEs, AS levels, your passion for learning, your love for your subject (if you have decided on a major), your extra-curricular activities and you as a person will all be considered. You'll need to demonstrate a match between what you have to offer and the type of institution you are applying to, so thorough research is essential.

Although you can apply for an undecided major, you will normally apply to a particular school within the university, for example, the School of Arts, School of Engineering or School of Management.

Application forms

From 1 August, the Common Application becomes available at www.commonapp.org. This is used by more than 500 universities, although each university involved still retains its own deadlines, administration fees and requirements. All other universities require direct applications, so you may have a number of forms to complete. Even if you're not using the Common Application, most applications are similar, so you will not have to start completely from scratch with each one. There tend to be more sections to complete and more space available than on the UCAS application, so it can result in quite a lot of work. You will be able to copy and paste information, as long as you remember to amend and target it each time.

Universities tend to offer separate deadlines for early-decision and early-action applications, often sometime in November. The benefit of applying early is that you are being considered before the majority of applicants and competing with fewer students, so you might have a better chance of an offer. On the downside, you'll need to sit any admissions tests early. Most institutions offer either early decision or early action; some offer neither.

The main difference between the two is that early decision is binding, whereas early action gives you the comfort of knowing you have an offer, but with no strings attached. You can only apply to one university as early decision and you are committing yourself to that university if they offer you a place. This demonstration of commitment can have its benefits for consideration by the university and for scholarships. You might choose early decision if you have your heart set on one specific university, but it could be risky if the amount of scholarship or financial aid you are offered will play a part in deciding where you study.

Regular admissions deadlines come a little later, often in December or January. Check individual institutions for full details.

Undergraduate admissions tests

You will need to check whether an admissions test will be necessary. Many universities will be looking for both good grades and strong admissions-test scores; this is particularly so if you are applying for academic merit-based scholarships (see Help with finances on page 209). Where an admissions test is required, the amount of importance placed upon the test scores varies between universities.

Most universities ask for the American College Test (ACT) or the Scholastic Assessment Test (SAT) for undergraduate-level study; both tests are designed to assess academic potential. If the university accepts both, you will be able to choose which test to sit. Although the tests are both well recognised and essentially achieve the same objective, the tests themselves are different and you may find that one will suit you more than the other. The SAT originally set out to measure aptitude, while the ACT was achievement-based, although both have changed since their inception.

The ACT includes more questions, so you end up with less time per question; it includes English, reading, science and higher maths. It comprises a single test, which may be more convenient, but is only available in limited locations across the UK. For the more competitive universities, you are likely to have to complete a supplementary 30-minute writing section (in addition to the nearly three-hour-long ACT test). It costs around $75 (£49), or around $90 (£58) including the written section.

The SAT comprises a reasoning test of nearly four hours, plus two or three subject tests for the more competitive universities. The test is widely available in the UK, but both tests are taken on different dates. It costs nearly $90 (£58) for the reasoning test, around $72 (£47) for the first subject test and $16 (£10) for subsequent basic subject tests.

It is essential to be prepared for these tests. Take a look at www.fulbright.org.uk/study-in-the-usa/undergraduate-study/admissions-tests and www.collegeboard.org to help you prepare.

Sitting a test in early autumn of year 13 in England and Wales, Y14 in Northern Ireland or S6 in Scotland, is ideal, as it gives you time to resit, if necessary. Some candidates choose to take their first test as early as the previous spring. Candidates need to register sometime between spring and mid-September. It is worth registering early as places can quickly fill up. You can register and find a testing centre through the ACT website, www.act.org, and the SAT website, www.sat.collegeboard.org.

Essays

Essays are likely to be based on your response to specific questions set by the university; make sure that you answer the questions fully and directly. They may want to find out about your skills and personality traits; why you want to study at this university; what are your goals; and what inspires you. Although you might choose to write on a subject related to your area of interest, you do not normally have to do so. The Fulbright Commission (www. fulbright.org.uk/study-in-the-usa/undergraduate-study/applying/ essays) has examples, video tips and useful handouts on this subject.

Examples of essay questions from University of Virginia.

- What is your favourite word and why?
- Describe the world you come from and how that world shaped who you are.
- What work of art, music, science, mathematics or literature has surprised, unsettled or challenged you, and in what way?

Transcripts

The transcript should include predicted grades from your current qualifications, but also your progress from year 10 (Y11 in Northern Ireland or S3 in Scotland) onwards. It could include GCSE or National 5s, details of any exams taken since then (AS levels and so on), results of mock exams or other internal assessments and any academic honours achieved. Where relevant, ask your school or college to include explanations for any anomalies in your academic record. Qualifications may also need to be explained and details of the institution incorporated.

The format of the transcript is generally chronological. It should be around a page in length and produced on official headed paper. You will need to work with your school or college to help them prepare this, directing them to sample transcripts, such as those on the Fulbright Commission website (www.fulbright.org.uk).

On the application form, you'll be asked for your GPA. The Grade Point Average cannot be officially converted from UK qualifications, so you should leave this section blank.

Recommendations

You will need to arrange two or three letters of reference or recommendations from staff who know you well; follow your chosen university's guidelines on whom to ask. The restrained and often modest tone taken in a UCAS reference might not be enough for a US university. Recommendations from US schools tend to be far more detailed and far more positive, so you will need to prepare your referee to really sell you. Refer potential referees to the Fulbright Commission website for tips and sample letters, www.fulbright.org. uk/study-in-the-usa/undergraduate-study/applying/reference-letters.

The EducationUSA website (www.educationusa.info) explains why you might choose to waive your right to see a copy of the recommendation.

> **“** A recommendation form may include a waiver where you can relinquish your right to see what is written about you. If this option is offered, most admissions officers prefer you to waive your right so that recommenders may feel more comfortable when writing their evaluations. Admissions officers usually interpret waived recommendations as more honest. **”**

Financial statement

How will you fund your studies in the USA? Your university will want to know, so you will need to complete any requests for evidence. You can use the evidence again when applying for a visa. You will need to show that you can at least cover the first year's costs, maybe even the costs for the length of the whole course. If you need financial assistance, you should include how much will be required. In most cases, a 'need-blind' admissions system means that your application will not be affected by this evidence.

Interview

These days, the internet and Skype are typically used for interviewing. You may be surprised to find yourself being interviewed by an ex-student. Alternatively, the interview may be with a member of admissions staff. They may come to the UK or may ask you to go to the States, in which case you could enquire about help with travel expenses.

You could be asked why you have chosen this university, how you will contribute and why you intend to study in the USA. They will want to know about your subject interests, whether you have any ideas about your major or what your strengths and weaknesses are.

To prepare, you should look over the research you did when choosing this university. You can read over the essays you sent and look at how you can expand upon what was written. You should prepare questions to ask of the interviewer, but make sure that any questions aren't already answered in the university's prospectus or website.

Offers

Early-action applicants get an answer in December or January, while regular applicants hear later in the spring. The response could be one of three options: accepted, wait list, or not accepted. Those accepted can choose to accept, decline or defer. (Deferring is rare, so you should always check the process with your university. Even if your university agrees, any offers for funding might not also be deferred.) A deposit of around $500 (£325) will secure your place.

If you are placed on a wait list, there is still a possibility that you will be offered a place; follow any instructions you receive about the wait-list process and keep your fingers crossed.

Your offer won't be conditional, but it is still important to work hard and do well. You may gain university credit or advanced standing from good UK qualifications.

Applying for graduate school

As with undergraduate admissions, students apply direct to their chosen universities. The Fulbright Commission suggests restricting applications to between four and six institutions.

The details of deadline dates, entry requirements and application fees will vary, although most will require some of the following:

- application form
- admissions test scores
- a few essays (of around 500 to 750 words)
- research statement
- transcript (details of your academic performance)
- two or three recommendations
- possibility of an interview.

There will be an application fee to pay of around $50 to $100 (£32–£64) per university.

Each application may be different but, rather like a job application, you should be able to adapt the information you provide, rather than starting from scratch each time.

Most universities will be looking for at least a 2:2 from UK undergraduate study, with the more competitive universities looking for considerably more. They will be looking at your all-round offer, not just academic achievements, but also the way you demonstrate a good understanding of your chosen university and how this matches you as an individual. US universities are also keen to know about your involvement in extra-curricular activities. Contact the universities direct to discuss their requirements.

Much of the information in the previous section on applying for undergraduate study will also apply to postgraduate applications (see page 197). Notable differences include the research statement and the different admissions tests.

Research statement

The research statement allows you to outline your areas of interest, specialism and plans for how and why you intend to complete your research. Here are some of the key points that you need to consider when writing a research statement.

- Sum up your current plans for research, understanding that they may well change as you refine your ideas or as other developments occur.
- Relate your plans to your chosen university department and professors.
- Demonstrate your intellectual skills, but without alienating the admissions staff who may be considering your application.

Graduate admissions tests

Most postgraduate options require an admissions test and there are a number of different tests to consider:

- Dental Admissions Test (DAT), www.ada.org/dat.aspx
- Graduate Management Admissions Test (GMAT), www.mba.com
- Graduate Record Exam (GRE), www.ets.org/gre
- Law School Admissions Test (LSAT), www.lsac.org
- Medical College Admission Test (MCAT), www.aamc.org/students/applying/mcat.

The cost of these tests can be quite substantial, with GMAT costing $250 (£162) and MCAT costing from $395 (£257). Some tests are available across the country, with others restricted to London, and the DAT currently only being tested in North America.

How the tests are used also varies, with some tests being a central factor in a successful application, while other tests are considered along with a variety of different aspects. In some cases, looking at how your scores compare to last year's averages can help to indicate your chances of success.

Preparation is vital, as the system tends to rely quite heavily on multiple-choice testing. Remember that you will be competing with US students who are used to this style of testing, so you need to know what to expect. See the individual test websites for sample papers or use the Fulbright Commission's 'Preparing for Admission Exams' page at www.fulbright.org.uk/study-in-the-usa/postgraduate-study/admissions-tests/preparation.

You could study . . .

Associate degree in Construction Management
Baton Rouge Community College, Louisiana
Two years
Apply by 18 August (financial aid applications by 15 April)

Annual fees $7,771 (£5,047)

Annual living costs (room and board) $7,459 (£4,844)

Bachelor's degree in Mathematics

University of Virginia (public)

Four years

Apply by 1 January (early-action application by 1 November)

Annual fees $42,184 (£27,397), merit scholarships are available

Annual living costs (room and board) $10,052 (£6,528)

Master's degree in Hispanic-American Studies

Rice University, Houston, Texas (private)

Two years

Apply by 1 January

Annual fees $40,665 (£26,410), financial aid available for international students

Annual living costs (room and board) $13,400 (£8,703)

Visas

If you plan to study in the USA and you aren't a US citizen or a permanent resident in the USA, you will need a visa. Find out about the rules and the procedures at Embassy of the US, London (http://london.usembassy.gov).

You should apply for your visa at a US embassy or US consulate before you leave the UK. There are two visa categories, F-1 Student Visa and J-1 Exchange Visitor Visa; F-1 is for students undertaking a full-time programme in the USA, while J-1 is for those on study-abroad programmes or exchanges. Your university will tell you which one to apply for. There are differences in restrictions on these two visas: whether you can work, for example (see page 212).

> 66 After you receive your visa you will need it upon entry to the USA and then again for opening accounts etc. After this you should store it carefully. Be aware of things that may impact on it, for example, if you decide to travel or get a job. 99
>
> *Simon McCabe, University of Missouri, USA*

Once you have been offered a place at a university and provided evidence as to how you will fund the first year of your studies, your institution will prepare a Form I-20 (F-1 visa) or Form DS-2019 (J-1 visa); you will need this to apply for your visa. The university will also send instructions as to how to apply. The process will involve a visa interview at the US Embassy in London or the US Consulate in Belfast, as well as completion of an online SEVIS I-901 form (requiring a $180 (£117) fee) and an online visa application or MRV (requiring a $160 (£104) fee).

If your application is successful, you will normally be admitted for the duration of your student status. You should check any visa restrictions and follow them to the letter, as breach of these conditions is an offence.

Costs and help with finances

Tuition fees in the USA can be considerably higher than across the rest of the world. However, weigh this up against a strong tradition of financial aid and things might not always be as expensive as first anticipated. One third of international undergraduate students in the USA have a scholarship as their main source of funding, while two-thirds of undergraduate students receive some form of financial support.

Costs

According to the College Board (www.collegeboard.org), the following average annual tuition fees are reported for 2014/2015:

- four-year, public institutions (out-of-state students): $22,958 (£14,910)
- four-year, private institutions: $31,231 (£20,283).

Fees for out-of-state students at two-year community college should be around $8,000 (£5,196) per year.

> If you are looking at ways to make US education more affordable, you could consider taking a year or two at a community college before transferring to a university.

You should allow in the region of $10,000 to $12,000 (£6,495 to £7,793) per year for accommodation, food, books and materials, travel and so on. Costs could be higher than this as they will vary depending on where you live and the type of lifestyle you lead. Universities will provide an idea of local living costs on their websites.

The USA comes in at number 24 of 119 countries on a cost-of-living ranking from Numbeo (www.numbeo.com). This suggests that its living costs are more reasonable than the UK, Canada, Australia, New Zealand and much of northern Europe.

Help with finances

According to the US-UK Fulbright Commission, over 900 universities support their international students by offering scholarships of over $10,000 per year, with many institutions offering considerably more than this amount.

While you cannot access the UK student loans and grants for overseas study, there may be some alternative options available. You should be researching universities and investigating funding concurrently, since your choice of university will impact on your options for certain scholarships or financial aid. Start early and consider that support will often be pulled from a number of sources:

- scholarships from universities
- scholarships from external bodies
- sports scholarships
- savings or personal loans from the UK
- financial aid.

Much of the additional funding you may be applying for comes direct from US universities. Scholarships are allocated based on a range of criteria: merit, achievements, financial need, talents or personal background (country of origin, gender or ethnicity). Use the admissions or financial aid pages on the university's website to find out which institutions offer scholarships to UK students. Keep in mind that, even if you are lucky enough to get a scholarship, it is unlikely to cover all your costs.

The amount of financial aid varies between colleges. For example, if you have the brains to get into Harvard and your family income is under $65,000 (£42,215) per year, then you would not have to pay anything. The threshold is $75,000 (£48,709) at MIT (Massachusetts Institute of Technology). Further financial aid is awarded on a sliding scale for family income over these amounts up to around $150,000 (£97,418).

You might be able to speed up your studies, and thereby reduce some of your costs, by taking additional courses each semester or gaining credit over the summer break.

Sports scholarships are a highly competitive option and you will need to start the process even earlier than for a mainstream application. Applicants must meet and maintain academic standards, while also having the sporting talent to participate at varsity (inter-university) level. Scholarships are awarded for a range of sports, with opportunities for UK students in soccer, golf, athletics or swimming, for example.

Certain sporting associations will require scores over a particular level on SATs or ACTs. You can make contact with university coaches direct or use the services of an agent, who will often charge a fee. Both EducationUSA and the Fulbright Commission have handouts on their websites taking you through each option.

There are a range of external bodies that offer scholarships, each with their own specifications and deadlines. Try this web page for more details of organisations you might want to contact: www. fulbright.org.uk/study-in-the-usa/undergraduate-study/funding/ external-funding-bodies.

The following websites will help you get started on your search for funding:

- www.educationusa.info
- www.edupass.org/finaid/databases.phtml
- www.iefa.org
- www.internationalscholarships.com.

Cultural differences

If you have watched enough Hollywood films, you may feel that you already know the USA. You may have heard of Thanksgiving and Spring Break and you probably have some ideas about campus life. Therefore you might not expect to experience culture shock when leaving for this western, English-speaking country. Although the changes won't necessarily be too extreme, it may still take a little while to adjust and feelings of homesickness and uncertainty are normal.

Meeting new people and making friends are important to help you start to feel at home. It may be tempting to stick with other international students, but if you want to get to know the real America, you will need to meet some Americans. As a nation, they are much more open than the Brits, so introduce yourself to hall mates and classmates or get involved with activities.

> **❝** Yale is, obviously, a top-class institution, but what drew me to it was the sense of community that I found there. Yale splits its students into colleges, akin to the ones at Oxbridge, which fosters a collaborative atmosphere for social and academic activities. **❞**
>
> *Stephanie Addenbrooke, Yale University, USA*

Drinking is less of a way of life than in the UK. The legal age is 21 and many university events, and even whole campuses, are dry.

Working while studying

It may be possible for you to work while you are studying in the USA, but it is essential to follow the rules to the letter. Remember that breaking employment law could lead to deportation. The information here should provide some of the basic details to get you started. For the latest rules and regulations, talk to the university's international office. You should check with them before taking on any work or voluntary commitments.

Full-time students on a Student Visa (F-1) can work 20 hours per week on campus. If you're on an Exchange Visitor Visa (J-1), you may request permission from your international office to work 20 hours per week on campus, but this is not guaranteed. You must have all appropriate paperwork, including SEVIS I-20, passport and Social Security Card – speak to your university for more information. Campus jobs might include library, cafeteria or office work. It makes sense to wait until you have had time to adjust to your new country before you start looking for work.

Other opportunities to work off-campus might be offered as part of your degree. Look out for Curricular Practical Training (CPT) or courses where an internship or practicum (practical work in a particular field) is required. Alternatively, Optional Practical Training (OPT) gives the option to work during or after university in an area linked to your field of studies.

Staying on after study

Once your course has finished, unless you have further study or Optional Practical Training lined up, it will be time to return to the UK. You normally get 30 (if you have a J-1 visa) or 60 (if you have a F-1 visa) days' grace at the end of your studies, which you could spend tying up your affairs or seeing some of this vast country. If you have any queries about when you should leave, try your university's international office.

Occasionally, some students get job offers which mean that they can stay on and eventually apply for a green card, giving the right of permanent residence. Alternatively, if close family are permanent residents of the USA, they may be able to sponsor you to stay on permanently. Don't go to the States banking on the chance to stay; these opportunities are the exception, rather than the rule. You can find out more at the website for the US Citizenship and Immigration Services, www.uscis.gov.

Pros and cons of study in the USA

Pros

- Some of the most highly rated universities in the world.
- More international students choose the USA than anywhere else.
- Opportunities for financial aid or scholarships for international students.
- Great facilities and campuses.
- English-speaking country.

Cons

- Few opportunities to stay on permanently.
- High university tuition fees.

Student story
Stephanie Addenbrooke, Yale University, USA

When it was time for Stephanie Addenbrooke to decide on her university subjects, she realised that it was going to be a difficult decision. 'The English higher education system asks students to decide on one subject for their studies, and solely study that subject for three or four years. While this was ideal for the majority of my friends, I felt constrained because I was interested in so much – I was not ready to make that decision. Also, the rise of tuition fees in England made me consider other options.

'The American liberal arts education is very broad and allows students to explore numerous interests. The colleges wish to graduate well-rounded students, and so there is a greater emphasis on getting involved outside of the classroom.'

Stephanie is studying a liberal arts degree and she hasn't had to decide on her major subject yet. 'The style of learning is very similar to A levels in that you are taking multiple subjects at once. Because of this, each of my classes feels very interdisciplinary. For example, there is a Math major in my English class, who brings a different perspective to the texts compared to a History major, for example.

'Yale is, obviously, a top-class institution, but what drew me to it was the sense of community that I found there. Yale splits its students into colleges, akin to the ones at Oxbridge, which fosters a collaborative atmosphere for social and academic activities. Also, Yale's admissions process is need-blind, which means that I was able to apply without worrying that my inability to pay would hinder my chances.

'Yale's grant system means that I am essentially only paying what I can afford to go to college. I have the opportunity to graduate with no or minimal debt – the complete opposite to my friends studying in the UK. Yale also includes a student job in its grant packet, which means I can work on campus in order to earn extra money. As well as the financial benefits of this, I will also have established a resumé and gained experience that will help me when looking for jobs post-graduation.

'The US university application process is very different to the system in the UK. It is considerably longer, involves standardised testing, and each school can ask their own application questions separate to the standard application. However, while this can be stressful and time-consuming, it means that your application is much more a representation of yourself. For the most part, US college admissions are holistic and consider you as a whole person, not just your grades. This was one of the most rewarding aspects of US college admissions – when I got admitted to Yale, I felt like they were admitting me, not my quantitative data.

'The process of applying for a visa was relatively stress-free – it was a lot of paperwork and involved a trip to the embassy, but in hindsight, it was not really something I felt like I needed to worry about.

'Yale is incredible in its support networks. All students, but freshmen especially, have so many resources at their fingertips that it is sometimes difficult to keep track! As an international, I receive even more support. The most helpful support network that Yale offered was the Office of International Students and Scholars' five-day orientation programme at the beginning of the semester. The international students were acquainted with Yale's campus ahead of everyone else, were assisted in practical issues such as getting a cell phone or bank account, and we were prepped for life in America.

'Yale tries to link you with support for all outlets. I have a writing partner who is helping me adjust to US college essays. All freshmen have a freshman counsellor who is there to help us become acquainted with college and with Yale. We also have more formal academic advisors, and then less formal "older siblings" in our residential colleges.

'I have had minimal difficulty adjusting to life here, but I think that's due to Yale's community aspect. I genuinely feel like I've been welcomed into some sort of family that is looking out for me. Also, I guess that Britain and America aren't too different culturally, so that hasn't been too much of an issue. One of the hardest parts was Family Weekend – a tradition that Yale has where parents can come and visit. My parents weren't able to go, and it was kind of awkward to be surrounded by everyone and their parents. The same goes for breaks when people go home. That being said, I have been inundated with offers of places to stay and Thanksgiving dinners. I was spoilt for choice!'

Stephanie's top tips

Accommodation

'If you get the option, I would recommend living with American students. Some schools offer international houses that some people find benefit in, but I have found living with Americans made my transition easier because they were able to help me with cultural (and even language) differences.'

Food

'The food is different! It was actually one of the hardest cultural shifts I experienced, mainly because it is something you can't really shy away from. I do get my parents to ship over some of the British classics once in a while, which is not only exciting, but sometimes pretty helpful! Americans all assume the only thing British people drink is tea, so expect to be asked about it frequently.'

Making friends

'Get involved, especially early on! The first couple of weeks will be spent with everyone getting to know each other – there is no stigma about asking for someone's name and introducing yourself, because no one knows anyone. Extra-curricular activities and classes are also a great way to meet people with common interests.'

Best sources of information

'The Fulbright Commission was my first source of information. I was one of the students on their Sutton Trust programme, which obviously lends itself to an insane amount of support. The College Day that they offered was of great help to me – I was able to meet representatives from multiple

US colleges, and get a feel for what study in the USA, and at the individual schools, would be like.'

Stephanie has already begun to experience some of the benefits of studying abroad. 'You automatically have something special and interesting that no one else does. Your professor and friends will initially remember you as the "one with the British accent". Yes, this can be frustrating, but it also makes for interesting conversation starters – people want to hear all about your background, and will try and untangle some of their predetermined perceptions of your country. I also know that upon graduating, I will have something to make me stand out on my resumé. After all, not everyone has the courage to study away from home for four years.'

Yale University (www.yale.edu) is a prestigious Ivy League university which includes five US presidents amongst its alumni.

Chapter 7

Studying in Canada

If you're looking to get more for your money than in the UK and considering a country with a good quality of life where you may be able to stay on afterwards, Canada has a lot to offer. As many as 2,499 UK students are already out there enjoying the benefits (OECD Education at a Glance 2014).

The education system

The education system in Canada is run by a separate Ministry of Education in each province or territory. Each region has consistent standards and it is fairly easy to move between them. Courses are taught in English or French although some institutions teach in both languages.

The academic year runs from September to May and is divided into two semesters. Fall term runs from September to December and winter term follows from January to May. Some institutions offer a trimester system, with an additional summer term starting from May onwards, although there may be more limited programme choice at this time. Although it is possible to join courses in the second (and sometimes the third) term, September intake is the most common.

University study

More than 10,000 undergraduate and postgraduate degree programmes are available at a range of public and private (not-for-profit) universities and university degree-level colleges. The majority of universities in Canada are public. Canada's education system is considered to be of high quality, with investment in research and development at universities in Canada almost twice that of any other G8 nation. Canada can also boast eight universities in the 2014–2015 Times Higher Education World University Rankings Top 200. Bachelor's, master's and doctoral degrees are comparable in level to those from the UK.

How to find a course

The official Study in Canada portal is a good starting point for your research; it features a course finder for international students and links to information from the 10 provinces and three territories, as well as links to the individual institutions, www.studyincanada.com.

The Association of Universities and Colleges of Canada (www.aucc.ca) features a course search, as well as university profiles, facts and figures, and information on quality assurance.

Accreditation and quality

You can check that your chosen institution is accredited by using the Directory of Universities, Colleges and Schools in the Provinces and Territories of Canada. You can find this at www.cicic.ca (Canadian Information Centre for International Credentials). The listing includes all public and accredited institutions, as well as some private establishments.

Undergraduate study

Bachelor's degrees from Canada take three or four years to complete. In some cases, an honours degree is part of the degree programme; in other cases, it is taken as an extra year of study. You will generally be looking at four years of study for an honours degree.

Four-year applied bachelor's degrees offer a more vocational option, combining academic study with the development of the more practical skills needed for employment. If you're looking to incorporate work experience, co-op programmes are similar to sandwich courses in the UK, providing the opportunity to work as well as gain academic credentials. It is worth noting that certain competitive fields, like medicine, may not always be widely available to international students; your university will be able to advise you of any issues.

Differences from education in the UK

A key difference in Canadian education is that the degrees tend to be much more general than you would expect in the UK, particularly when compared to England, Wales and Northern Ireland. Although there will be certain programmes you must study to achieve your major, you will have the option to study a range of additional subjects. For the first two years you might be choosing programmes from general sciences or general arts, for example, before starting to specialise.

> ❝ My best subject in school was maths and so that's what I decided to study. However, I have always had a wide range of interests so I wanted the flexibility to do other things as well. ❞
>
> *Lauren Aitchison, University of Waterloo, Canada*

Higher education in Canada takes place in universities, university colleges and community colleges. Some universities are research-intensive, with others focusing purely on teaching, in contrast to the UK, where all universities tend to carry out both teaching and research. The institution's website (or the institution's staff) should reveal what type of institution it is.

Associate degrees

Some students may choose to take their first year and second year
at a community college, studying for an associate degree, before
transferring to a university to achieve a bachelor's degree. In
some cases, community colleges and universities work together
to provide a joint programme. Colleges tend to offer applied
(rather than purely academic) studies, smaller classes (university
classes can be large, particularly in years one and two) and lower
tuition fees. There is some snobbery and colleges are sometimes
considered to be the second choice to university. Associate degrees
take two years on a full-time basis and are broadly equivalent to a
Certificate of HE in the UK.

Entry requirements

Much as in the UK, each university sets its own admissions
requirements and publicises the minimum qualifications required.
High-school graduation in Canada is at a similar level to A levels
or Advanced Highers in Scotland; universities will generally be
looking for applicants educated to this level. Community colleges
may have slightly lower entry requirements. Your institution will
be able to tell you more, including whether they have any additional
requirements, for example, for competitive or specialist subjects.

If you intend to study in French, the institution will talk to you
about the level of French they require and whether an assessment
of your skills will be necessary.

Postgraduate study

Postgraduate courses are available at some, but not all,
universities in Canada and include master's and doctoral degrees.
Postgraduate study in Canada includes coursework, although less
than at undergraduate level, alongside research. The courses tend
to be based around seminars and will involve large amounts of
structured reading, particularly in the early years.

Most master's degrees take two years to complete and don't always require completion of a thesis. Doctoral degrees (for example, PhDs) last between four and seven years, with a dissertation forming an essential component of the qualification. It is sometimes possible to move straight from an undergraduate honours degree to a doctoral degree. In these cases, the doctoral degree will often incorporate the master's degree.

What we know as 'postgraduate study' in the UK is more commonly known as 'graduate study' in Canada and the USA.

For those intending to follow a regulated profession like law, medicine or social work, a licence to practise is granted following success in academic study and a relevant internship.

Entry requirements

Institutions will normally require an honours degree for progression to postgraduate study, although some exceptions are made for those with substantial work experience. Three-year degrees from the UK (and other parts of the European Higher Education Area) should meet the general entry requirements for postgraduate study in Canada.

Academic recognition

Your chosen institution may already know and understand the UK qualification you are applying with; in which case, they may accept your certificates without further evaluation. If the qualification is unfamiliar, or if they are less experienced at dealing with international qualifications, you may need to pay to have your qualification evaluated. Talk to the admissions staff to see whether evaluation is required, as you may save yourself some money if you don't need this service. The Canadian Centre for International Credentials (www.cicic.ca) will provide further information on how to proceed.

Applying

Your first step when applying should be to contact the international office requesting application documentation. They should send you information about the application procedure and timescale, along with requirements for the evaluation of qualifications, the costs of study and the visa-application processes.

Alberta, British Columbia and Ontario each have a centralised application service, while Quebec has a number of different regional systems. You will find that many individual institutions require direct application. Applications may be paper-based or online. Applications will incur a fee, often well in excess of the £23 required by UCAS. If you are applying to a number of universities in various provinces, you may have to pay more than once. Remember to factor in this cost when working out the costs of study. Careful research and narrowing down your choices should help to reduce these costs, and the additional work required by multiple applications.

Application deadline dates vary between provinces and between individual institutions. International applicants are normally required to apply between December and early spring for September start, in the autumn for January start, and around January for start dates in the summer. Graduate application deadlines may be earlier, particularly for the more competitive courses.

Start planning for your application a good year in advance. Bear in mind that evaluation of qualifications, the need to sit admissions tests (for postgraduate study) and the time taken for international post may slow the process down considerably. You should expect a decision around four or five months after the deadline date, although this will also vary between institutions.

The application form

The application form itself is likely to be quite a small part of the application process, requiring basic information about the applicant's:

- personal details
- contact details
- education
- test scores
- relevant professional experience (where applicable)
- referees.

Further documents required in support of an application could include:

- transcript
- letter of intent/statement of purpose
- essay or sample of writing
- letters of reference
- proof of immigration status.

A CV, medical form and portfolio may be required for certain courses. Similarly, a criminal records check will only be required in certain cases.

There will be an initial deadline date for the application and a later date for the provision of the supporting documentation. Some institutions won't consider an application until all documents are received, so send all documents promptly to improve your chances.

Transcript

A transcript is an academic record produced by your school, college or university. It might include details of your education and progress from year 10 in England and Wales, year 11 in Northern Ireland or S3 in Scotland. It will include exam and mock-exam results, internal assessment results and predicted grades; it should include any special awards or recommendation, as well as an explanation of any problems or anomalies in your educational attainment.

Letter of intent or statement of purpose

This is a key part of the application and may determine whether you are accepted. Use the statement to explain your interest, any relevant experience and what you hope to achieve with the qualification. You need to demonstrate your suitability and your potential. Try to analyse your experiences and remember to back up any claims you make about your strengths with examples. Explain any discrepancies or gaps in your education.

At postgraduate level, you should incorporate an outline of the research you intend to undertake. Consider what interests you about this area of work, how you intend to approach the research and illustrate how the research will fit in with the focus of the department.

The statement needs to be well written and free from spelling and grammatical errors. Two typed A4 pages should be sufficient.

Letters of reference

A letter of reference should be a positive document that provides details of your skills, strengths and achievements; a detailed, targeted letter is much more helpful than a general one. You will need to find two or three academic staff who know you well and can comment on your capabilities and really sell you.

Provide your referee with details of the courses you are applying for, along with a copy of your statement and transcript. You could suggest some of the key skills you would like them to draw attention to.

The referee will need to illustrate their own academic competence and background. The referee should provide specific examples of your strengths, since any claims should be backed up by relevant evidence. It may be useful for your referee to compare your achievements and skills to others that they have taught.

Give your referees around one month to compile the letters. It is helpful to gently follow them up to check that the letters have been completed. Thank them for their efforts; you may need to use their services again.

Tips, sample references and standard reference forms are available on university websites. See the University of British Columbia, www.grad.ubc.ca/prospective-students/application-admission/letters-reference, and McGill University, www.mcgill.ca/law-admissions/undergraduates/admissions/documents/#LETTERS, for some examples.

Admissions tests

Canada does not have a standardised university entrance exam; universities have their own admissions requirements. In most cases, UK students shouldn't need to take admissions tests for undergraduate courses.

Entrance exams required by Canadian graduate schools include the GRE (Graduate Record Examination), which can be taken across the world (www.ets.org/gre). It is available as a computer-based test in the UK and costs US$195 (£127). Other tests include the Graduate Management Admissions Test (GMAT) for business studies (www.mba.com), LSAT for Law School (www.lsac.org) and MCAT for Medical School (www.aamc.org/students/applying/mcat).

Different universities use the results from these tests in different ways. In some cases, the result will be a deciding factor; in others, the result will be just one of a number of considerations. Ask your chosen institution how they use the results and what kinds of scores previous applicants have achieved.

You are likely to do better in these tests if you are prepared for the style of questioning and any time limits for completion. Books and courses are available to help you prepare. You can take tests like the GRE more than once, but the costs can end up being quite substantial if you do so.

What next?

If you are successful in gaining a place at a Canadian college or university, you will be provided with a letter of acceptance. The next step will be to apply for a study permit.

You could study . . .

Associate of Arts degree Creative Writing
Camosun College, Victoria, British Columbia
Two years
No application deadline dates for international students
Annual fees C$13,000 (£6,736)
Homestay (room and board) from C$850 per month (£440)

Bachelor of Arts and Sciences (Hons)
McMasters University, Hamilton, Ontario
Four years
Apply by 1 April via OUAC International (www.ouac.on.ca)
Annual fees C$23,464 (£12,158)
Monthly living costs from C$900 (£466)

MSc Biological Science

University of Alberta, Edmonton, Alberta

Two years

Application deadline dates vary by department

Annual fees C$8,651 (£4,483)

Monthly living costs from C$1,000 (£518)

Visas

A study permit is required for anyone who will be studying for more than six months in the country; you will need to apply to the Canadian High Commission in London. To gain a study permit, you will need to prove that you can pay your tuition fees plus living costs of around C$10,000 (£5,182) per year. You will also need to be in good health and without a criminal record. Follow all instructions carefully and allow from around six weeks for processing. There is a processing fee of C$150 (£78).

There are different immigration requirements if you study in Quebec, where a *certificat d'acceptation du Québec* (CAQ) from the Immigration Service of Quebec is required prior to entry to Canada. See www.immigration-quebec.gouv.qc.ca/en/immigrate-settle/students/index.html.

If your chosen university or college welcomes lots of international students, the staff should be experienced in supporting applicants through the immigration procedures.

Further information on the procedures and how to apply can be found at www.cic.gc.ca/english/study/index.asp.

Costs and help with finances

Canada promotes itself as being more affordable for international students than the USA, Australia and New Zealand.

Costs

Tuition fees across the provinces and territories of Canada vary. According to Imagine Studying in Canada (the Council of Ministers of Education), university tuition fees range from around C$8,000 to C$26,000 (£4,145 to £13,472) per year, with college fees of between C$5,500 and C$15,000 (£2,850 and £7,772) per year.

Overall, international undergraduate students paid annual tuition fees averaging C$20,447 (£10,595) per year in 2014/2015. International full-time postgraduate students paid an average of C$13,934 (£7,220) per year (www.statcan.gc.ca).

> **66** The cost of study has been a lot more expensive but now that the fees in the UK have gone up, the difference is much less. The fees are approximately C$8,000 (£4,145) per semester. I also received an entrance scholarship and a second scholarship in my second year. **99**
> *Alex Warren, University of British Columbia, Canada*

Some research-based postgraduate study is subsidised and the fees can be lower than undergraduate fees. To calculate more specific costs for the courses and institutions you are interested in, the Imagine Studying in Canada website has a useful cost calculator at www.educationau-incanada.ca/educationau-incanada/template-gabarit/step-etape.aspx?lang=eng.

To compare the cost of living in Canada to the rest of the world, try the Numbeo Cost of Living Ranking at www.numbeo.com. Canada is ranked number 20 of 119 countries, indicating that it is cheaper than the UK, Australia and New Zealand.

Help with finances

If you're looking for a scholarship to help offset the costs of international study, be prepared to start your research early, more than a year ahead. Consider how you will support yourself, as scholarships are limited, highly competitive and may not cover the full costs of your studies.

Talk to your chosen university about any scholarships they offer and take a look at the Canadian government's website as a starting point, www.scholarships-bourses.gc.ca/scholarships-bourses/non_can/opportunities-opportunites.aspx?lang=eng.

Scholarships include the Vanier Canada Graduate Scholarships and Trudeau Scholarships. There are more opportunities for postgraduate than undergraduate study.

Other sources of information include:

- Commonwealth Scholarships: http://cscuk.dfid.gov.uk/apply/scholarships-uk-citizens
- Scholarships Canada: www.ScholarshipsCanada.com.

Cultural differences

Canada is considered to be a tolerant and multicultural society and it welcomes students from across the world. Canadian culture shares much with its neighbour, the USA, but there are differences. The province of Quebec is French-speaking and culturally quite different from the rest of the nation. Parts of Canada show a particularly British influence, including Toronto and Victoria.

Adjusting to the sheer size of Canada can be a shock, as well as getting used to the long, cold winter in much of the country.

> **❝** I knew it was cold in Canada but the UK really doesn't prepare you for a Canadian winter. I wish I knew to invest in a good winter coat and pair of snow boots! **❞**
>
> *Lauren Aitchison, University of Waterloo, Canada*

Citizenship and Immigration Canada has some helpful information on culture shock, as well as on adjusting to life and the weather in Canada at www.cic.gc.ca/english/newcomers/after-life.asp.

Working while studying

Full-time degree-level students can work on campus at their university or college without any special permission. Some new rules came into force in June 2014 making it easier to work off-campus; students are now allowed to work off campus without a special permit for up to 20 hours per week during term-time, and full-time in the official holidays. If you are taking a spouse or partner with you, they can apply for a work permit too.

Citizenship and Immigration Canada should tell you all you need to know about working while studying, co-op programmes and internships, and working after graduation, www.cic.gc.ca/english/study/work.asp.

Staying on after study

The Canadian authorities have a number of programmes that allow students to stay on in Canada after completion of their studies. Remember that these schemes change from time to time and may even have changed by the time you complete your studies.

Post-graduation work permit programme

Graduating students can apply for a permit of up to three years, depending on the length of their studies, see www.cic.gc.ca/english/study/work-postgrad-who.asp.

Canadian experience class

Graduating students have the opportunity to apply to stay on in Canada permanently; you will need to meet various conditions including at least one year's Canadian work experience in a managerial or professional occupation or the skilled trades. See www.cic.gc.ca/english/immigrate/cec/apply-who.asp for details.

Provincial nominee programme

If you are considered to offer the skills, education and experience to make an immediate economic contribution to your province, you may be able to gain residence under this scheme, www.cic.gc.ca/english/immigrate/provincial/apply-who.asp.

If you are leaving Canada, you can still remain connected through the Global Canadian Alumni Network. The nearest Canadian embassy or High Commission will be able to tell you more.

Pros and cons of study in Canada

Pros

- Good quality of education.
- High investment in research and development.
- Opportunities to stay and work after graduating.
- Possibility of emigrating after graduating.

Cons

- Certain competitive fields may not always be widely available to international students.
- Different systems in place in the different provinces.

Student story
Dharmesh Vyas
University of Saskatchewan, Canada

For Dharmesh Vyas, studying in Canada was the obvious next step after sixth form. 'I have always been curious about living in different places, exploring different climates and ultimately meeting new people. I had just finished the International Baccalaureate program and so I felt being an international student and citizen would help me understand and look at the world in a different way. I had friends and family tell me time and time again that the people in Canada are super friendly and, since I've been here, I've found that there is always that warmth and welcome you receive so you don't feel like an outsider.'

Luckily for Dharmesh, he coped well with the lower Canadian temperatures. 'It was obviously something I had never been exposed to – nothing as cold as here – and I was always curious as to how people still functioned when it got cold. Before I moved, the coldest I'd ever felt was probably -6 C. So you could probably imagine my surprise when we hit -40C (I loved it though).

'The reason I chose the University of Saskatchewan was that I liked the program here. Like the other universities in Canada, I still had the freedom to choose what I wanted to major in and I didn't have to decide before starting; I had more time to sift through my options and find something I liked.

'The university application process was very simple and easy. The university website outlined it all in a step by step process. Looking at it now, it's even easier than it was when I did it five years ago. The websites have updated, the information required is all there and if you ever have a question, they'll respond to you within a few days as well. They're there to help you and I definitely felt like I was treated well.

'Applying for a student visa was a bit more stressful. It was a case of gathering the documents, proving you have the funds, explaining why you wanted to study abroad rather than in your home country. The CIC website (Citizenship and Immigration Canada, www.cic.gc.ca/english) was somewhat overwhelming with the amount of information they needed, but breaking it down and going through it slowly helped. My parents also helped with a lot of that as well.

'Before I arrived, I had emails and letters coming to me in the UK. The university sent a brochure about accommodation and student life and preparing for the climate – something I thought was a bit strange at the time, but now I can definitely understand why. They granted me a scholarship which helped with funding as well.

'Adjusting to life overseas at the beginning was difficult in the sense that your best friends and family are far away. At the same time, you get used to it and become very independent. Figuring out things like banking, health coverage and car insurance are all things you need to do, but you always have someone to help you whether they're a friend or someone working for the university.

'It's always important to remember that living somewhere and travelling somewhere are two different things and adjusting anywhere will have ups and downs, although I certainly wouldn't classify any of my experiences as negative experiences.'

Dharmesh felt well supported with his academic decisions and progress. 'In order to make sure I was moving in the right direction with my studies, I had the option to book appointments to meet with university counsellors. Once I got to know the professors and had a declared major, I always had their support and I have definitely maintained contact with my professors even after graduating. They not only helped me settle in as an international student, but also encouraged me and helped me build my character and my opinions.

'Once I was accepted into a degree program or college, I had free rein over what I could study; however, each major has certain compulsory classes which form the core material for the degree. Although I ended up with a degree in Regional and Urban Planning, I had the option of doing things such as Physiology and Pharmacology, Physics, Biology, Chemistry,

Women and Gender Studies or English, to name a few. This way of studying definitely keeps you well rounded. It also allows you to build your schedule according to times that suit you (the times were scheduled with different professors and you picked what worked with the other classes you wanted to take).

'You were assigned a time at which you could sign up for classes and you would have to work out a schedule to get the classes you want. Sometimes you ended up adjusting your schedule because you couldn't get into the class, or you needed authorisation from a professor or an override to take the class even if it was full. It got stressful the further into the degree you got (especially your last semester), where the class is full and you can't get in. At those times, meeting with the heads of department helped and there were times when you could get replacement classes to cover the core subject requirements.'

'Another benefit was that I could speed my degree up by taking classes in the summer. I ended up finishing my degree in three years rather than four and I was also able to get transfer credit for university classes from my International Baccalaureate classes in the UK; A Levels work the same.'

Dharmesh's top tips

Accommodation

'It's always important to pick the right roommate – I heard horror stories from some other friends, so it's always important to respect boundaries and also to not be afraid to make your point. Also, set up your ground rules at the start – if splitting costs for groceries with a roommate works for you, then fine.'

Food

'I am vegetarian so I initially struggled with finding food. Of course, you can just cook everything at home, which I still do. But going out, I had a few issues with menus because I could maybe eat one thing on a massive menu. This has improved a lot in the past few years and eating out has become much more vegan/vegetarian-friendly.'

Insurance

'I took out car insurance in Saskatoon. The car insurance company, SGI (Saskatchewan Government Insurance) was great. Car insurance amounted to C$120 (£62) (give or take) a month and I used to get it done for three to four months at a time.'

Living costs

'Rent came to about C$500–600 (£259–£311) a month (split with a roommate); though the price really does vary according to the area you're in, proximity to places like shopping centres, the university etc. Groceries have been going up, but I could manage on about C$40–50 (£21–£26) for about two to three weeks and just buying the stuff I run out of as I go. As a student, it's important to remember that you will more than likely be spending a lot of money on coffee – especially closer to the times when you have all-nighters with friends.'

Working while studying

'I found that on-campus jobs worked best for me. The first job I got on-campus was with a professor in the Biology Department and I was helping him with research; he was also my genetics professor so that was great. Then I worked at the language centre which was my main job for two and a half years of my three years at university. I juggled three jobs at one time on campus while still going to class and that was definitely stressful. Two was manageable, but you're here to study so work comes second.'

Making friends

'Making friends was actually very easy. People were so nice and polite and people I met on my first day in an orientation session are really good friends now. You aren't always with the same people in different classes and it's always a good idea to have friends in different classes too – they help you and you help them; so when you're up at 3am doing an essay you should've done a few days ago, they're probably going through the same thing too. The further into your major you get, the more consistency you'll see in the faces of people and then you'll more or less know who you work well with (and who you don't).'

Lifestyle and culture

'The lifestyle and culture is a bit different. People are very relaxed. Skiing and snowboarding are often topics of conversation, as is hockey – all of which I knew very little about to begin with. Bars and night life were also different from back home, but a lot of that also has to do with growing up with friends and people for 18 years and then not having them around.

'The three-day weekends throughout the year (generally there was one every month) were usually very boring and that was mainly because all my friends went home to their cities and towns so there wasn't anyone around; that always just turned into an opportune time to mingle with other international students and possibly even take trips to other cities and the mountains.'

Travel and transport

'Travelling within Canada is quite expensive. At times it's even cheaper to go to another country. Public transport within Saskatoon was a huge adjustment coming from London where buses and trains are readily available. Buses come every thirty minutes until 6.30 and are far less frequent thereafter; there was also no train. That was the biggest adjustment and so it got to a point where I did need to get a car.'

Options for after you finish your studies

'After finishing, you have the option to apply for a Post Graduate Work Permit and work, or just go home once you're done. It's always important to have done your research with CIC prior to this and send in your applications in a timely manner. You do not want to get stuck or caught out on a technicality because you sent in an application after your deadline.'

Dharmesh has now graduated from university and is working for a Municipal Government. 'I wanted to gain some work experience with my degree and knowledge from the University of Saskatchewan. I do plan on going back into studies at a later date and the options are endless – whether I move to a different province or country (or even move back home), I know I have many options available and many places to explore.

'The best thing about studying overseas is you get exposed to a different culture, different people and you get to explore what you may otherwise never get around to doing. We could stay in the same place and some are perfectly content with that. Others either need to or want to move around to find what they're passionate about. In that sense, I feel the best part of studying overseas is being able to figure out what you want to do for yourself.'

The University of Saskatchewan (www.usask.ca) started off in 1907 as an agricultural college. It is now a public, research-based university offering over 200 academic programmes.

Chapter 8
Studying in Australia

What makes UK students choose to travel halfway around the world to experience study in Australia? Perhaps it's down to the combination of good-quality education, great lifestyle and reasonable entry requirements. Many UK students are already convinced, with 1,408 of them enrolled in Australia when the last checks were made (OECD Education at a Glance 2014).

The education system

A significant difference between the UK and Australia is the academic year; in Australia, this runs from February to November. Universities tend to run a two-semester year with semester one running from February to June and semester two from July to November. It is possible to start most courses in July, although some courses, including medicine and dentistry, are only available to start in February. The long summer holiday runs from December to February.

University study

The style of teaching tends to be slightly different from that in the UK, focused on practical learning to encourage independent thought and discussion. The approach is less formal, but equally challenging. You will need to share your views on subjects and may even be assessed on your class participation. In fact, you will probably be assessed in a range of different ways, in recognition of the fact that individual students learn in different ways.

Independent study and the development of critical thinking are encouraged, much as in the UK. You might find that you have more contact hours and a closer link with the lecturers than you would generally get in the UK.

Nearly all of Australia's universities are public, with only a few private universities. Undergraduate and postgraduate study can be offered at both pass and honours level.

How to find a course

You could start your search with the official Australian government site, www.studyinaustralia.gov.au. Use the handy study wizard to research courses or institutions, check entry requirements and create a shortlist. Study in Australia also includes a mini-site for students from the UK at www.studyinaustralia.gov.au/uk.

Accreditation and quality

It is fairly straightforward to ensure that you will be studying with an approved provider. The institutions that are approved to offer degrees and other higher-education qualifications can be found on the AQF (Australian Qualifications Framework) Register at www.aqf.edu.au/register/aqf-register.

Australia also has an Act in place to ensure that institutions taking on international students support them adequately; this might include helping students adjust to life in Australia as well as helping them to meet their learning goals. Go to www.cricos. deewr.gov.au to discover the list of institutions that meet these requirements.

> **❝** I find it seems to be more personal than at UK
> universities. Our class is quite large, but somehow
> you still manage to feel a personal connection with the
> lecturers; they really try to get to know you and give you
> great feedback on assignments and how you're going
> throughout the year. **❞**
>
> *Kadie O'Byrne, Murdoch University, Australia*

Academic recognition

If your institution takes lots of international students, they may
understand your UK qualifications and accept you without the
need to compare their standard to those offered in Australia. If the
qualification is not known to them, they may ask you to have your
qualifications assessed.

Undergraduate study

Undergraduate study tends to take three to four years in
Australia, with a strong emphasis on coursework. Certain courses,
like medicine, can take as long as six years. Unlike the UK,
ordinary or pass degrees are the norm, generally taking three
years. Access to an honours degree is reserved for those who
have achieved particularly well. A bachelor's degree (honours)
would normally take at least four years and requires independent
research and the completion of a thesis.

The system allows for more flexibility than you get in much of
the UK. You choose a major and study a fixed number of relevant
courses, but you will also have the chance to study a range of
elective courses in different subjects. You might start off majoring
in one subject and end up graduating with a major in a different
subject, based on your interests and abilities as you proceed
through your studies.

A degree with honours is achieved after completing an ordinary bachelor's degree with high achievement. It is different from an honours degree.

Vocational education

TAFE (Technical and Further Education) and VET (Vocational Education and Training) colleges may also offer some higher-education courses. They tend to offer more vocational courses that prepare you for an industry or trade. Vocational higher-education qualifications include associate degrees and AQF advanced diplomas, both of which are similar in level to HNDs or foundation degrees in the UK.

Entry requirements

If you have passed three A levels or equivalent study, then you should meet the general entry requirements for degree-level study in Australia. Certain university courses require particular grades and specific subjects to have been studied previously, while some courses will require a selection test or audition. On the whole, grade requirements tend to be slightly lower than in the UK. Programmes like medicine and dentistry are competitive, requiring high-achieving applicants with some relevant experience. Associate degrees or advanced diplomas may have lower entry requirements, although they may require specific experience or relevant previous study.

> **❝** The grading process is different. Instead of getting a first, 2:1, 2:2, you are awarded high distinction, distinction, credit or pass on each of your assignments, exams or units. **❞**
>
> *Vicky Otterburn, Murdoch University, Australia*

Postgraduate study

A range of different graduate qualifications are available,
including graduate certificates and diplomas, master's degrees and
doctorates.

- Graduate certificates (one semester) and diplomas (two
  semesters) are the shortest postgraduate options. They
  are of a similar level to postgraduate certificates and
  diplomas in the UK and can be used as a bridge to the
  study of a new subject at postgraduate level.
- A master's degree by coursework (or taught master's)
  tends to take two years. It may include a minor thesis.
- A master's degree by research generally takes one year
  after a bachelor's (honours) degree, or two years after an
  ordinary or pass degree.
- Doctor of Philosophy (PhD) takes from three years.

The length of your postgraduate study depends on your academic
background and the subject you choose to study.

Entry requirements

The successful completion of an undergraduate degree is the
standard entry requirement for postgraduate study in Australia.
For some courses, you may also be required to demonstrate
relevant work experience or previous research.

Entry requirements vary between institutions and their
departments. The institution will be able to tell you more or you
can browse institutions at www.studyinaustralia.gov.au.

Applying

There are some centralised admissions services in Australia, but
in the vast majority of cases, international offices require direct

applications. Alternatively, some students opt to apply via an Australian educational agent (see page 101).

Closing dates fall in the autumn for courses starting in February. You need to apply to university in good time to give yourself a chance to get a visa and to sort out all the other aspects of a move overseas. Certain courses, like medicine and dentistry, require a much earlier application; likewise, if you're applying for a scholarship as well, you may need to start the process much earlier. Ideally, you should be preparing for your application a good year in advance.

The application form

Contact your chosen institution requesting information about the application process and an application form. Application forms can often be completed online. If paper-based, the application might be sent direct to the institution. Alternatively, you may choose to deal with an agent or local UK representative, depending on the requirements of the university or college.

The application process is more straightforward than the UK system. When applying direct to an institution, you will choose a first preference for your course, along with second and third options. The institution may charge you a fee to apply, ranging from around A$50 to A$100 (£25–£50). Certain fees may be waived when applying online or through some educational agents.

Other documents

Alongside the application, you will be asked to provide an academic transcript with details of any qualifications gained, as well as details of units and unit grades. Proof of existing qualifications will be needed. If you are applying before your qualifications have been completed, you are likely to receive a conditional offer and will have to provide proof of qualifications once the results come out.

Some courses, but not all, require a personal statement and an accompanying academic reference.

Admissions tests

In some cases, an admissions test will be required. Your institution will tell you more.

If a test is required, please make sure that you are prepared. Although you may not be able to revise, preparing yourself for the style and time constraints of the test can make a big difference.

Undergraduate admissions tests

Applicants to medicine, dentistry and health-science courses at certain universities may be required to sit either the UMAT (Undergraduate Medicine and Health Sciences Admission Test, www.umat.acer.edu.au) or the ISAT (International Student Admissions Test, www.isat.acer.edu.au). Both are available in the UK.

Postgraduate admissions tests

Postgraduate tests used in Australia include:

- the Law School Admissions Test (LSAT), www.lsac.org
- the Graduate Australian Medical Schools Admissions Test (GAMSAT), www.gamsat.acer.edu.au.

If an interview is required as part of the admissions process, you may be interviewed online or over the phone.

What next?

If your application is successful, you will receive an offer letter. Once the offer is accepted and the required tuition fees are paid (generally the fees for one semester), you will be sent an electronic confirmation of enrolment (eCoE). You will need this document to apply for a visa.

You could study . . .

Bachelor of Marine and Antarctic Science
University of Tasmania, Hobart
Three years
Apply at least three months before semester start date
Annual fees A$23,168 (£11,429)
Annual living costs A$13,500–A$19,000 (£6,876–£9,677)

Master of Environment (coursework)
Australian National University, Canberra
2 years
Apply by 12 December for February start
Annual fees A$33,168 (£16,893)
Weekly living costs from A$370–A$570 (£188–£290)

PhD Humanities and Communication
University of Western Sydney
Three years
Apply by 15 November for February start
Annual fees A$24,100 (£12,274)
Annual living costs A$18,610 (£9,478)

Visas

In order to apply for a student visa, you will need your eCoE and the ability to financially support yourself throughout the course; this includes the cost of tuition fees, return air fare and A$18,610 (£9,478) living costs per year. Remember, you may need more money than this to live on.

A further condition is adequate health insurance whilst you are in Australia. You will also need to meet certain health requirements and may be required to show evidence of your good character.

> The new streamlined visa process (SVP) means that applications for degrees at participating universities require less evidence and are processed more quickly.

This information is a basic introduction to the visa process; contact the Australian High Commission in London (www.uk.embassy.gov.au) for the latest application procedures and fees information. You should be able to apply online and fees are currently set at A$535 (£272). You shouldn't apply more than four months in advance and should normally expect your application to be processed within four weeks. Ask your institution if you need further support; they are likely to have experience in this process.

Further information on applying for a study visa can be found at www.immi.gov.au.

Costs and help with finances

Even the cheapest Australian undergraduate degrees cost more than those on offer in England, while the most expensive courses far exceed English fees. Scottish, Welsh and Northern Irish students will pay more in Australia than at home. So Australia is not a cheap option, but it does have some great benefits in terms of quality of education, lifestyle and opportunities.

Costs

Fees vary between different universities. According to www.studyinaustralia.gov.au, you can expect to pay annual tuition fees as follows:

- bachelor's degree – A\$15,000 to A\$33,000
  (£7,640–£16,807)
- master's and doctoral degree – A\$14,000 to A\$37,000
  (£7,130–£18,844).

Lab-based courses and those requiring specialist equipment are likely to be at the higher end of the fee scale, with courses in arts or business towards the lower end. Courses such as medicine and veterinary science will be significantly higher. Remember to consider the cost of books, materials and field trips too.

All students in Australia pay a student-service fee of up to A\$286 (£146) for campus services and student societies. Some universities incorporate this within tuition fees for international students, so check with your institution whether an additional payment is necessary.

The strong Australian dollar means that the cost of living in Australia is currently higher than in the UK, although it also means that earnings are higher too. Australia is currently listed at number six out of 119 countries on a cost-of-living ranking for 2015 at www.numbeo.com.

It is a requirement of the visa that you have adequate health insurance; the cost of overseas student-health cover (OSHC) starts at a few hundred pounds per year. According to the Australian Department of Health and Ageing, the average cost of minimum cover is A\$437 (£223) for 12 months. Visit www.studyinaustralia. gov.au/en/Study-Costs/OSHC/Overseas-student-health-cover for more details.

The following average weekly costs are provided by www.
studyinaustralia.gov.au:

- accommodation: A$80 to A$400 (£40–£204)
- groceries and eating out: A$80 to A$200 (£40–£102)
- utilities (including internet): A$80 to A$150 (£40–£76)
- public transport: A$10 to A$50 (£5–£25)
- entertainment: A$50 to A$100 (£25–£51)

The Australian Trade Commission quotes average monthly living costs of A$1,400 to A$1,900 (£713 to £968). To find out about finances and budgeting in Australia, go to www.moneysmart.gov. au/managing-my-money.

Help with finances

If you're hoping for a scholarship to help fund your studies in Australia, you need to start early and get ready to prove yourself, as competition is fierce. Scholarships are hard to come by and often don't cover all the costs, so think about how you will support yourself.

You can make a start by using the scholarship database on www.studyinaustralia.gov.au. You should talk to your university about any scholarships that they offer.

You could also take a look at the following websites:

- www.australiaawards.gov.au
- www.kcl.ac.uk/artshums/ahri/centres/menzies/ scholarships/index.aspx
- http://cscuk.dfid.gov.uk/apply/scholarships-uk-citizens.

Cultural differences

You will soon discover how multicultural Australia is; with one in four of its population born overseas, you are sure to come across other British people. Adjusting to Australia includes adjusting to its extremes of weather and its vast size. Find out about the climate in the different states and territories when you are deciding where to study.

The way of life in Australia is a bit different too; things are generally more informal and the good weather means that there is more time to enjoy life outdoors.

> **❝** The Australian lifestyle is great! Everyone is so friendly, welcoming and laid back. Sport is a big part of the Aussie lifestyle; there are heaps of regular sports clubs and great facilities to use all year around. In the summer, people have BBQs regularly; you don't rush around because of the heat and spend a lot of time at the beach or around a pool with friends. There are lots of music festivals and events on offer. **❞**
>
> *Vicky Otterburn, Murdoch University, Australia*

Working while studying

The opportunity to start working as soon as you start your studies is a definite benefit of study in Australia. For new students gaining a student visa, there is no need to apply for extra permission to work 40 hours per fortnight in term time. You are permitted to work unlimited hours during holiday periods. Remember: there will be serious consequences if you break the conditions of your visa. The Australian Government Department of Immigration and Citizenship (www.immi.gov.au) has the most up-to-date and detailed information.

There are a range of opportunities in pubs, bars, restaurants and shops, but you will need to balance your study and your work. The national minimum wage is A$16.87 (£8.59) per hour, although some junior employees may get paid less than this.

You will need a Tax File Number (TFN) from the Australian Tax Office (www.ato.gov.au) to work and to open a bank account.

Staying on after study

Australia is keen to welcome international students and has introduced a number of changes to make it even more attractive. In early 2013, a new post-study work visa was launched. International students with a bachelor's degree or master's degree by coursework from an Australian university, and who are granted a visa, are now able to work for two years in Australia in any type of job. Students with a master's degree by research are able to sign up for three years' work and doctoral students for up to four years.

For those considering staying on a more permanent basis, Australia has a skilled migration programme targeting those who can contribute to the economy. The requirements and occupations needed vary, so choosing a course of study because it is on the skilled-occupation list is not a guarantee of success; the list may well have changed by the time your course is completed. For the latest details, see the Department of Immigration and Citizenship website at www.immi.gov.au/skilled/general-skilled-migration.

> **❝** There are many ways to stay after you have
> finished studying: applying for residency, applying
> for a work visa or a sponsorship by a company based on an
> employment opportunity. The studying is the easy part,
> finding the job is much harder, so many more people are
> going to university these days and it is much more
> competitive for places in the workforce. **❞**
>
> *Vicky Otterburn, Murdoch University, Australia*

Pros and cons of study in Australia

Pros

- Strong reputation for higher education.
- Reasonable entry requirements.
- Good pay for part-time work.
- Possibility of emigrating if you have the right skills.

Cons

- High cost of fees.
- High living costs (while the Australian dollar is strong
  and the pound is weak).

Student story
Joshua Jackson, SP Jain School of Global Management (Singapore and Sydney, Australia)

Josh Jackson took a big step when he decided to study abroad. 'I wasn't sure what I wanted to do for university. The headmistress of my school announced one morning in assembly that an institution was offering the possibility of 100% scholarship on fees and accommodation for four years. The new Global Bachelor's of Business Administration course required two years study in Singapore and ended with two years in Sydney, Australia.'

Getting a scholarship to cover his tuition fees resulted in a huge saving. 'The full cost of study would be about US$20,000 (£12,981) a year.'

Josh found the application process to be fairly straightforward. 'I had to write a short essay about myself. After that there was a written task with three questions that I needed to complete in a certain amount of time. Following that, I had an interview on Skype with one of the professors. The interview was very short and informal as I had met the professor around six months before on a week-long "bridge to BBA" event the university ran. This was a five-day event where students were invited to stay in university accommodation, meet the staff and spend some time in SP Jain and Singapore.

'The university sorted out the visa for Singapore for me. A few days after we arrived, the university staff took us to the immigration office where we were given the visa. For Australia, we had to apply for the visa ourselves but the university provided us with a code we needed once we had paid the tuition fees. A few days after the application went through, I was instructed to have a medical at one of a small number of panel doctors in the UK. Around seven working days after the medical, my visa was granted and I was able to fly over.

'Sorting out of the Singapore visa was the single most useful thing the university did. They also put me in touch with a current student who could answer my questions and the head of the student council emailed all the new students to give them some information before they came.

'Since I arrived, I feel the university does not help very much. They helped us get health insurance in both countries and the former dean and student counsellor were very helpful to the students in every way possible, but other than that we are very much on our own. The most important aspect of this is that although the master's degree graduates often get 100% placement, there is currently no facility in place to help us get jobs when we graduate, which many find very concerning.'

Josh has coped well with adjusting to life on two new continents. 'In the two and a half years I have been away I have had about two nights where I felt homesick, but other than that I have enjoyed the experience greatly. Some of my peers have felt very out of their comfort zone and struggled somewhat, but there are people from almost all round the world so finding someone quite similar to you is not too hard.'

He explains about some of the differences in teaching and learning that he has experienced. 'Due to the small size of the institution I actually have a very close relationship with all of my professors.

Classes rarely, if ever, exceed 30 students whereas I have friends in the UK who have lectures with 400 or more students. I think this is a huge benefit, as well as the fact many professors teach master's degree students as well and so are very highly qualified and knowledgeable.'

Joshua's top tips

Accommodation

'Staying on-campus is always useful at first for making friends. Staying off-campus is usually cheaper, sometimes by quite a long way, but normally less convenient.

'I have stayed on-campus in both countries. In Singapore, the city is so small and transport so cheap it doesn't matter where you stay, but in Sydney the city is very expensive. I stay in Wentworth Point, near the Olympic Park, and it is very removed from the city centre. Travelling up to central Sydney takes over an hour, and almost two hours to reach the east coast of the city.'

Food

'The cuisine in Singapore is a huge mix of different cultures, mostly traditional Asian Chinese but also influenced by Indian and western food. They also have most of the large fast-food chains as well (McDonald's, Subway, KFC etc). Traditional Singapore hawker centres are a great place to go to eat like the locals. The food is cheap and quick but good and tasty as well, almost like a Singaporean version of fast food!'

Insurance

'Our school provided us with health insurance policies in both Singapore and Sydney. In Sydney it was mandatory to have health insurance to get the visa.'

Living costs

'Singapore was very cheap compared to where I live in England. At the time I was there, it was around two Singapore dollars to one British pound, but you could get a fast-food meal for around S$5. Going out to the movies and drinking was also cheaper.

'Australia is about as expensive as London as far as I can tell, though I have only been here for a few months. I buy almost everything non-branded, eat at home every day and rarely go out drinking.'

Financial support for study

'I have a 100% scholarship on my tuition fees but pay for accommodation. This is conditional on the basis that I get within the top 25% of the class throughout the year.'

Working while studying

'In Singapore I did not have to work, but I was told the pay was not very good as there is no minimum wage. Working in Australia is pretty good though. I am able to work 20 hours a week during term time and an unlimited amount during the holidays. The pay is far better than England for unqualified jobs. However, there do seem to be a few licences around that you need to get before working. For example, I needed to pay A$100 (£51) to get a "Responsible Service of Alcohol" (RSA) licence.'

Making friends

'Making friends was never that hard. Everyone is in the same position, away from home and starting a new chapter of their life. Many had never studied away from home before, and almost everyone had never studied in a different country to their home.'

Lifestyle and culture

'The lifestyle in Singapore is very metropolitan, busy, and Asian; they are more traditional, hierarchical and family oriented. It is definitely a hybrid between typical Western and Eastern lifestyles, a good stepping stone between England and Malaysia, for example.

'Australian lifestyle and culture is very like England's, but more relaxed and with a slightly heavier influence on sport and relaxation.'

Travel and transport

'Public transport in Singapore was very good and cheap. Taxis were cheap as well and very useful when you couldn't use public transport.

'In Sydney, though, the transport is not as good and quite expensive. The buses are still quite costly, especially for a student. Getting to the city is quite a hassle and taxis are very expensive.'

Options for after you finish your studies

'I am not very sure about options after I finish, though both places seem a little easier to get a job after graduation than England. The pay in Singapore is not that great in comparison, but in Australia you get paid very well and there are more job opportunities than in England.

'The best things about studying overseas have been experiencing a new culture and travelling; seeing a completely different way of life, cuisine and society has been truly amazing. As I am in each place for two years, I really get a feel for it as opposed to going on holiday somewhere for a few weeks. The travelling has been amazing as well. Going from Singapore to Indonesia, Malaysia and Thailand is as simple as visiting France, Germany or Spain from England, and often cheaper! There are so many travel opportunities in Australia as well that I am very much looking forwards to experiencing.

'Overall, studying abroad is completely what you make of it. You really have to go out there and immerse yourself in the place you are studying to fully enjoy it. If you keep yourself to yourself and only look at why it is worse than home, you won't enjoy it.'

SP Jain (www.spjain.org) was originally established in Mumbai, India in 1981 and now has campuses in Dubai, Sydney and Singapore and achieves high global rankings for its MBAs.

Chapter 9

Studying in New Zealand

New Zealand might seem like a long way to go for an education, but many international students choose the country for its safety, quality of life and the option to settle after studies. According to a 2014 survey, over 6,800 UK students are already studying there.

New Zealand is a little larger in area than the UK, but with a population of only 4.5 million.

The education system

Much as in Australia, New Zealand's academic year runs from late February to November. The academic year incorporates two semesters, each lasting 12 weeks. You can expect breaks mid-semester and at the end of semester one, with a longer summer break after semester two (from November to February). It may be possible to join certain courses in July or as part of a summer school between November and February.

At all levels, students in New Zealand are encouraged to develop independent thought and defend their ideas in discussion and debate. Most taught courses are assessed by means of exams and classroom activities, which could include essays, assignments, presentations, projects and practical work. Make sure that you get involved in class activities; your participation may be assessed here too.

All eight of New Zealand's universities are publicly funded. There are also a range of other institutions with degree-awarding powers: polytechnics, colleges of education and wānanga.

- Polytechnics, or institutes of technology, originally specialised in technical or vocational studies, but now offer a range of subjects and research activities.
- Colleges of education, for the most part, offer studies in the fields of early-years, primary and secondary education.
- Wānanga provide mainly vocational educational opportunities that include Māori tradition and culture.

There are also private training establishments offering degree-level education.

How to find a course

Take a look at New Zealand Education (www.studyinnewzealand. com) to search for programmes at universities, institutes of technology, and polytechnics. The site also features a scholarship search option, as well as useful information about study and life in New Zealand.

Accreditation and quality

New Zealand has strong quality systems for education. In order to verify that your course or provider is accredited, you can search for approved qualifications and recognised institutions at the New Zealand Qualifications Authority website (www.nzqa.govt.nz/ search).

Five of New Zealand's eight universities can be found in the 2014–2015 Times Higher Education World University Rankings Top 400, with one of its universities featured in the Top 200.

As an international student so far from home, you need to know that you will be well supported. The New Zealand Ministry of Education has a code of practice that all institutions accepting international students must adhere to. The code requires clarity and accuracy in the information you receive before you apply; ensures that international students have access to welfare support and information on life in New Zealand; and explains grievance procedures, should things go wrong. It should help you to make an informed choice on where to apply and give you a realistic idea of the support you can expect once you arrive.

Undergraduate study

Bachelor's degrees in New Zealand tend to take three years to complete, although some subjects take longer, up to six years for a Bachelor of Medicine. Students must successfully complete each year before moving on to the next. High achievers may opt for an additional year of study to gain an honours degree, or choose a course of at least four years with honours already incorporated.

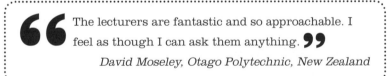

The lecturers are fantastic and so approachable. I feel as though I can ask them anything.

David Moseley, Otago Polytechnic, New Zealand

You can often be flexible in the direction your academic studies take you, having the opportunity to try out a range of subjects. It is not unusual for the major subject you choose when you apply to end up being different from the major subject you graduate in.

Your university will guide you through the process of choosing the right core and elective subjects to achieve a major in your desired subject.

> Stage 1 or 100-level courses are taken in the first year, stage 2 or 200-level courses in the second year, and stage 3 or 300-level courses in the third year.

It is possible to transfer credit and move between different institutions at tertiary level.

Vocational education

Qualifications in technical and vocational education are available at polytechnics, institutes of technology or in the workplace; some opportunities are available through universities and wānanga. Level 6 national diplomas could be compared to qualifications like HNDs or foundation degrees in the UK. If you decide to move from a national diploma to a relevant degree, it may be possible to transfer credit or to gain exemptions from the initial stages of the degree programme.

Entry requirements

Entry requirements in New Zealand tend to be lower than in the UK, as the smaller population means less of a demand for places. The grades required tend to reflect the academic level you will need to cope with the demands of the course. In most cases, you will need to have gained three A levels, or equivalent; some universities ask for three Cs at A level and there are additional grade requirements for certain courses.

At the University of Auckland, New Zealand's highest-ranking university, students need to achieve a minimum of CCC at A level (excluding General Studies) to be considered for entry. There are additional course-specific requirements, for example, a minimum of CCC for Bachelor Education (Teaching), BBC for Bachelor Architectural Studies, and BBB for Bachelor (Hons) Engineering. They are not currently accepting international applicants for direct entry to Bachelor Medicine, Bachelor Optometry or Bachelor Pharmacy, instead applicants will be considered based on first year results from BSc Biomedical Science. If you are applying with alternatives to A levels, contact the university's international office via www.auckland.ac.nz/uoa/is-contact-auckland-international.

Postgraduate study

At postgraduate level, you might choose to study for a:

- postgraduate certificate
- postgraduate diploma
- master's degree
- doctoral degree.

All of these are of a comparable level to the same qualifications in the UK. Postgraduate certificates take one semester to complete, with postgraduate diplomas taking one year. Master's degrees tend to take two years (or less, if you have achieved an honours degree) and can be based on the completion of a thesis or have more of a focus on coursework. Doctorates would normally take three years to complete.

If you are not ready for postgraduate study, perhaps because of your achievements at undergraduate level or maybe because you are changing subject, you could consider a graduate diploma.

Entry requirements

An undergraduate degree from a recognised institution is required to undertake postgraduate study in New Zealand. You generally need a master's degree to join a doctoral degree, although applicants with a bachelor's (honours) degree with a first or upper-second classification may also be considered.

Distance learning

New Zealand has a range of distance-learning providers offering education at degree level, including the Open Polytechnic of New Zealand (www.openpolytechnic.ac.nz) and Massey University (www.massey.ac.nz/massey/learning/distance-learning). Most tertiary institutions offer blended learning, delivering their education in a range of different ways (including online) to meet their students' needs.

Applying

Institutions in New Zealand require direct application, so the first step should be to contact the international office at the universities where you would like to study. They will provide all the information you need on how to apply and show you how to access the relevant application forms. They may charge an application fee. Some students choose to use the services of an agent, rather than dealing direct with the institutions.

Ideally, you should start the research process more than a year in advance, to allow time to apply for scholarships, apply for a visa and make the arrangements to move. You should plan to make contact with the universities at least six to eight months beforehand. Closing dates for applications to start in semester one (February) normally fall between September and December; to join programmes in semester two (July), you should apply by April or May. Restricted-entry or competitive courses

often have an earlier closing date and some may only have a
February intake.

The application form

The application forms tend to be a lot shorter and simpler than the
UCAS form in the UK. You will need to provide personal details,
information on your previous and current academic studies and
your career plans. You will be asked for a first and second choice
of degree, along with details of your intended major(s).

Applications are paper-based or online. If they are online, you will
still need to allow time for certified or witnessed documents to be
posted or couriered to New Zealand.

Other requirements

Other documents required include academic transcripts (with
details of education and qualifications) and certificates. Academic
references and written statements may be requested, along with
portfolios and other evidence for certain courses. The institution
will also ask for a copy of your passport. Copied documents often
need to be certified or witnessed by someone in the legal profession
or in another position of responsibility.

In addition, postgraduate applicants may need to provide two
references and a CV, and may be asked to submit a research
proposal.

In some cases, an interview over the phone or online may be
necessary for undergraduate and postgraduate applicants.

Academic recognition

If your qualifications are unfamiliar to the international office, you
may need to pay for an International Qualifications Assessment
through the New Zealand Qualifications Authority: www.nzqa.

govt.nz/qualifications-standards/international-qualifications/apply-for-an-international-qualifications-assessment.

What next?

If your application is successful, you will receive an offer of admission. The next step will be to apply for a visa.

You could study . . .

BSc Geology

University of Otago, Dunedin

Three years

Apply by 31 October for February start

Annual fees NZ$27,200 (£13,284)

Annual living costs NZ$15,000–NZ$17,000 (£7,326–£8,302)

MA Pacific Studies

University of Canterbury, Christchurch

Two years

Apply from October for February start

Annual fees NZ$26,600 (£12,990)

Average weekly living costs NZ$494 (£241)

PhD Mechanical Engineering

University of Auckland

Three to four years

Applications accepted throughout the year

Annual fees NZ$6,503 (£3,176)

Annual living costs NZ$20,000–NZ$25,000 (£9,767–£12,210)

Visas

Once you have accepted an offer of admission and paid your tuition fees (or the appropriate deposit), you can start to apply for a student visa. You are also likely to have to provide a chest X-ray, police certificates (or criminal records check) and accommodation details, along with evidence of funds for living costs and air fare home. For courses of over nine months, you will need access to NZ$15,000 (£7,326) (as at February 2015) per year to cover your living costs alone; you may need more than this to live on. You will also need to take out adequate health insurance to cover you during your stay in New Zealand.

> **"** I found the experience of applying for a visa for New Zealand a little daunting at first, especially as there were several different types of visa which you could apply for. However, with helpful advice from my tutor at the University of Birmingham and from properly reading through the information provided on the website, the process was pretty simple. You had to prove that you had enough money to fund yourself for the year, which could be challenging for some, but because I had savings from a part-time job it was fine for me. I applied for my visa quite early on and it took about three weeks for it to arrive; however, I know of some people who had some problems such as the date of return on the visa being wrong and the visa not actually being placed in the passport! So it is really important to make sure that you apply for your visa well ahead of leaving for the country, but also to check the visa information once you get it back. **"**
>
> *Madeleine Prince, Cawthron Institute, New Zealand*

> When you apply for a visa for an undergraduate or postgraduate degree lasting over two years, if you hope to work, tick the boxes under 'variation of conditions' requesting permission to work up to 20 hours a week during the academic year and full-time during the Christmas and new-year holidays.

For full details of how to apply, rules and regulations and the latest fees, go to Immigration New Zealand (www.immigration.govt.nz). Further information can be found at the New Zealand High Commission in London (www.nzembassy.com/unitedkingdom). You should allow four to six weeks for processing, although many applications are processed within 25 days. The fee is currently £140.

Most international offices have lots of experience in helping students through these processes. They will know the problems that previous applicants have encountered and should support you to make a successful application for a visa.

Once you have a visa, you will need to follow certain requirements in order to retain it, such as attending your course and achieving certain standards. Your visa will only last for a maximum of one academic year, so you will need to reapply for subsequent years of study. You may be able to renew it online through your institution in subsequent years.

Costs and help with finances

New Zealand is unlikely to offer a cheaper option for education at undergraduate level; some of the cheapest university undergraduate fees in New Zealand are comparable in cost to the most expensive in the UK. At postgraduate level, the costs can be higher than in the UK, although there is an incentive to study PhDs, making New Zealand a very attractive proposition.

Costs

Individual tertiary institutions set their own fees, which will vary depending on the course you choose. According to Study Options (www.studyoptions.com), annual tuition fees for undergraduate study range from NZ$20,000 to NZ$26,000 (£9,769 to £12,698). Fees for courses at polytechnics or institutes of technology may be lower than NZ$18,000 (£8,792) per year, making them a more affordable option.

Postgraduate tuition fees for international students can be as much as NZ$32,000 (£15,628) per year. However, international PhD students pay the same fees as students from New Zealand, starting at around NZ$6,000 (£2,930) per year.

Although you will be required to prove access to NZ$15,000 (£7,326) per year for visa purposes, New Zealand Educated suggests allowing as much as NZ$20,000 (£9,768) for living costs. In comparison to the rest of the world, New Zealand is ranked number seven of 119 countries on a 2015 cost-of-living ranking at www.numbeo.com; the UK is listed just below at number ten.

Remember to budget for medical and travel insurance; international students are legally obliged to hold this throughout their period of study in New Zealand.

Help with finances

A range of scholarships are available, although you will need to compete with other applicants. Apply early, follow all the guidelines and be prepared to supplement any scholarship with other sources of funding; most scholarships will not cover all costs. Scholarships include the Commonwealth Scholarship and Fellowship Plan, and international doctoral research scholarships.

You can search for scholarships at www.studyinnewzealand.com/ get-started/find-scholarships. This searches options including national and university-specific awards. Talk to your university or polytechnic about the range of scholarships they administer.

Take a look at the Commonwealth Scholarships website for details of their scholarships, awards and fellowships, http://cscuk.dfid. gov.uk/apply/scholarships-uk-citizens.

Cultural differences

New Zealand is a multicultural nation with an informal way of doing things. One in seven New Zealanders is Māori, so their language and culture forms an important part of the national identity. In New Zealand, you can expect an outdoor lifestyle with the opportunity to get involved with sports and a range of cultural activities.

Although there will be similarities to the UK, don't assume that life will be the same; there will be cultural differences. It is helpful to find out about the culture and way of life in New Zealand in order to prepare yourself for a successful transition. Talking to other people who have already made the transition can be helpful. There are many websites for expats that might help in this process. Your university's international office may be able to help too.

Working while studying

If you have ticked the relevant boxes on the student visa application (variation of conditions), you may be allowed to work up to 20 hours per week during academic term, and full-time during the summer holidays. Make sure you have permission before you start working and follow the visa requirements to the letter. Your right to work can normally be found on your student visa. You can apply for a variation of conditions at a later date, if necessary.

> **❝** Obviously getting a part-time job is useful; however, the reason you are on this year abroad is to study. I would advise making studying your top priority; make sure that the part-time job doesn't get in the way of that (or even in the way of socialising with your new-found friends). Sometimes a part-time job can hinder other exciting opportunities such as visiting other parts of the country at the weekend. It all depends which you feel is more important.**❞**
>
> *Madeleine Prince, Cawthron Institute, New Zealand*

Don't assume that you will find work immediately. It can be hard to find the right job to fit in with your studies and your visa requirements. You will also need to consider how you balance your academic studies and your working life. Take a look at Student Job Search for opportunities in your area, www.sjs.co.nz. You will need an Inland Revenue Department (IRD) number too. Find out more at www.ird.govt.nz/how-to/irdnumbers.

Staying on after study

If you hope to stay on in New Zealand after finishing your studies, there are a number of schemes currently in operation. The government is keen to retain young people with the right skills and knowledge to contribute to the New Zealand economy. If you hope to emigrate, you may decide to choose your subject based on skills-shortage areas at the time you apply; don't forget that these lists are subject to change and may well be different by the time you complete your studies.

If you don't have a job offer, you have the following options.

- **Post-study work visa**

  Recent graduates from tertiary institutes in New Zealand can apply for a visa of up to 12 months giving them time to search for a skilled job (and to work on a temporary basis while searching). Amongst other requirements, you will need to provide evidence that you can support yourself financially. On finding a skilled, long-term job, you can apply for a visa under the Study to Work category for two to three years.
- **Skilled migrant category visa**

  This is a points-based residence visa, with points gained for a job offer, experience, qualifications and so on.

There are a number of options if you are offered a job considered to be in a shortage area.

- **Essential skills visa**

  The essential skills visa allows those with a job offer to work in New Zealand on a temporary basis (provided a New Zealander cannot be found to do the job).
- **Long term skills shortage list (LTSSL) work category**

  If offered a job on the LTSSL, you can apply for a 30-month work visa; after two years, holders of this visa can apply for a resident visa.

- **Skilled migrant category visa**
  A job offer will enhance the points you can gain on this points-based residence visa.

For information on all these options and more, see www. immigration.govt.nz/migrant. The information is complex and subject to change. Your university may be able to put you in touch with relevant sources of support for this process.

Pros and cons of study in New Zealand

Pros

- Range of internationally recognised qualifications.
- Support for international students.
- Reasonable entry requirements.
- Possibilities to stay on and work afterwards.

Cons

- Current costs of living.
- Far from home.

Student story
Anwar Hussain Nadat
University of Auckland, New Zealand

Anwar Hussain Nadat had wanted to be a primary teacher for some time when his research into suitable courses led him a little further away than he'd first anticipated. 'I started to look at the courses available in the UK and, the more research I did, the more I felt that these courses were not what I was looking for. I then decided to look at courses abroad and targeted countries which would also allow me to be qualified in the UK. I wanted to broaden my horizons and the chance to experience a whole new setting and adventure was too good to refuse.'

So what convinced Anwar that New Zealand was the right setting for him? 'I love the natural side of the earth and enjoy watching the landscapes, which New Zealand has plenty of. I also have relatives in New Zealand and knowing you have familiar faces around provides a security net which wouldn't have been available elsewhere. It is a big move so I researched New Zealand over the course of a year to make sure that it was the right fit for me.

'I knew I had to find a university in Auckland as this is where my relatives are based. Once I learned that University of Auckland is the most highly ranked university in New Zealand, I started to focus on this institution and found out about their Graduate Diploma in Primary Teaching. I used an organisation called Study Options who are based in the UK and help prospective students to apply for universities in Australia and New Zealand. I also enquired with my relatives in Auckland as they had studied at the university. This all helped to give me an overall picture which convinced me that this was the right institution for me.

'The cost is a little bit more than in the UK. The PGCE course in the UK costs £9,000 and this year the Graduate Diploma was NZ$31,000, roughly working out to £15,000, so £6,000 more in fees. However, as an international student it is compulsory to have both health and travel insurance which is added to your course fee along with the student services fee, so in total it cost me

NZ$33,080 which was about £16,000 as the exchange rate was high. Overall it adds up to about £7,000 to £8,000 more.

'The application process was straightforward although it did take a number of months. Study Options were fantastic in assisting me with my application. They sent me an application which I filled in in May. They checked through the form and then sent it on to the university. There was no application fee which was a bonus. In June, the university notified me that my application was being processed. In July, I was asked to complete a Maths and Literacy test online. I found the Maths test to be very similar to the Professional Skills Test we have in the UK; however, the Literacy test was different as I was given an article to write a summary about, rather like a mini essay.

'After this, the application process became very slow and I did not hear anything back until October when I was given a conditional place based on passing an interview and having a clean police check. I had to obtain a Police Certificate for immigration from ACRO and this has a small cost to it.

'I completed my interview via Skype around mid-October and it lasted roughly 30 minutes. I had previously asked the university what to expect so I was able to prepare. Finally, after seven months I got the final confirmation of my place. The university does have an online application portal, which was very helpful to know how far along your application was. Study Options took a lot of pressure and worries off me as they found the answers to any enquiries I had.'

Anwar went through the fast-track visa scheme, so getting a visa ended up being a bit quicker than getting a place on the course. 'I needed one year's visa and I received it within 10 days; however, there was a lot of preparation behind it. The full year's fee has to be paid in full and the receipt needs to go with the application. This means that you don't have the option to spread your costs. As my course also has an early start date in January (rather than a normal start date in late February), any future student would have to have the money ready by at least November to get the visa in time. If the visa is not in place, the university cancel your place. Immigration New Zealand also ask for evidence that you have sufficient money to sustain you during your study – NZ$15,000 (£7,326) for the whole year or NZ$1,250 (£610) a month.'

In addition to support from Study Options, Anwar also received help from the University of Auckland. 'I received a lot of key information and support via email. I received a list of books and resources that I had to buy as well as details of where to buy them. I was sent an online orientation module to complete and this was very helpful as it included local transport and how to access your timetables and accommodation.

'The Faculty of Education also sent me an itinerary of the induction so I knew exactly what I had to do and where I had to be which is always helpful when arriving into a new country and institution.

'The university also gave information on how to open a bank amount. ANZ, one of the major banks, offer an international student account and actually have a branch on the university campus. I was able to open the bank account here in the UK and deposit money into it. It was a major relief not to carry that amount around with me during the flight and have it safe and ready waiting for me in NZ.

'I am pleased to say that I have so far not had any difficulties in adjusting to life in New Zealand. As the language is the same and there are similarities in culture, it's just like being home, plus you get the chance to watch plenty of UK TV programmes.

'The education is a lot more practical and also a lot is focused on self-building. The NZ curriculum is very flexible and the child's achievement is at the heart of it, which feels different compared to the results-based approach in the UK. I have recently started my placement in a school and it has reminded me of the times when I was in school and when learning was fun.'

Anwar's top tips

Living costs

'You generally need in excess of NZ$20,000 (£10,000). Accommodation in Auckland is expensive and students pay roughly NZ$5,000 a year in accommodation. There is the option of renting one-bedrooms outside the main CBD; however, a train or bus would be needed to get to the main CBD.'

Food

'Compared to prices in the UK, it works out the same or, in some cases, a little bit more expensive. There are plenty of restaurants and takeaways but these can be expensive.'

Insurance

'As part of my course fees I paid for both health and travel insurance as this is the requirement of the New Zealand government. If you do not have these, your visa application can be delayed and the university can withdraw your offer.'

Transport

'There is a massive import of Japanese cars, so it is easy to get hold of a second hand or new car. The transport system is not the greatest and you can see the work and effort that has been put behind it to raise its profile. A journey in a car which would take 15 mins takes one hour in a bus. Everyone prefers to drive.'

Financial support

'There is no help for postgraduate study available so everything is self-funded; however, some universities do offer doctorates at the same price to both domestic and international students.'

Working while studying

'You are allowed to work 20 hours per week on your visa, but due to the nature of my course and its intensity, I have not been able to find the time. There are plenty of companies who will hire international students.'

Lifestyle and culture

'The local New Zealand people are very friendly and I have been able to make new friends and settle in quickly. The lifestyle and culture is very relaxed compared to the UK and you also have a feel of living in a UK of the past.'

Although he's only been away for a short while, Anwar is really enjoying his time in New Zealand. 'I would not mind staying here for a few more years, perhaps applying for teaching jobs in Auckland. As part of our course we have workshops helping us to attain teaching posts near the end of the year and the international office helps us with getting registered in New Zealand, which is helpful to know.'

He believes the experience of studying abroad is already starting to pay off. 'I am benefitting from the opportunity to explore and gain a new understanding of the perspectives of life and culture. Home is always where the heart is, but it's also good to step outside the box and see things differently and this is something I have been able to do. I hope to use this experience to make me a well-equipped individual who can offer a different perspective to everyday life.'

University of Auckland is New Zealand's largest university with over 40,000 students. It is a top 200 university in the Times Higher Education World University Rankings 2014–2015.

Chapter 10
Studying in Asia

There are plenty of reasons to consider studying in Asia. Asia's economy is continuing to grow faster than other regions, investment in universities in Asia has been huge over recent years and its universities are fighting for position in the world league tables. Twenty-four Asian universities appear in the Times Higher Education World University Rankings 2014–2015.

Hong Kong

Hong Kong is a special administrative region of China, offering a cosmopolitan lifestyle and a gateway to China. As Hong Kong was under British rule for many years, English is still an official language. Street signs and announcements on public transport are in English, Cantonese and often Putonghua (Mandarin).

Now under Chinese rule, Hong Kong has its own currency and political system and a separate identity from the rest of China.

Higher education in Hong Kong

Hong Kong offers a four-year bachelor's degree. Both ordinary and honours degrees are available, along with associate degrees at a lower academic level. Master's degrees will take one to two years, and doctorate degrees a minimum of three years to complete.

If you are interested in opportunities in China, you will find that degrees from Hong Kong are compatible with Chinese qualifications. Beginners' courses in Cantonese and Putonghua will be available; some programmes even offer the chance of a year in Beijing or Shanghai.

The academic year runs from early September to May, with orientation activities taking place in late August. The year is split into two equal semesters. Hong Kong features 19 degree-awarding institutions made up of a combination of nine public and ten private establishments. Higher education is split between universities, polytechnics and technical institutes.

To find out more about studying in Hong Kong or to search for a course or an institution, go to Study HK (http://studyinhongkong. edu.hk/eng).

Applying

Entry requirements vary, but satisfactory performance at A level should meet the general requirements for undergraduate-level study. For example, the University of Hong Kong (currently placed just below King's College London and just above University of Manchester on the 2014–2015 Times Higher Education World University Rankings Top 200) asks for a minimum of three passes at A level (not including English or Chinese language) to meet the general academic requirements. However, that is not the full story, as the International General Academic Requirements document (www.als.hku.hk/admission/applying-or-admission-info/ hong-kong-students/non-jupas/entrance-requirement) indicates: 'Competitive applications should have good or excellent grades in all three subjects. Actual grades will be dependent on the degree programme and the number and quality of applications that year.' There may be additional subject requirements and you will need

GCSE English Language at grade C. The University of Hong Kong also looks for evidence of second-language ability (evidenced by a grade E or better at GCSE) and state that they 'value all-roundedness'.

An honours degree is required for entry to postgraduate study.

Application deadlines vary, but may be as early as December or as late as May for a September start. Applications should be made direct to your chosen university and are likely to include:

- personal statement
- reference
- predicted grades plus previous educational achievement
- research statement (for postgraduate research).

Costs

According to Study HK, annual tuition fees range from HK$90,000 to HK$265,000 (£7,530 to £22,172).

Accommodation in university halls of residence is reasonably priced, but space is at a premium in Hong Kong and private rental can be astronomical. According to Study HK, on-campus living accommodation costs from HK$5,000 to HK$15,000 per semester, while off-campus accommodation costs a similar amount per month (HK$8,000 to HK$15,000). Most institutions prioritise accommodation for international students; some universities even guarantee it.

> ❝ Accommodation is small (this is Hong Kong after all, where space is in short supply); however, you get used to it and it is all the space you need.❞
>
> *Warren Mitty, Hong Kong Polytechnic University*

When weighing up living costs, Study HK estimates, 'HK$30,000–HK$50,000 (£2,510–£4,183) per year for additional costs, including food, leisure, transportation, and personal items, depending on how extravagantly you plan to live.' Hong Kong comes in at number 26 of 119 countries on a cost-of-living ranking for 2015. Compare that to the UK, which is listed at a pricier number 10 (www.numbeo.com).

Scholarships are available, although opportunities are limited and most, although not all, are restricted to those displaying academic excellence. See Study HK for a list of scholarships or talk to your institution for further details.

Four of Hong Kong's 19 degree-awarding institutions can be found in the Times Higher Education World University Rankings Top 200 2014–2015.

You could study . . .

BBA (Hons) Financial Services
Hong Kong Polytechnic University
Four years
Apply by 16 March
Annual fees HK$120,000 (£10,040)
Monthly living expenses from HK$4,199 (£351)

Master of Laws (Chinese Law)
University of Hong Kong
One year
Apply from December
Annual fees HK$135,000 (£11,295)
Annual living expenses from HK$64,200 (£5,371)

Visas

Once you have been accepted and have found a place to live,
you can then apply for a student visa. This should be arranged
through the university which will normally act as your local
sponsor to support the visa application. You'll need to provide
proof of academic qualifications, proof of accommodation and
proof of finances. There is no specific amount required by the
Hong Kong Immigration Department; your university will be able
to give you an idea of appropriate amounts to cover academic and
living costs.

For more information on visas, go to www.immd.gov.hk. The
application can take up to eight weeks to be processed and will
need to be renewed every year. Your institution will be able to
support you through the process.

Working while studying

Although a student visa doesn't normally allow work alongside
study, there may be opportunities to take internships, campus-
based work or work during the holidays. Talk to your university
about these procedures and whether you can apply for a 'no
objection letter' allowing certain conditions of employment.

After you complete your degree, you can apply for a 12-month stay
without a job offer.

Pros and cons of study in Hong Kong

Pros

- High proportion of highly ranked institutions.
- A gateway to China.
- English as an official language.
- Chance to experience a different culture.
- Modern, efficient and cheap public transport.

Cons

- Private accommodation is small and expensive.
- Air pollution and humidity.
- Densely populated.

Japan

At the last count, 424 UK students had chosen Japan as their study destination (OECD Education at a Glance 2014). The Japanese government is keen to attract more international students and is investing in higher education and extending the study options available in English.

The Global 30 group of universities was set up to boost the number of international students in Japan. They offer a range of degrees taught in English.

- Doshisha University
- Keio University
- Kyoto University
- Kyushu University
- Meiji University
- Nagoya University
- Osaka University
- Ritsumeikan University

- Sophia University
- Tohoku University
- University of Tokyo
- University of Tsukuba
- Waseda University.

Find out more, including links to all these universities, at Japanese Universities for Motivated People (JUMP), visit www.uni.international.mext.go.jp.

Higher education in Japan

Currently, most institutions in Japan require proficiency in Japanese, but there are some exceptions. A number of Japanese universities offer master's and doctoral degrees in English, although the options are more limited at undergraduate level. JASSO (Japan Student Services Organisation) has a list of university degree courses offered in English, see www.g-studyinjapan.jasso.go.jp/en/modules/pico_lang_top/index.php?content_id=16.

There are far more private than public universities. Japan has some international universities and overseas universities with campuses in Japan. Five of Japan's universities have made it into the Times Higher Education World University Rankings Top 200 for 2014–2015. This includes the University of Tokyo, the most highly ranked of all the Asian universities.

The academic year starts in April and is run as a two-semester system, April to September, and October to March, with holidays at intervals throughout the year. It should take you four years to complete a bachelor's degree; the first two years offer more general studies, while the final two years allow you to specialise. Study at master's level tends to take two years, with a further three years required for a doctorate.

You should apply direct to your chosen university; you may be required to sit an entrance exam.

Costs

Study in Japan (www.g-studyinjapan.jasso.go.jp) suggests average monthly costs, including fees, of JPY138,000 (£752). The cost of living in Tokyo will be higher, so you should check individual universities for local costs. The Study in Japan website also has lots of information on scholarships, living and accommodation costs.

University accommodation is substantially cheaper than private rented accommodation, so check whether your chosen university will guarantee accommodation for you. In private accommodation, in addition to rent, there are deposits and 'thank you' money to be paid, which can be around four months' rent (and sometimes more).

Japan has a reputation for being expensive, although its costs remain below those of many European countries; it is ranked number 21 out of 119 countries on the cost-of-living ranking (www.numbeo.com).

You could study . . .

BA Liberal Arts (Japanese Society and Global Culture)
Doshisha University's Institute for the Liberal Arts, Kyoto
Four years
Rolling admission (apply from 1 September for April entry)
Annual fees JPY1,129,000 (£6,150) (including admission and facilities fees)
Monthly living expenses JPY120,000 (£654)

MA International Development
International University of Japan, Niigata (private)
Two years
Apply by 16 February for April entry

Annual fees JPY2,100,000 (£11,440) (including admission fees)

Minimum monthly living expenses JPY94,000 (£512)

Visas

You will need a student-visa in order to study in Japan; your university will act as a sponsor for the visa process and should obtain a certificate of eligibility for you. This will need to be processed at the Embassy of Japan (www.uk.emb-japan.go.jp).

In the UK (or the country where you are resident) Student-visa holders need the approval of their university and the immigration office to be able to work.

For information on study in Japan, go to www.studyjapan.go.jp/en.

Pros and cons of study in Japan

Pros

- A culture which combines tradition and cutting-edge technology.
- Drive to increase numbers of international students.

Cons

- Language barrier outside the classroom.
- Relatively few western students at present.
- The need to factor in additional fees for study and accommodation.

Malaysia

Malaysia has hundreds of higher-education institutions to choose from and strong links with the UK. Many overseas universities have chosen to base campuses there, including institutions

from the UK such as the University of Nottingham, Newcastle
University (Medicine) and University of Reading.

Other institutions offer degrees incorporating UK qualifications.
For example, BEng (Hons) Electrical and Electronic Engineering
from INTI International College, Penang is awarded by University
of Bradford.

Higher education in Malaysia

The academic year in Malaysia has changed to a September
start to bring it into line with the northern hemisphere; certain
courses also have intakes in January or May. In Malaysia, a
bachelor's degree takes three to four years to complete, with the
exception of courses like medicine and dentistry, which take five
years. A master's degree will take between one and three years
and can be coursework-based, research-based, or a combination.
A minimum of two years' subsequent study can lead to a doctorate.

Courses taught in English tend to be restricted to private or
international universities at undergraduate level. At postgraduate
level, there should be English-medium options at public
universities too. Only selected private institutions approved by the
Ministry of Home Affairs are open to students from overseas; you
will need to check that your chosen university has the appropriate
permissions to recruit international students. All public
universities can recruit from overseas.

Study Malaysia (www.studymalaysia.com) has a course search,
along with useful information about education, costs and the
country itself.

Applying

International applicants will need to apply direct to their chosen
institutions, either online or via a paper application. A personal
statement will be a key component of the application. You should

apply by the required deadline date and at least six months before you are due to commence your studies.

You could study . . .

BA (Hons) Finance, Accounting and Management
University of Nottingham Malaysia Campus, Semenyih
Three years
Application deadline 28 November for February start
Annual fees RM41,040 (£7,303)
Monthly living expenses RM1,500–RM2,000 (£267–£356)

MSc Science, Technology and Sustainability
University of Malaya, Kuala Lumpur
From one and a half years
Apply by May for September intake
Annual fees RM7,014 (£1,249)
Monthly living expenses RM1,000 (£178)

Visas

Your university will apply for a student pass on your behalf. Once the student pass is granted, you will then be able to apply for a visa. Following some recent changes to immigration rules, you may need to obtain a visa in advance, rather than on arrival in the country. More information is available from the Malaysian High Commission in London at www.kln.gov.my/web/gbr_london/home or Study Malaysia at www.studymalaysia.com.

Costs

Tuition fees vary from institution to institution. Study Malaysia suggests that undergraduate fees range from RM33,000–RM140,000 (£5,876–£24,923) (for pharmacy) at private universities and from RM50,000–RM450,000 (£8,901–£80,110) (medicine) at overseas university branch campuses. NB These costs are for the entire programme, not per year. The annual average undergraduate tuition fee is RM20,000 (£3,560).

Postgraduate research degrees at public universities cost from RM1,800–RM6,000 (£320–£1,068) per year at master's level, and RM2,700–RM8,000 (£481–£1,424) for PhDs.

The fees for a UK degree might be only slightly lower in Malaysia, but if you choose to study overseas, you will benefit from the lower cost of living and the international experience. Living costs are considerably lower than in the UK, with a suggested budget of RM1,200 (£214) per month. Malaysia is rated number 88 out of 119 countries on a cost-of-living index for 2015 (www.numbeo. com), making it the cheapest country featured in this book. Information on funding and scholarships can be found at www. studymalaysia.com, Commonwealth Scholarships (http://cscuk. dfid.gov.uk/apply/scholarships-uk) and from your institution.

Pros and cons of study in Malaysia
Pros

* Reasonable tuition fees for Malaysian degrees.
* Opportunity to gain degrees from USA, UK and Australia in a country with a low cost of living.
* Chance to experience a different culture.
* Tropical climate.

Cons

* No world-renowned Malaysian universities.
* Need approval of your institution before you can work during term-time.
* Not all universities are open to international students.

Singapore
Neighbouring Singapore may be small, but it is a hot spot for financial services, an important trading centre in the heart of Asia

and home to the world's busiest port. Its education system is well recognised around the world and comparable in level to education in the UK. English is widely used, particularly for education and business, and most courses are taught in the language.

Higher education in Singapore

The academic year runs from the beginning of August to early May and is divided into two semesters. Bachelor's degrees are available at ordinary level (after three years' study) and with honours (after four years). Most master's degrees take one year, with a minimum of three years required to complete a PhD.

Singapore has four autonomous public universities:

- National University of Singapore
- Nanyang Technological University
- Singapore Management University
- Singapore University of Technology and Design.

As an alternative, Singapore Institute of Technology, a publicly funded institute of technology, provides an industry-focused university education.

You will find one private university, SIM University, along with a number of other private institutions, polytechnics and international universities with a campus in Singapore.

Singapore might only have a handful of universities, but two of them can be found in the Times Higher Education World University Rankings Top 200 2014–2015.

To find out about university options, you could start with Ministry of Education Singapore, www.moe.gov.sg/education/post-secondary, where you'll find a handy guide to post-secondary education. Contact Singapore (www.contactsingapore.sg) has a lot of information on living in Singapore.

Applying

At undergraduate level, universities will be looking for good passes in three A levels, so you should be aiming to apply with grades at C or above. In some cases, particularly if you're applying before you know your results, the universities will require the SAT or ACT admissions tests. (For more information on the SAT and ACT, see the US-UK Fulbright Commission website, www.fulbright.org.uk/study-in-the-usa/undergraduate-study/admissions-tests.)

At postgraduate level, you are likely to need a 2:1 in an honours degree combined with GMAT (www.mba.com) or GRE (www.ets.org/gre) admissions tests for specific subjects. See individual universities for entry criteria and test requirements.

Applications should be made direct to the university's admissions or international office. Undergraduate applicants can select up to five potential courses. As part of the application, you might have to write a short essay on your achievements or reflect on any positions of responsibility. Postgraduate-research applicants will need to write a research proposal. At both undergraduate and postgraduate level you will need to provide references.

The university will charge you an application fee from around S$20 (£10). You can apply from September or October.

At the National University of Singapore, you will not be eligible for competitive courses like dentistry and medicine if you apply with predicted grades. If this is the case at your chosen university or with your chosen course, wait until you have your actual grades to make the application; this might mean waiting for the next intake, but can also result in exemption from certain admissions tests.

Costs

Tuition fees in Singaporean universities are high, but are subsidised by the government through the tuition-grant scheme. This scheme is open to international students on the condition that you work for three years after graduation for a Singaporean company; this can be deferred for specific reasons including further study. You can find out more at the Ministry of Education website (www.moe.gov.sg) or from your university.

The National University of Singapore (ranked above the London School of Economics and Political Science and the University of Edinburgh on the Times Higher Education World University Rankings Top 200 2014–2015) charges fees for undergraduate degrees ranging from S$28,600 to S$129,200 (£13,654 to £61,682) (for medicine and dentistry). These fees fall to between S$15,700 and S$48,400 (£7,500 and £23,121) when the tuition grant is included.

At postgraduate level, Nanyang Technological University suggests typical fees of S$16,700 (£7,978) for a coursework-based master's degree; this includes the tuition grant (or service obligation). Without a tuition grant, you would be looking at fees of S$27,800 (£13,280). Additional fees may be payable for the students' union, exams and health services.

Scholarships are available and can be searched for at the Ministry of Education website (www.moe.gov.sg) or discussed with your university. Some loans may be available.

> 66 Singapore was very cheap compared to where I live in England. At the time I was there, it was around S$2 to £1, but you could get a fast food meal for around S$5 (£2.50). Going out to the movies and drinking was also cheaper, though drinking was only marginally so. 99
>
> *Joshua Jackson, SP Jain Global School of Management, Singapore and Australia*

The National University of Singapore estimates on-campus living costs of S$1,180 to S$2,320 (£564 to £1,108) per month.

Singapore falls at number 8 of 119 countries listed on a cost-of-living ranking (www.numbeo.com), so is considered slightly more expensive than the UK at the moment.

You could study . . .

Bachelor's degree in Public Policy and Global Affairs
Nanyang Technological University
Four years
Apply from 1 October
Annual fees S$15,700 (£7,500) with tuition grant, S$28,680 (£13,700) without
Estimated monthly living expenses from S$1,460 (£697)

MSc Chemical Engineering
National University of Singapore
18 months
Apply by February for August intake

Annual fees S$29,950 (£14,306) with tuition grant, S$37,800 (£18,050) without

Estimated monthly living costs from S$1,180 (£563)

Visas

You will need a Student's Pass to study in Singapore. Your university will register you on the Immigration and Checkpoints Authority online registration system (SOLAR) and you will then need to complete an online application. There is no required amount of money that you need to provide evidence of, so you should talk to your university about an advisable amount. You won't receive the student pass until you arrive in Singapore, so you will first be granted a social-visit pass at the airport.

Find out more at the Immigration and Checkpoints Authority (www.ica.gov.sg) or the High Commission for the Republic of Singapore in London (www.mfa.gov.sg/london).

Working while studying

International students can work up to 16 hours per week under certain conditions and with the approval of the university or polytechnic that you are studying in. You would need to talk to your institution to request a letter of authorisation.

On graduating, if you are successful in finding a job, you will need to obtain an employment pass before you can start working. For more details, see the Ministry of Manpower (www.mom.gov.sg).

Pros and cons of study in Singapore

Pros

- Chance to experience another culture.
- Modern city-state with a high standard of living.
- Tropical climate.

Cons

- Densely populated.
- Competitive entry.
- Need approval of your university before you can work in term-time.

China

The Chinese government is investing heavily in its higher education and is keen to attract international students; around 35,000 European students were studying in China in 2012 according to information from the China Scholarship Council. The growth of China as an economic force means that awareness of Chinese culture and language is likely to be an important asset.

The British government is also keen that UK students develop their understanding of China; its Generation UK project offers internships and scholarships towards short-term study in China. Find out more at www.britishcouncil.org/china-education-generationuk.htm.

How to find a course

You could start your search at Campus China (www.campuschina. org). You can also search for degree programmes on the CUCAS (China's University and College Admission System) website, www. cucas.edu.cn. Once your search brings up a list of courses, you can select those taught in English. The Chinese Ministry of Education also holds a list of English-taught programmes in Chinese higher education, as well as information on scholarships; visit www.moe. edu.cn. You'll find more opportunities at postgraduate level rather than at undergraduate level.

Three of China's universities feature in the Times Higher Education World University Rankings Top 200 2014–2015.

Higher education in China

The academic year runs from September to mid-July and international students should apply between February and April.

Bachelor's degrees normally take four years to complete, master's degrees take two to three years, and doctorates take from three years; all are similar in level to those offered in the UK.

Traditionally, the style of teaching in China has been more teacher-centred than in the UK. You may find that this is less of an issue on English-taught courses aimed at international students.

Applying

A level study is generally required for undergraduate courses, with a bachelor's degree (plus two references) required for master's study, and a master's degree (plus two references) for doctoral study.

Applications can be made direct to universities or online through CUCAS. If applying through CUCAS, additional documentation (copy of passport, academic transcripts and police certificates (or criminal records check), for example) can be scanned or clearly photographed for submission. CUCAS charges a service fee of US$50 to US$150 (£32 to £96) for up to six applications. The exact fee depends on your chosen institution. Institutions also charge an application fee before they will issue the school-admission notice required for a visa; they will normally take a further four to eight weeks to process an application.

You could study . . .

Bachelor's degree in Food Quality and Safety
Jinan University, Guangzhou
Four years
Apply by 30 June
Annual fees RMB30,000 (£3,110)

Annual living expenses RMB25,200–RMB32,400
(£2,612–£3,359)

Master of Laws

Peking University, Beijing

Two years

Apply by 20 March for September start

Annual fees RMB80,000 (£8,293)

Annual living expenses approximately RMB26,400–RMB33,600
(£2,737–£3,484)

Visas

For study in China of over six months, you will need an X-visa. You can apply through the Chinese Embassy. Go to www.visaforchina.org for more details.

Costs

CUCAS advises of tuition fees around US$3,300–US$49,900 (£2,143–£6,429) per year and average monthly living expenses of around RMB4,500–RMB5,000 (£466–£518) in metropolitan areas like Shanghai or Beijing. Costs in many other cities are likely to be lower, at around RMB1,500–RMB3,500 per month (£155–£362). Some sources suggest higher average costs than this and costs will vary depending on the type of lifestyle you want to lead. China is listed as number 82 of 119 countries on the Numbeo cost-of-living ranking for 2015; making it one of the cheapest countries for cost of living featured in this book.

> **"** The city of Ningbo itself was much cheaper than the UK and the cost of living was a fraction of what I would spend in the UK. **"**
>
> *Lewis McCarthy, University of Nottingham Ningbo, China*

Full and partial scholarships are available through the China Scholarship Council (www.csc.edu.cn/Laihua). If you are proficient in a Chinese language, you may be eligible for a Chinese Government Scholarship. Search for scholarships on the Ministry of Education website (www.moe.edu.cn) and through CUCAS (www.cucas.edu.cn).

There are age restrictions for international students hoping to study higher education and apply for certain scholarships in China.

- Undergraduate applicants should be under 25.
- Master's degree applicants should be under 35.
- Doctoral applicants should be under 40.

Pros and cons of study in China

Pros

- An increasingly powerful world economic force.
- Investment in higher education.
- Chance to experience a new culture.

Cons

- Language barrier outside the classroom.
- A new setting for international students.
- Issues around censorship and political restrictions.

Saudi Arabia

Although most courses are in Arabic, there are opportunities in English at certain Saudi universities and around 165 UK students are already studying in the country (OECD Education at a Glance 2014). Saudi Arabia's first international university, King Abdullah

University of Science and Technology (www.kaust.edu.sa), opened in 2009 and offers postgraduate courses taught in English.

Higher education in Saudi Arabia

Public and private universities in Saudi Arabia are overseen by the Ministry of Higher Education. Bachelor's degrees run for a minimum of four years, master's degrees take two years, and doctorates from three years. Qualifications are of a similar level to those in the UK. For a list of universities, go to the Ministry of Higher Education website at www.mohe.gov.sa. Some institutions are not open to women.

Life in Saudi Arabia

Saudi Arabia is a Muslim country where Islamic law is strictly enforced. Life differs greatly from that in the UK; mixed gatherings are not customary and alcohol is not permitted. Recreation activities for men centre on sport, with many activities for women restricted.

Applying

Applications should be made direct to your chosen university.

Costs

Tuition fees vary, with individual universities setting their own. Scholarships and fellowships are available; talk to your chosen university about what is on offer.

Saudi Arabia is listed at number 76 of 119 countries on the Numbeo cost-of-living ranking for 2015 (www.numbeo.com). The UK is at number 10.

You could study . . .

Master's degree in Applied Mathematics and Computational Science
King Abdullah University of Science and Technology, Thuwal
Two years

Apply by April

Full fellowships awarded covering tuition fees and living expenses

Visas

Once you have been offered a place, you should then start the process of applying for a visa or entry permit. For details, go to the Ministry of Foreign Affairs website at www.mofa.gov.sa or www.saudiembassy.org.uk.

Pros and cons of study in Saudi Arabia

Pros

- Investment in higher education.
- Chance to experience a new culture.

Cons

- Saudi universities (and Middle Eastern universities in general) are not well represented on the world university rankings.
- Social and recreational activities may be restricted, particularly for women.

Qatar

If you're interested in the Middle East, but prefer the familiarity of a UK or US degree, you could take a look at Qatar. Qatar's Education City is a huge complex of education and research facilities and includes universities from the USA, France and the UK. Find out more at the Qatar Foundation for Education, Science and Community Development at www.qf.org.qa or at Education City at www.myeducationcity.com.

As it is a hub for elite international universities, your experience will vary according to which institution you choose. You can opt for a UK degree or choose a degree from another country. The tuition fees, style of teaching and who will award your degree will be determined by your chosen university.

> 66 My visa was organised by UCL Qatar and was very straightforward, apart from some mandatory health checks and appointments, which all expatriates moving to Qatar must undertake after they arrive in Doha. Support upon arrival was particularly helpful, starting with a "meet and greet" at Doha airport, and followed by lots of induction activities.99
>
> *Benedict Leigh, UCL Qatar*

Student life is likely to be different in Qatar, where the sale of alcohol is limited and modest dress is expected. Social activities might be more focused on campus activities, cultural events and shopping malls rather than all-night clubbing.

You could study . . .

MA Archaeology of the Arab and Islamic World
UCL Qatar, Doha
Two years
Apply by 1 May
Annual fees QAR123,900 (£22,102)
Approximate monthly living expenses QAR1,500 (£268)

Pros and cons of study in Qatar
Pros

- Investment in higher education.
- Chance to experience a new culture.

Cons

- Different student life.

Student story
Lewis McCarthy, China

'I thought studying overseas would be a great opportunity to spend time living in a different country and culture. I decided not to take a gap year after my A levels and thought that by taking a degree that included a year abroad, I could combine the experiences of gap year travelling with academic study.'

He was interested in China from the start. 'I chose to learn about China as it is a very different culture to the UK and Europe – the country is also growing in economic and political influence. I believe an understanding of China enhances my career prospects and differentiates me from other graduates.

'I looked at various universities and a range of courses, but it was Nottingham's degree in Management with Chinese Studies that fit me best. A key factor was that Nottingham has its own campuses in China and Malaysia, the opportunity to study at those was too good to pass up. Crucially, I could study at a world-class British university abroad, while other universities only offered programmes abroad at "partner" universities. A further important consideration was that it was a three-year course, rather than the four-year courses offered elsewhere. This meant I potentially saved a year's worth of student borrowing.'

This wasn't the only way that Lewis managed to cut the cost of learning. 'At Nottingham's campus in Ningbo, the fees and accommodation were around half the price. The city of Ningbo itself was much cheaper than the UK and the cost of living was a fraction of what I would spend in the UK.'

Application for his year out was straightforward, with everything either dealt with or supported by the University of Nottingham. Even applying for a visa wasn't too problematic. 'The application was a relatively long winded process, but the staff in the Chinese visa centre were exceptionally helpful.

Even though I had not filled in part of my form, they telephoned me and, with my permission, completed it on my behalf so it didn't need to be sent back to me again. They also processed and mailed the visa and passport back quickly.'

When he first arrived in China, he found that he wasn't quite as prepared as some fellow students. 'I felt Nottingham could have provided more support, I think part of the problem was that my course was officially part of the Business School, not School of Contemporary Chinese Studies. I got the impression when arriving that those on the Chinese Studies course had been given more guidance and clue as to what to expect.'

But Lewis didn't let this hold him back and he adjusted well to life in China. 'When I first arrived, everything seemed so new, different and interesting that it felt more like a holiday than living somewhere else. By the time that feeling had worn off, I was already settled and accustomed to most things. Still, I know some people who did experience homesickness, miss certain food and get irritated by cultural differences: people not queuing and no concept of personal space, for example.'

Lewis went on to have such a positive experience in China as an exchange student that, after graduating, he went back to China to study Mandarin at Shanghai Jiao Tong University. 'Living in Shanghai was considerably more expensive than Ningbo; however, it was still cheaper than the UK. Rent in Shanghai is roughly half that in London. The cost of study in Shanghai was £2,000–£3,000 – however, the Chinese government offered various non-means-tested scholarships that covered all of these costs plus accommodation, as well as providing a small stipend for living.

'The university application process was simple, I applied by downloading forms via their website, filled them in and emailed back. Once they had confirmed that they had space on their course, I paid some fees via a bank transfer and that was it!

'Shanghai didn't provide much support. I was emailed welcome packs, but beyond that it was up to me. This was not a problem. The city is cosmopolitan and easy to navigate, there were many helpful students on campus who assisted me when I asked or looked lost.

'On the Chinese language course you are left to your own devices, although the school does occasionally have events that you can attend. That said, the staff and teachers were all very helpful, they were forthcoming in offering their contact details in case we (the students) ever needed help or things explaining in Chinese. On campus there were also sports facilities that were free to use without the need to book, such as a running track, football field, tennis courts, outdoor gymnasium etc.'

There were some differences to get used to, particularly the style of teaching. 'The teaching differs hugely, the emphasis is on rote learning, a lot of information may be covered in a lesson and you are expected to put in several hours outside class time to learn and memorise what is covered in class.'

Lewis has faced a few negative experiences along the way. 'Pickpocketing, having food stolen while on a train and witnessing mass brawls have all occurred in the two years I have spent in China. However, providing you are aware of risks and use some common sense you should be fine. There are risks in any country. On the whole, China is probably the country that I have felt safest in for travelling, living and walking home late at night.'

So what tips would Lewis give to other students thinking of studying in China?

Accommodation

'If you search for private accommodation in China, as I did the second time I went there to study, be prepared to look at many houses each day with estate agents whisking you off by car or bike for viewings. If possible, try to be clear about what you want and where you want to live. There should be someone in the office who speaks a little English, otherwise you can use Google or Baidu Translate.'

Food

'Don't be squeamish! As long as you're not vegetarian, be willing to try everything. The food is possibly the biggest thing to get used to in China. It is nothing like western versions of Chinese food. Expect to see all body parts of animals (nothing is wasted) and lots of different tastes and types of cooking. In China, it is customary to share several dishes per meal rather than have a single dish each.'

Living costs

'If you are making food yourself, try to buy meat and vegetables from the same place as the Chinese do – usually markets – it will be infinitely cheaper than western supermarkets which have imported products that are generally very over-priced.

'If you want to live a western lifestyle in China, be prepared that it might cost more than you think, and potentially more than it would in the UK. Rent and travel will be much cheaper but buying western food and drinking in (some) bars could be more expensive, maybe this is more of a problem in Shanghai, rather than other cities. I didn't find it a problem in Ningbo.'

Scholarships

'China Scholarship Council (www.csc.edu.cn/Laihua) and Hanban (http://english.hanban.org) offer some excellent scholarships.'

Working while studying

'It is illegal to undertake any work on a study visa in China. There is always demand for English teachers and it pays anywhere between £10–£20 an hour. Just check the conditions of the visa you are on.'

Lifestyle and culture

'Chinese culture stretches back nearly five thousand years and the Chinese are very proud of their culture. Reading about the culture and history is a good way of preparing yourself and understanding some things when you arrive, just expect it to be different from how you imagine. It is very different from the UK.

'The lifestyle is great, a bit of disposable income can go quite far in China and you can go out for meals and eat at nice restaurants relatively cheaply. Foreigners are well respected within China and you should not have problems with locals, many will be warm and chatty, eager to make new friends.'

Travel

'You don't need to speak as much Chinese as you think to be able to travel in China. All of the tourist areas will have English translations and if you travel to areas that are off the well worn track, passersby will often help you if you seem lost.

'It is a country the size of a continent, so be aware that customs and lifestyles may be marginally different in other places across China. The food will certainly change as each region has its own preferred tastes and delicacies.'

Options for after you finish your studies

'There are work options, such as teaching after you study. It is also fairly easy to find work in international or Chinese companies. A grasp of Mandarin will put you in a much stronger position, but it is not always deemed compulsory.

'During the time abroad, you will be exposed to so many different opportunities and possibilities that you would not receive at home, travelling to different areas and regions, eating local delicacies, work opportunities, homestays with local friends etc.

'Meeting new people will also give you different perspectives on your own views and a much better insight into local culture, history and customs than can be taught in class. Meeting new people doesn't simply extend to those of the locality that you are studying in either, some of my closest friends now are compatriots and international students who I studied abroad with.'

Lewis recommends www.echinacities.com and www.shanghaiist.com to help you find out more about life in China.

Chapter 11

Studying in the rest of the world

You might imagine that you wouldn't find students from the UK studying right across the globe; well, prepare to be surprised. Although a less common choice than Australia or the States, some UK students opt for South Africa or Brazil as their place of learning. This chapter introduces you to some of the countries you might not have considered for your studies.

South Africa

Why South Africa? The Rainbow Nation offers diversity, culture and an outdoor lifestyle combined with a great climate and low cost of living. According to the most recent figures, more than 797 UK students are currently taking advantage of what the country has to offer.

Higher education in South Africa

Higher education is offered at universities, universities of technology, and comprehensive universities. Traditional universities offer academic study, while universities of technology focus on practical or vocational options; comprehensive universities offer both. There are a variety of private universities in South Africa. The languages of English and Afrikaans are both used.

Bachelor's degrees take at least three years (up to six years for medicine), with an additional year of study to achieve an honours degree. A master's degree takes at least one year, while doctorates require a minimum of two years' research.

The academic year runs from February to November. Higher Education South Africa (www.hesa.org.za) has links to all the public universities, where you can browse the courses on offer.

South Africa has one university in the 2014–2015 Times Higher Education World University Rankings Top 200, and three in the top 400.

Applying

Applications should be made direct to your chosen institution by the deadline date they specify. The institutions will often charge an application fee. They will advise you how to get a certificate of exemption to validate your international qualifications. Two A levels plus three GCSEs at grades A* to C (or four Scottish Highers plus one National 5) should meet the general requirements for undergraduate programmes in South Africa. For further details, see the South African Matriculation Board website (www.he-enrol. ac.za/qualification-country). There will be additional requirements for specific subjects. A bachelor's (honours) degree should meet the general entry criteria for a master's degree.

While postgraduate-research programmes may be flexible about when you can apply, you will need time to apply for a study visa and to prepare for the move. South African post can be slow, so you should apply as early as possible. Deadline dates for undergraduate and taught postgraduate courses vary; expect to apply in the autumn if the course starts in February, maybe earlier if you're also applying for a scholarship.

Costs

Fees vary depending on what you study and where. For example, the University of the Witwatersrand charges between ZAR64,940 and ZAR116,280 (£6,487) per year for its undergraduate courses. For private board and lodging local to the university, you should expect to pay around ZAR63,500 (£3,542) per year. This also includes the costs of books, stationery and local travel. The international office will be able to tell you more about the costs at your chosen university.

> 66 My tuition fees were more than in the UK as I was an international student. However, that was more than compensated for by the relatively low cost of living in Cape Town compared to London. For this reason, my overall cost of living and studying in Cape Town for a year and a half was about 50% less than it would have been had I studied in London. 99
>
> *Nick Parish, master's student, South Africa*

In a 2015 cost-of-living ranking produced by www.numbeo.com, South Africa is listed at number 89 of 119 countries, making it one of the cheapest countries featured in this book.

You could study . . .

BA Cultural and Heritage Tourism
University of KwaZulu-Natal, Durban
Three years
Apply by 30 September for February start
Annual fees US$10,024 (£6,507)
Annual university residence fees from ZAR15,463 (£863)

MBA

University of Cape Town

One year

Apply by 30 September for February start

Annual fees ZAR334,180 (£18,642)

Monthly living expenses ZAR11,000 (£614)

Visas

Once you have received a written offer, you will need to apply for a study visa at the South African High Commission (www.southafricahouseuk.com). There is a £35 processing fee and an expected turnaround time of 30 working days. You will need to prove that you can support yourself financially and will be asked for a medical report and a police certificate (or criminal records check), as well as proof of medical cover. The visa will need to be renewed every year.

Further information

If you need further information, you'll find Study South Africa, a helpful guide for international students, on the International Education Association of South Africa website (www.ieasa.studysa.org).

Pros and cons of study in South Africa

Pros

- Great climate.
- Low cost of living.
- Outdoor lifestyle.

Cons

- Crime rate.

The Caribbean

A number of UK students head off to the Caribbean for their studies, particularly for medical or dental programmes, with over 70 medical schools listed there. Many opt for international universities with a base in the Caribbean that prepare students for a medical or dental career in countries like the USA, Canada or the UK. This list includes St George's University Grenada, Ross University, the American University of the Caribbean, and Saba University School of Medicine. St George's recruits from the UK and prepares students for medical practice in a number of countries, including the UK, whereas the other institutions tend to have more of a North American focus.

At St George's University, if you choose to study medicine, you could be looking at total fees over four years of US$246,000 (£159,686). You'll also need to budget for living expenses of around US$7,500 to US$9,000 (£4,869 to £5,842) per year. There are scholarships on offer which may assist with costs. The university has intakes in August and January and you should apply direct.

There are also local universities offering courses, most notably the University of the West Indies (UWI), a regional university representing 15 countries with four sites across the Caribbean. Its fees at undergraduate level are around US$15,000 (£9,737) per year, with the exception of medicine, which is around US$28,000 (£18,176).

Undergraduate degrees tend to take three to four years, followed by a two-year master's degree and a three-year PhD. Make sure you check the validity of any professional qualification with the relevant professional body. If you intend to practise medicine in the UK, you should check requirements with the General Medical

Council. For a list of the relevant professional bodies in the UK, see the website of the National Contact Point for Professional Qualifications in the UK at www.ecctis.co.uk/uk%20ncp.

Unfortunately, there isn't one single source of information to find recognised universities in the Caribbean. You could use the High Commission websites in the UK; for example, the Jamaican High Commission in the UK, at www.jhcuk.org/citizens/universities, lists UWI, University of Technology, and Northern Caribbean University. You could also use accreditation organisations like the University Council of Jamaica, the Barbados Accreditation Council, and the Accreditation Council of Trinidad and Tobago. Find contact details for these and other accreditation bodies at CANQATE (Caribbean Area Network for Quality Assurance in Tertiary Education), www.canqate.org/Links/RelatedLinks.aspx. Once you are sure that your university is recognised and accredited, you can go to their website for the latest information on courses, fees and how to apply.

You could study . . .

BA History

University of the West Indies, Mona Campus, Jamaica
Three years
Annual fees US$15,000 (£9,737)
Living expenses not provided, hall fees from JA$161,650 (£911) per academic year

Master of Science in Biology

Northern Caribbean University, Manchester, Jamaica
Two years
Annual fees approximately US$10,000 (£6,491)
Living expenses not provided, accommodation with meal plan from US$3,300 (£2,142) per academic year

Pros and cons of study in the Caribbean

Pros

- Tropical climate.
- Low cost of living.
- Chance to gain medical training relevant to more than one country.

Cons

- A range of education systems on offer with no single reliable source of information.
- High costs for medical and dental studies.

Hopefully, the information about these countries will have whetted your appetite and given you a starting point for your research. Of course, the countries profiled here are not the only options open to you; many other countries are keen to attract students from the UK. If you are interested in studying elsewhere in the world, you can use the information in this book (see Chapters 2, 3 and 4) to help ensure that the education you opt for is the right step for you.

Student story
Justin Axel-Berg, University of São Paulo, Brazil

'I originally left the UK a few years ago during the financial crisis after I had graduated and was unable to find a job that I wanted. Instead, I qualified as an English teacher and started travelling. I always had the intention of returning to study and when the opportunity arose I took advantage of the fact that there was a top-class university on my doorstep.

'I decided I wanted a change from Asia, which I know well and have lived in before, and Australia, in which I studied during my degree. Brazil has a dynamic and exciting economy with lots of opportunity for foreigners. It has a deserved reputation for being friendly, exciting and warm.'

With a first degree from University of Sussex, Justin is now enrolled to a Mestrado (master's degree) in International Relations. 'The Universidade de São Paulo (USP) has consistently been rated the best institution in Latin America, with a very strong research tradition and excellent reputation. All degree courses in federal and state universities in Brazil are completely free to all applicants, with a good chance of receiving a scholarship for living expenses while you study through one of the funding bodies.'

However, there is a downside to study in Brazil. 'In order to do anything in Brazil, Portuguese language is a pre-requisite, and that includes, for the time being anyway, university. The university offers language courses to foreign students while you study, which are of good quality, and they are also currently launching an online distance-learning programme, so you will be able to pick up some Portuguese at home before you leave. It's not an insurmountable challenge, but it is a challenge nonetheless. People are always willing to help you out with it and will happily share class notes with you in case you missed anything. Essays can be submitted in English if you prefer.'

Justin found the application process to be fairly straightforward. 'I had to sit the GRE exam, which I did in London, although it is also possible at other locations across the UK. I then wrote up a research proposal and a CV and sent it via email along with the application form. The procedure does vary from course to course, so it's best to check their website.

'While I was waiting for my documents to arrive I was in constant contact with the university by phone and by email, and they took a real personal interest in getting me to Brazil safe and well.

'The process of applying for a visa was quick, but a little bit complicated. Firstly you must register and complete a form on the federal police's website before booking an appointment at the consulate. Unfortunately, my university acceptance letter was caught in a postal strike so I was rather delayed in getting documents sorted, but once I got to the consulate they were friendly and helpful and the whole process took well under a week from giving them my passport to receiving my visa. Once you arrive in Brazil you then have to go to the police to register and get your Brazilian ID card (RNE), which takes about six months to arrive.'

Justin praises the academic support he has experienced since starting at the university. 'My academic advisor is excellent, and here they tend to take a much more hands-on approach to support than in the UK. He is constantly sending me interesting events to attend or things to read. I would say that education in Brazil is much more tutor led; Brazilian students have their hands held much more than in the UK. There is also more of a focus on personal and career development alongside research than in the UK.'

Although he is an experienced traveller and has studied overseas before, Justin did have to make some adjustments. 'There are always little things that surprise me. Although Brazil is superficially very European, in reality it most definitely isn't. People's outlook on life is different, what people say versus what they mean is very different. Also the fact that, in a polite way, Brazil functions in a kind of irrational bureaucratic chaos can be difficult to adjust to; things simply don't work in the way that you expect.'

On the whole, there have been very few negative experiences. 'Perhaps a few too many afternoons sitting in the policia federal trying to register my documents. Despite São Paulo's violent reputation, it's really quite a safe place. I've lived here for three years now, travelling all over the city at all times of night and day and never come to harm anywhere.'

Discovering the latest information about study in Brazil can be a challenge.

'The information is unfortunately a bit scattered at the moment as UK and international students are so few. It's best to contact the university and ask for information. Gringoes (www.gringoes.com) is a good guide to living in Brazil with a very supportive forum.'

Justin's top tips

Accommodation

'USP cannot guarantee accommodation because of the size of the student body, but private sector provision is excellent and catered towards students in either "republicas" (shared houses) or individual kitchenettes or studio flats both next to the campus and further into the city. It'll be very hard to sort anything out before you arrive though, so plan on starting in a hostel for a couple of weeks'.

Food

'Brazilian food is delicious, heavy on meat and beans, as represented by the famous feijoada (bean and meat stew). Fresh fruit juices are everywhere and made of a vast array of things you'll never have heard of. São Paulo also has the best sushi outside of Japan as a result of the huge Japanese population, and the Italian food and especially the pizzas are fantastic.'

Insurance

'As a student you may use the public healthcare system. It is probably recommended to have your own private insurance too, but personally I haven't bothered, and every time I've needed the doctor I've been well looked after.'

Living costs

'São Paulo is not a cheap city to live in. People come to Brazil expecting the third world and finding the first. Expect to spend up to BRL700–BRL1000 (£158–£226) per month on a room. I pay more than this because I live in my own apartment in the city. Food is often roughly the price of the UK, although savvy shoppers buy in street markets where it is much lower. Alcohol is reasonably priced. All electronics and other non-consumables are absurdly expensive (200–300% of UK price); bring your iPhone and laptop with you from home.'

Financial support for study

'Both CAPES and FAPESP give generous scholarships which will go a long way towards supporting you as you study. They are widespread and not terribly difficult to get. The university also offers postgraduates the opportunity to monitor and assist courses in return for money.'

Working while studying

'Working is not possible on a student visa, although there is a burgeoning market for international students tutoring English privately all over the city.'

Making friends

'It's Brazil: everyone wants to stop and chat with people passing by. It's extremely easy to make friends and Brazilians are very welcoming warm people who treat foreigners very well.'

Lifestyle and culture

'Brazil is a lot more laid back than the UK and a lot more informal and relaxed. People live for the beach, and it is easily accessible from SP at the weekends. São Paulo is the cultural capital of Brazil and the amount of art, especially street art, is phenomenal, as is the range of music and fashion available in the city. There is something here for everyone, but you might have to search for it.'

Travel and transport

'The traffic is terrible. Really bad. However, the buses are very regular, clean, safe and cheap (BRL1.50 or 35p for 2 hours travel as a student) and the metro, although limited, will cover everywhere you will want to go as a foreigner. It is also cheap, quick, safe and very clean.'

Options for after you finish your studies

'Brazil is expanding rapidly, and has technical needs in almost every field at the moment. It also has a specific need for bilingual people with some expertise. If you're planning to do almost anything in Brazil, a qualification from USP will get you there.

'I am getting married here in Brazil this year, and planning afterwards to either look for a job in an NGO, in university administration or carry on and do a doctorate. Possibly a combination of the above.'

So how would Justin reflect on his experiences so far? 'Living in beautiful Brazil, being exposed to another culture in a deep way not open to most travellers or even expats and learning to view the world through another culture is fascinating and an experience I wouldn't trade for the world.'

University of São Paulo is the highest ranked university in South America according to the Times Higher Education World University Rankings 2014–2015. It has 86,000 students and over 15,000 staff.

Chapter 12
Further research and resources

Before you go

UK National Academic Recognition and Information Centre (NARIC)
www.ecctis.co.uk/naric/individuals
Information on the comparability of international qualifications

National Contact Point for Professional Qualifications in the United Kingdom (UKNCP)
www.ecctis.co.uk/uk%20ncp

Foreign and Commonwealth Office
www.fco.gov.uk
Find an embassy or seek travel advice by country

Prospects Country Profiles (postgraduate focus)
www.prospects.ac.uk/country_profiles.htm

U-Multirank
www.u-multirank.eu
Compare international universities based on your own chosen criteria

iAgora

www.iagora.com/studies

Students review and rate their international universities

SteXX

www.stexx.eu

Students review and rate their European universities

Association of Commonwealth Universities

www.acu.ac.uk

Citizens Advice

www.citizensadvice.org.uk

For information on how studying overseas might affect your status in the UK

HM Revenue and Customs

www.hmrc.gov.uk

Information on tax when you return to the UK

International course search

Find a master's/MBA/PhD

www.findamasters.com

www.findanmba.com

www.findaphd.com

International Graduate

www.internationalgraduate.net

Search for postgraduate opportunities worldwide

International university league tables

The Times Higher Education World University Rankings

www.timeshighereducation.co.uk/world-university-rankings

QS Top Universities
www.topuniversities.com/university-rankings

Academic Ranking of World Universities
www.shanghairanking.com

Financial Times Business School Rankings
http://rankings.ft.com/businessschoolrankings/rankings

Costs and funding

Numbeo
www.numbeo.com
Cost-of-living comparison

Expatistan
www.expatistan.com
Cost-of-living comparison for cities worldwide

Professional and Career Development Loans
www.gov.uk/career-development-loans/overview

International Student Identity Card (ISIC)
www.isic.org
Student discounts worldwide

Student Finance England
www.gov.uk/student-finance/overview

Student Awards Agency for Scotland
www.saas.gov.uk

Student Finance Wales
www.studentfinancewales.co.uk

Student Finance Northern Ireland
www.studentfinanceni.co.uk

Marie Curie Scheme
www.ukro.ac.uk/mariecurie/Pages/index.aspx
Fellowships and grants for research

Commonwealth Scholarships
http://cscuk.dfid.gov.uk/apply/scholarships-uk-citizens

Insurance
European Health Insurance Card (EHIC)
www.ehic.org.uk

Endsleigh Insurance
www.endsleigh.co.uk/Travel/Pages/study-abroad-insurance.aspx

STA Travel Insurance
www.statravel.co.uk/study-abroad-travel-insurance.htm

Blogs and diaries
Third Year Abroad, The Mole Diaries
www.thirdyearabroad.com/before-you-go/the-mole-diaries.html

Samuel Knight in Groningen
www.samstudyingabroad.tumblr.com

Residence Abroad Blogs (University of Manchester)
www.llc.manchester.ac.uk/undergraduate/residence-abroad/blogs

Maastricht Students
www.maastricht-students.com

The University of Nottingham in North America
http://universityofnottinghamnorthamerica.blogspot.co.uk/

Short-term study overseas

Study China

www.studychina.org.uk

INTO China

www.intohigher.com/china

IAESTE

www.iaeste.org

Fulbright Commission

www.fulbright.org.uk/study-in-the-usa/short-term-study

Summer schools at US universities

EducationUSA

www.educationusa.info/5_steps_to_study/short_term_programs_
step1_research_your_options.php

Third Year Abroad

www.thirdyearabroad.com

Distance learning

International Council for Open and Distance Education (ICDE)

www.icde.org

Study Portals (search for a distance-learning course in Europe)

www.distancelearningportal.com

Distance Education Accrediting Commission (USA)

www.deac.org

Educational agents and marketing consultancies

A Star Future

www.astarfuture.co.uk

Study Options

www.studyoptions.com

The Student World

www.thestudentworld.com

Degrees Ahead

www.degreesahead.co.uk

Mayflower Education Consultants

www.mayflowereducation.co.uk

PFL Education

www.preparationforlife.com

M & D Europe

www.readmedicine.com

Pass 4 Soccer Scholarships

www.pass4soccer.com

Study International

www.studygo.co.uk

Admissions tests

Scholastic Assessment Test: SAT

www.sat.collegeboard.org

American College Test: ACT

www.act.org

Undergraduate Medicine and Health Sciences Admission Test: UMAT

www.umat.acer.edu.au

International Student Admissions Test: ISAT

www.isat.acer.edu.au

Special Tertiary Admissions Test: STAT

www.acer.edu.au/tests/stat

Graduate Management Admission Test: GMAT

www.mba.com

Graduate Record Exam: GRE

www.ets.org/gre

Dental Admissions Test: DAT

www.ada.org/dat.aspx

Law School Admissions Test: LSAT

www.lsac.org

Medical College Admission Test: MCAT

www.aamc.org/students/applying/mcat

Graduate Australian Medical Schools Admissions Test: GAMSAT

www.gamsat.acer.edu.au

Health Professions Admission Test (Ireland): HPAT

www.hpat-ireland.acer.edu.au

Studying in Europe

Study Portals

www.studyportals.eu

Search for courses and scholarships in Europe

STUDYING ABROAD

PLOTEUS (Portal on Learning Opportunities throughout the
European Space)
www.ec.europa.eu/ploteus/home_en.htm

A Star Future
www.astarfuture.co.uk/what_to_study.html
Search for courses taught in English in Europe and beyond

EUNICAS
www.eunicas.co.uk
Search for courses taught in English

EURAXESS
www.ec.europa.eu/euraxess
Research opportunities in the EU

PromoDoc
www.promodoc.eu/study-in-the-eu
Doctoral study in the EU

European Commission, University in Europe
www.ec.europa.eu/youreurope/citizens/education/university

European Commission, Study in Europe
www.ec.europa.eu/education/study-in-europe

Eurodesk
www.eurodesk.org.uk
Information on European work, study, travel and volunteering

Europass
www.europass.cedefop.europa.eu
Documents to make your qualification and skills easily understood
across Europe (CVs, diploma supplements and so on)

Erasmus

www.britishcouncil.org/erasmus-about-erasmus.htm

Austria

www.oead.at/welcome_to_austria/education_research/EN

Belgium

www.highereducation.be (Flemish community)

www.studyinbelgium.be (French community)

Czech Republic

www.studyin.cz

www.msmt.cz (Scholarships)

Denmark

www.studyindenmark.dk

www.optagelse.dk/admission/index.html (Danish Co-ordinated Application System, KOT)

www.su.dk/English/Sider/foreign.aspx (State Educational Support, SU)

Estonia

www.studyinestonia.ee

Finland

www.studyinfinland.fi

www.studyinfo.fi (applications to universities and universities of applied sciences)

France

www.campusfrance.org/en

www.cnous.fr (National Centre for University & Student Welfare, student life and student costs)

Germany

www.study-in.de/en

www.hochschulkompass.de (HochschulKompass, institution search) www.daad.de (German Academic Exchange Services, DAAD)

www.uni-assist.de/index_en.html (uni-assist, application service for international students)

Hungary

www.studyhungary.hu

Ireland

www.educationireland.ie

www.hetac.ie (Higher Education and Training Awards Council)

www.icosirl.ie (Irish Council for International Students)

www.qualifax.ie (course search)

www.postgradireland.com (postgraduate search)

www.cao.ie (Central Applications Office)

www.pac.ie (Postgraduate Applications Centre)

Italy

www.study-in-italy.it

Latvia

www.studyinlatvia.lv

Lithuania

www.lietuva.lt/en/education_sience/study_lithuania

www.skvc.lt/en/content.asp?id=235 (Lithuanian Centre for Quality Assessment in Higher Education)

The Netherlands

www.studyinholland.nl

www.studyinholland.co.uk

http://info.studielink.nl/en/studenten/Pages/Default.aspx

(Studielink for applications)

www.duo.nl/particulieren/international-student/student-finance/
how-does-it-work.asp

(Department of Education, grants and loans)

Norway

www.studyinnorway.no

www.nokut.no (Norwegian Agency for Quality Assurance in HE, NOKUT)

Poland

www.studyinpoland.pl

Portugal

www.dges.mctes.pt/DGES/pt (General Directorate for HE)

Slovakia

www.studyin.sk

Slovenia

www.slovenia.si/en/study

Switzerland

www.swissuniversity.ch

www.crus.ch/information-programme/study-in-switzerland.html?L=2

Spain

www.universidad.es/en

www.educacion.es (Ministry of Education)

www.uned.es (UNED, for evaluation of qualifications)

Sweden

www.studyinsweden.se

Studying in the USA

Fulbright Commission

www.fulbright.org.uk

EducationUSA
www.educationusa.info

College Board
www.collegeboard.org

College Navigator
www.nces.ed.gov/collegenavigator

National Association of Credential Evaluation Services (NACES)
www.naces.org

Common Application
www.commonapp.org

Hobsons Virtual Events
www.hobsons.com
US virtual student fairs

Scholarships and financial aid

Edupass
www.edupass.org/finaid/databases.phtml

International Education Financial Aid
www.iefa.org

International Scholarships
www.internationalscholarships.com

US Citizenship and Immigration Services
www.uscis.gov

Studying in Canada

Study in Canada
www.studyincanada.com

Association of Universities and Colleges of Canada
www.aucc.ca

Canadian Information Centre for International Credentials
www.cicic.ca

Citizenship & Immigration Canada
www.cic.gc.ca/english/study/index.asp

Immigration Québec
www.immigration-quebec.gouv.qc.ca/en

Statistics Canada
www.statcan.gc.ca

International Scholarships
www.scholarships-bourses.gc.ca/scholarships-bourses/index.
aspx?lang=eng
www.cbie-bcei.ca
http://cscuk.dfid.gov.uk/apply/scholarships-uk-citizens
www.ScholarshipsCanada.com

Studying in Australia

Study in Australia
www.studyinaustralia.gov.au
www.study-in-australia.org/uk

Australian Qualifications Framework
www.aqf.edu.au

Australian High Commission in London
www.uk.embassy.gov.au

Department of Immigration & Citizenship
www.immi.gov.au

International Scholarships
http://cscuk.dfid.gov.uk/apply/scholarships-uk-citizens
www.australiaawards.gov.au
www.kcl.ac.uk/artshums/ahri/centres/menzies/scholarships/index.aspx

Finances and budgeting
www.moneysmart.gov.au/managing-my-money

Australian Tax Office
www.ato.gov.au

Studying in New Zealand

New Zealand Education
www.studyinnewzealand.com

New Zealand Qualifications Authority
www.nzqa.govt.nz/search

Universities New Zealand
www.universitiesnz.ac.nz

Immigration New Zealand
www.immigration.govt.nz

New Zealand High Commission in London
www.nzembassy.com/united-kingdom

Student Job Search
www.sjs.co.nz

Inland Revenue Department
www.ird.govt.nz/how-to/irdnumbers

Studying in Asia

Hong Kong
Study in Hong Kong
http://studyinhongkong.edu.hk/eng

Hong Kong Immigration Department
www.immd.gov.hk

Malaysia
Study Malaysia
www.studymalaysia.com

Singapore
Contact Singapore
www.contactsingapore.sg

Ministry of Education
www.moe.gov.sg

Immigration and Checkpoints Authority
www.ica.gov.sg

High Commission for the Republic of Singapore in London
www.mfa.gov.sg/london

Ministry of Manpower
www.mom.gov.sg

China

Campus China
www.campuschina.org

China's University and College Admission System
www.cucas.edu.cn

Chinese Ministry of Education
www.moe.edu.cn

China Scholarship Council
www.csc.edu.cn/Laihua

Chinese Embassy
www.visaforchina.org

Japan

Study in Japan
www.studyjapan.go.jp/en

JUMP (Japanese Universities for Motivated People)
www.uni.international.mext.go.jp

JASSO (Japan Student Services Organisation)
www.jasso.go.jp

Embassy of Japan in the UK
www.uk.emb-japan.go.jp

Saudi Arabia

Ministry of Higher Education
www.mohe.gov.sa

Ministry of Foreign Affairs

www.mofa.gov.sa

Royal Embassy of Saudi Arabia in London

www.saudiembassy.org.uk

Qatar

Qatar Foundation for Education, Science and Community
Development

www.qf.org.qa/education

Education City, Qatar

www.myeducationcity.com

Studying in the rest of the world

The Caribbean

Jamaican High Commission in London

www.jhcuk.org/citizens/universities

Caribbean Area Network for Quality Assurance in Tertiary
Education (CANQATE)

www.canqate.org/Links/RelatedLinks.aspx

South Africa

Higher Education South Africa

www.hesa.org.za

South African Matriculation Board

www.he-enrol.ac.za/qualification-country

South African High Commission in London

www.southafricahouseuk.com

Glossary

Academic transcript

A record of academic progress from around Y10 (Y11 in NI, and S3 in Scotland) onwards, including exam results, unit grades, internal assessments, academic honours and explanations for any anomalies.

American College Test (ACT)

The ACT is used to determine academic potential for undergraduate study.

Associate degree

A two-year programme of higher education, often in a vocational subject such as hospitality or health.

Bologna process

A system to make higher education comparable and compatible across the EHEA, through use of mutually recognised systems and a clear credit framework.

Community college (USA)

These colleges offer two-year associate degrees, with the possibility of transferring to a university to top up to a full degree; a cheaper option than going straight to a US university.

Co-op programme

Period of paid work experience linked to a university course, rather like a sandwich course in the UK.

Core

The compulsory foundation for university study (used in North America and a number of other countries); students choose from a broad range of subjects.

Diploma mobility

Taking an entire degree overseas, as opposed to a study-abroad or exchange programme.

Diploma supplement

A detailed transcript of attainment in higher education, recognised across the EHEA and beyond.

eCoE (electronic confirmation of enrolment)

The eCoE is issued by Australian colleges and universities as proof of enrolment and is required to apply for a student visa.

ECTS

European Credit Transfer and Accumulation System, aiding the transfer of students between institutions.

EHEA

European Higher Education Area; the countries where the Bologna process is utilised.

Elective

An optional course taken at university.

English medium

Education with English as the language of instruction.

Europass

Helps people to study, work or train across Europe, by presenting skills and qualifications in a standardised format that is easily understood in a range of countries.

Freshman year

First year (USA).

Frosh

Another name for a fresher or freshman. Frosh week is similar to freshers' week in the UK.

Graduate Australian Medical Schools Admission Test (GAMSAT)

Used to determine academic potential for postgraduate medical courses.

Graduate Record Exam (GRE)

Used to determine academic potential for postgraduate study.

Junior year

Third year (USA).

Letter of intent

A statement demonstrating why you should be considered for your chosen course, used by the universities to distinguish between applicants. It may also be described as a letter of motivation, a statement of purpose or a personal statement.

Letter of motivation

A statement demonstrating why you should be considered for your chosen course, used by the universities to distinguish between applicants. It may also be described as a letter of intent, a statement of purpose or a personal statement.

Letter of recommendation

Reference letter to a potential university, most often (but not always) from a member of academic staff who can comment on your ability and potential.

Major

Your main subject area, for example, history, engineering or nursing.

Mid-term

An exam taken midway through the academic term.

Minor

A secondary subject area or a specialism of your major.

Nollning (Sweden)

The introduction of new students to university life, much like freshers' week in the UK.

Numerus clausus (Germany)

A competitive system for courses that have more applicants than places.

Numerus fixus (the Netherlands)

A fixed number of places are available on a course.

OECD

Organisation for Economic Co-operation and Development.

Orientation

Events and activities for new students, like freshers' week in the UK.

Personal statement
A statement demonstrating why you should be considered for your chosen course, used by the universities to distinguish between applicants. It may also be described as a letter of intent, a letter of motivation or a statement of purpose.

Polytechnic (New Zealand; Finland)
An institution providing professional or work-related higher education, in conjunction with business and industry; also known as a university of applied sciences.

Research-intensive or research-based university
An institution involved in extensive research activity and doctoral education.

Research proposal or research statement
The outline of an applicant's plans for research, including area of interest and rationale.

Scholastic Assessment Test (SAT)
Used to determine academic potential for undergraduate study.

Semester
The two periods into which the academic year is divided in some countries.

Senior year
Fourth year (USA).

Sophomore year
Second year (USA).

Statement of purpose

A statement demonstrating why you should be considered for your chosen course, used by the universities to distinguish between applicants. It may also be described as a letter of intent, a letter of motivation or a personal statement.

Study-abroad programme

A term often used to describe an exchange programme or short-term overseas study.

Tertiary education

Education following secondary level; it includes university education, as well as other post-18 education such as vocational training.

UNESCO

United Nations Educational, Scientific and Cultural Organization.

University college (Denmark, Norway and Sweden)

An institution providing professional undergraduate degrees in areas like engineering, teaching or business.

University of applied sciences (Finland and the Netherlands)

See Polytechnic.

Wānanga

An educational establishment in New Zealand that teaches degree-level courses in a Māori cultural context.

Index of advertisers